A LIFE IN TWILIGHT

Also by Mark Wolverton

THE DEPTHS OF SPACE

THE SCIENCE OF SUPERMAN

A LIFE IN TWILIGHT

The Final Years of
J. ROBERT OPPENHEIMER

MARK WOLVERTON

St. Martin's Press
New York

www.stmartins.com

Book design by Jonathan Bennett

The photographs are reprinted by permission: frontispiece by J. Robert Oppenheimer Memorial Committee; Part 1 by Bettmann/Corbis; Parts 2, 3, and 4 by J. Robert Oppenheimer Memorial Committee; Part 5 by American Institute of Physics Emilio Segre Visual Archives, Physics Today Collection.

Library of Congress Cataloging-in-Publication Data

Wolverton, Mark.
 A life in twilight : the final years of J. Robert Oppenheimer / Mark Wolverton. — 1st ed.
 p. cm.
 ISBN-13: 978-0-312-37440-2
 ISBN-10: 0-312-37440-2
 1. Oppenheimer, J. Robert, 1904–1967—Last years. 2. Physicists—United States—
Biography. I. Title.
 QC16.O62W65 2008
 530.092—dc22
 [B] 2008025766

First Edition: November 2008

10 9 8 7 6 5 4 3 2 1

In memory of my mother and father

CONTENTS

A LIFE IN TWILIGHT

LAW OFFICES

BINGHAM, COLLINS, PORTER & KISTLER

HERBERT M. BINGHAM
LINTON M. COLLINS
*WILLIAM A. PORTER (ON LEAVE)
H. DONALD KISTLER
ROGER ROBB
ROBERT M. BOOTH, JR.
KENNETH WELLS PARKINSON
♦(IN GOVERNMENT SERVICE)

TOWER BUILDING
WASHINGTON 5, D. C.

CABLE ADDRESS
"BINGHAM"

TELEPHONE

July 2, 1954

Per Previous Release
ALL INFORMATION CONTAINED
HEREIN IS UNCLASSIFIED
DATE 6-9-99 BY _____
HQ# 90-2608

Honorable J. Edgar Hoover
Federal Bureau of Investigation
Department of Justice
Washington 25, D. C.

Dear Mr. Hoover:

Now that the Oppenheimer case is closed, I would like
to say a word to you about the work of the Federal Bureau of
Investigation.

I do not know how many leads Mr. Rolander and I set
out, or how many requests for information we made, but I am
sure there were dozens of each. In every case, the response of
the Bureau was immediate and effective. Every lead was thor-
oughly investigated and every request for information was com-
pletely answered. As a result, every scrap of available evidence
was presented to the Personnel Security Board. For example, on
the last day of the hearing, we read in evidence a copy of a
letter which had been obtained in Paris only three or four days
previously.

Having had some experience in such matters I do not
speak lightly when I say that the work of the Bureau in this
case was magnificent.

With kindest personal regards, I am

Sincerely yours,

Roger Robb

RR:mt

EX-123

RECORDED - 69
INDEXED - 69

100-17828-1839

PRELUDE

O n a bright and very warm morning in the first week of July 1954, Dr. J. Robert Oppenheimer arrived at his office in Fuld Hall and settled in for a routine day of attending to the business of running the Institute for Advanced Study in Princeton, New Jersey.

The role was as comfortable and familiar to him as the cushioned leather chair that cradled his thin frame. Just as he had been twelve years ago at Los Alamos, he was in charge of a collection of brilliant intellects, among the most stellar produced by humanity, including Albert Einstein himself. Although perhaps it would be a mistake to say that he was "in charge" of them. One didn't tell geniuses such as Einstein, Kurt Gödel, John von Neumann, Freeman Dyson, and the others gathered at the Institute what to do or how to think. Indeed, that was totally at odds with the avowed purpose of the Institute, which was to serve as a sanctuary, an oasis of intellectual freedom and tranquillity in a tumultuous world, a monastic retreat where the world's most incandescent minds could pursue their muses and their work in whatever direction and at whatever pace they desired.

Only in the crudest and most prosaic sense was Oppenheimer the "boss" of such people. He was the administrator, yes, with all the political and nuts-and-bolts responsibilities that position required, but in a larger sense he was a facilitator, a father confessor, a font of both encouragement and criticism, a voice from on high and a collaborator in the intellectual trenches, the overarching guiding spirit of the place.

And yet he was further removed from and less involved in the true work of the Institute than he had ever been at Los Alamos, where he had been the sun

around which all the frenetic, time-critical effort to build the bomb had revolved. Many of the younger Institute members, who might be there on appointments of a year or so, rarely saw Oppenheimer and spoke with him even less often, their direct interaction with him coming only perhaps in the form of a withering Oppenheimer remark during their presentations at an Institute seminar. Despite the many cocktail parties he hosted at his home, Olden Manor, and the social events of the Institute, Oppenheimer had never been one for casual socializing; although the Institute lunchroom was remarkably egalitarian and relaxed in atmosphere, with eminent Nobel Prize winners easily sharing tables and gossip with callow graduate students, you would never find the director among them. Partly it was intentional; he felt that some sort of proper distance had to be maintained between the director's office and the general Institute populace. But it was also simply his personal nature.

Now, however, as Oppenheimer stuffed his ever-present pipe full of his favored walnut tobacco and swiveled around in his chair to regard the brilliantly green and immaculately kept grounds of the Institute campus through the windows that lined his office, he was more alone and isolated than ever before. Eleven years ago his quiet academic life of research and teaching had taken an abrupt and wholly unpredictable turn: he had been thrust into leadership of the most important, most secret, and most life-and-death scientific gamble in history: the Los Alamos laboratory of the Manhattan Project that built the world's first atomic bomb.

And after that gamble paid off more spectacularly and more successfully than anyone could have hoped, he had been swept up into the heady sphere of national and international policymaking. He had served as a distinguished adviser and consultant to various governmental committees and agencies, most prominently as chairman of the General Advisory Committee of the Atomic Energy Commission, the AEC's august board of scientific advisers. He had been the key scientific expert behind the early efforts to bring atomic weapons and energy under international control through the United Nations, the main behind-the-scenes author of the Acheson-Lilienthal Plan, the first serious attempt to bring the bomb under international control. He lunched with prime ministers and presidents, shared cocktails with ambassadors and kings, all of whom eagerly sought his counsel and listened to his words raptly, as though he were an oracle bringing the precious secrets of atomic energy down from heaven itself. And he had been privy to the jealously guarded secrets of his own government, entrusted with things known only to the most select handful.

He had enjoyed influence and power and fame, but aside from those perhaps grossly egotistical satisfactions, he also had a profound satisfaction that few people ever have the privilege of experiencing: of knowing that he, personally, was making a difference in the world. His advice might not always be heeded, his opinions not always accepted, his judgment not always uncontested, but he knew that through his own efforts, he had done things that could change the world for the better.

And now that was all over.

He had been tossed aside, discarded, disregarded. Worse, he had been disgraced and tarred with a label that in McCarthy's America was practically indelible: security risk. The government that he had served for so long, the country that he loved so deeply and for which he had derailed the course of his entire life and scientific career, had decreed that he could no longer be trusted, in a secret Atomic Energy Commission proceeding that had become painfully public.

Yet, paradoxically, the same powers that deemed him undeserving of trust had also loudly affirmed his loyalty. Many of Oppenheimer's friends and supporters pointed out the apparent contradiction in such a position. Obviously, if one is disloyal to one's country, one is also a security risk and unworthy of that nation's trust. But if Oppenheimer's loyalty was beyond question, then by what twisted logic could he also be considered a risk to his country's security?

There was only one way that such a verdict made sense, and in its cruel implications it was even more painful: to be found loyal and yet untrustworthy could mean only that a person lacked the moral sensitivity and basic common sense to tell right from wrong, harmless from dangerous, innocent remarks from lack of discretion. It meant that you were naïve, clueless, unable to hold your tongue, a person whose loyalty was blind and thoughtless rather than based on deeply held convictions and the fundamental strength of one's character. It meant, in the crudest sense, that one was basically an idiot—as Oppenheimer had indeed called himself during his security hearing, whether in wry self-disparagement or profound, agonizing honesty.

Oppenheimer realized, perhaps better than any of his aggrieved colleagues and other defenders, that the defining chapter of his life had now come to an end with the final judgment of the AEC. There would be no more special privileges, no phone calls from presidential advisers; the stratospheric days of power and glory were truly over. He was again merely a scientist and academic administrator, one who still enjoyed great respect and prestige in those circles, but also

a figure who would be shadowed by a dark cloud to everyone outside those worlds and to the public at large.

He was a victim, a martyr, a marked man at age fifty, and somehow he had to find a way to start his life over and build something new on the wreckage of all that had just been destroyed, to forge a fresh path without everything that had just been taken away from him.

July 8, 1954

RECORDED - 69 100-17828-1839

Mr. Roger Robb
Tower Building
14th and K Streets, N. W.
Washington 5, D. C.

EX-123 Dear Mr. Robb:

 I have received your letter of July 2,
1954, and have noted your complimentary remarks
concerning the work of the Federal Bureau of
Investigation during the investigation of
Dr. J. Robert Oppenheimer. Your comments in
this matter are sincerely appreciated.

 I would like to take the opportunity
to congratulate you on the excellent manner in
which you handled the Oppenheimer case as
Special Attorney for the Atomic Energy Commission.
I feel confident that the successful outcome of
the case was greatly enhanced by your most able
presentation and direction.

 Sincerely yours,

 J. Edgar Hoover

JEM:epa

Tolson
Boardman
Nichols
Belmont
Glavin
Harbo
Rosen
Tamm
Tracy
Mohr
Winterrowd
Tele. Room
Holloman
Miss Gandy

MAILED 8
JUL 8 - 1954
COMM-FBI

68 JUL 26 1954

THE EDGE OF MYSTERY

Venturing cautiously back into the public spotlight: Oppenheimer explains some basic quantum physics to Edward R. Murrow on *See It Now*.

We will have to accept the fact that no one of us really will ever know very much. This is why we shall have to find comfort in the fact that, taken together, we know more and more.

—J. ROBERT OPPENHEIMER, "A SCIENCE IN CHANGE," BBC REITH LECTURES, 1953

FEDERAL BUREAU OF INVESTIGATION

UNITED STATES DEPARTMENT OF JUSTICE

FBI, NEWARK 11/18/54 AIRTEL

Transmit the following Teletype message to:

DIRECTOR, FBI (100-17828)

DR. J. ROBERT OPPENHEIMER, IS-R. FOR INFO OF BUREAU, AGENT OF

NEWARK OFFICE, WHILE ON O.B. AT INSTITUTE FOR ADVANCED STUDY,
OFFICIAL BUSINESS

PRINCETON, N.J., ON 11/17/54, OBSERVED DR. OPPENHEIMER CONFERRING

WITH EDWARD R. MURROW AND THIRD UNIDENTIFIED INDIVIDUAL.

PURPOSE OF CONFERENCE WAS NOT DETERMINED.

 HOSTETTER

END

ALL INFORMATION CONTAINED
HEREIN IS UNCLASSIFIED

Mr. Belmont

RECORDED-35

EX-124

Approved: _____ Sent_____ M Per_____
 Special Agent in Charge

1

The Scientist and the Reporter

The G-men had been watching J. Robert Oppenheimer for a long time. Over ten years, in fact, ever since he had been named scientific director of the Manhattan Project by its leader, Brigadier General Leslie R. Groves. At first the surveillance had been conducted by Army intelligence, who followed the scientist around in government-issue sedans, noting his movements and meetings, verifying he did what he said he was going to do and noting whenever he departed from schedule, such as when he spent a night with a former girlfriend in Berkeley in the summer of 1943. Occasionally the Army types were complemented in their watchdogging by J. Edgar Hoover's FBI men, who sometimes got into little turf wars over who was supposed to watch what and when. Both the military and FBI dutifully tapped Oppenheimer's phones and intercepted and read his mail as a matter of course.

During the war at least, Oppenheimer wasn't alone as an object of such scrutiny. Everyone who lived in Los Alamos or worked on the Manhattan Project was watched and monitored and surveilled, and the constant security measures became a source of running jokes among the project personnel, if not also frequent irritation. Some waggish project people liked to tweak the nose of the security stalwarts. Richard Feynman, a bongo-playing physicist, routinely planted secret messages in letters to his wife and opened safes at Los Alamos to leave taunting

messages inside for security officers. For most, it was simply an accepted, if unfortunate, necessity of wartime life in a top-secret enterprise.

Oppenheimer's case was different, though. Not only was he the leader of the scientists, he had an extensive leftist background, with a formerly Communist wife, brother, and sister-in-law, just for starters. Although he wasn't alone in such associations among the Manhattan Project scientific elite, he was the most prominent of those who went on to move in lofty government circles after the war, and arguably the most influential of all the atomic scientists. Obviously such a man continued to bear watching, thought some high governmental officials.

And so the surveillance of J. Robert Oppenheimer continued, sometimes only cursorily, other times more intensively, even after he left the Manhattan Project and continued as a scientific and policy adviser to his government, even after he was officially disgraced and expelled from any connection with the government, the military, or political powers that be. Perhaps he wasn't a Soviet agent, some reasoned, but what if he decided to defect? What terrible damage could he do?

Such logic impelled retired admiral Lewis Strauss, chairman of the Atomic Energy Commission and the man who had been instrumental in stripping Oppenheimer of his security clearance and destroying his political influence, to demand that Hoover's FBI keep the scientist under its watchful eyes, even as Hoover himself thought the need for such surveillance was long past and had become a drain on Bureau resources that could be better employed elsewhere.

For the agents assigned to the Oppenheimer detail, watching the disgraced physicist must have become a stultifyingly boring assignment by the end of 1954. Instead of chasing Soviet agents or Mafia kingpins, here they were, stuck watching the administrator of the world's biggest refuge for eggheads. So they were no doubt intrigued by the arrival at the Institute of the famous broadcaster Edward R. Murrow, another public figure who had been under FBI scrutiny. Unfortunately, without any bugs in Oppenheimer's office to let the Feds listen in to the meeting, the agents had to report that the "nature of the conversation is unknown."[1]

As it turned out, the agents didn't have to worry. They, along with everyone else in the country, would find out "the nature of the conversa-

tion" on a Tuesday evening in early January 1955, and it had been perfectly innocuous. Oppenheimer and Murrow hadn't been planning the overthrow of the government or the establishment of a Communist spy ring at the Institute, or even debating the finer points of *Das Kapital*. They had merely been discussing the details of an upcoming broadcast of Murrow's famous—or to some, infamous—television program, *See It Now*. Murrow and his producer/partner, Fred W. Friendly, the "third unidentified individual" noted by the FBI agent, wanted to do an episode featuring the Institute for Advanced Study, and the three men had been going over the necessary arrangements.

For Murrow and Friendly, 1954 had been almost as difficult and fateful a year as for Robert Oppenheimer. A month before the beginning of Oppenheimer's security hearing, in March 1954, Murrow had dared to directly and openly attack Senator Joseph McCarthy on *See It Now* in a devastating broadside that proved to be one of the signal events that led to McCarthy's downfall. A few days before the hearing convened, McCarthy responded to Murrow on *See It Now,* and several weeks later began the Army-McCarthy hearings—watched by millions of Americans, including Oppenheimer himself during the brief breaks in his own ordeal—that led to the Senator's censure by the Senate in December 1954. Murrow and Friendly paid dearly for their courage, facing not only the inevitable personal attacks from McCarthy and his supporters, but the more intimate fallout that landed on other members of their *See It Now* team, leading to resignations, firings, and even a suicide.

Thanks to their own strength of character and the grudging support of their network, Murrow and Friendly had survived the battles of 1954, slightly bloodied but still defiant, still eager to pursue the controversial and dangerous. But not every *See It Now* was intended to be as incendiary as the McCarthy show, nor did every episode deal with even remotely political or controversial subject matter. Some episodes simply provided fascinating glimpses of noteworthy individuals, gave an insider's tour of some previously unseen place, or reveled in the possibilities of the new technology of coast-to-coast television broadcasting. The January 4, 1955, *See It Now* broadcast was originally planned to be nothing more than one of these quieter, calm, noncontroversial episodes. It would turn out to be something quite different.

The original inspiration came not from Murrow, but from Friendly.

Putting together a weekly live television broadcast has never been an easy matter, and it was even less so in the early 1950s; the *See It Now* team worked long hours almost continuously from one week to the next, doing interviews, gathering material, writing and rewriting, viewing and editing film footage in marathon sessions that inevitably included nights and weekends. Caught up in the madness, Friendly's wife, Dorothy, forced him to promise to take a break once in a while, perhaps on a Wednesday here and there, after the Tuesday-night broadcast and before the rush began to put together the following Tuesday's show. On one of Friendly's brief Wednesday sabbaticals, he and Dorothy drove down from New York to visit some friends in Princeton, who took Friendly around to see the local sights, including the Institute for Advanced Study. Friendly recalled, "Its director, Dr. Oppenheimer, took us on a tour, and in the course of it gave us a blackboard explanation of the quantum theory in response to a question of Dorothy's. Neither of us understood the equations that danced before our eyes, but we were stimulated by the grace and drive of this man, whose need to teach even embraced a couple of mathematical morons. It seemed to me a waste that more people were not exposed to Oppenheimer's erudition and charm."[2]

But Friendly had the perfect means to bring that erudition and charm to a vast audience. He called Murrow later the same day, and they decided to do a *See It Now* on the Institute, featuring interviews with Oppenheimer, Einstein, Niels Bohr, and whatever other famous denizens of the place cared to make themselves available. As Murrow later put it, the Institute was unique in that "you find a Nobel Prize winner every time you open a door." It would be a perfect subject for *See It Now,* a show whose raison d'être was to show its audience people and places they wouldn't see elsewhere.

"For someone who knows as little about the Institute for Advanced Study as I do, I find I am doing a considerable amount of lecturing about this establishment and its purpose," Friendly wrote to Oppenheimer after his visit. "Thus far, of course, my only audience has been my senior colleague, Ed Murrow. We would both like to attempt to do a television report on the Institute and its people, and our only problem is to convince you and your associates that we would not do violence to the purpose and ethics that motivate your work."[3] Oppenheimer gave

his cautious approval, and soon after, Friendly returned to the Institute with Murrow to begin planning the program, as duly noted by the FBI.

With the blessing of Oppenheimer and the Institute board of trustees in their pocket, Murrow and Friendly expected no great difficulties. Over the years, they had dealt with personages as varied as congressmen, housewives, corporate presidents, Air Force generals, and movie stars, and had even slugged it out in the trenches with America's most feared demagogue. What trouble could there be from a group of the world's most brilliant intellects in the tranquil surroundings of Princeton? They soon discovered that in some ways, dealing with McCarthy had actually been simpler than the new task they had set for themselves. McCarthy, at least, never passed up a chance to make himself heard, and then in the clearest, most vociferous manner possible. Not so with the faculty of the Institute.

To begin with, the unquestioned superstar of the Institute himself, Albert Einstein, declined to participate, despite the fact that he respected and admired Murrow and complimented him on the McCarthy show. It wasn't an unusual move by the self-effacing scientist, who tended to shun the spotlight in his later years and chose his opportunities for public appearances and statements carefully. Murrow and Friendly were disappointed, but they still had an entire collection of geniuses from which to choose, including a physicist who was second only to Einstein in the scientific pantheon and who happened to be visiting the Institute for a few months, the Danish Nobelist Niels Bohr, who was more than willing to sit for Murrow's cameras.

On December 16, 1954—one week shy of a year since Oppenheimer had been told by Strauss of the suspension of his AEC clearance—Murrow and the *See It Now* crew encamped at the Institute for Advanced Study to shoot the program, one way or another. "The first few days of shooting went badly; we had obviously gotten into something over our heads," Friendly admitted.[4] Just how over their heads they were was made painfully clear by Murrow's interview with Bohr.

Unquestionably one of the greatest minds of the century, one of the founding fathers of the quantum theories that had revolutionized science, Bohr was also famously obscure in manner. In his thick, impenetrable Danish accent, he mumbled, he digressed, he jumped ahead, he

explained his thoughts in technical terms so opaque that at times he seemed to be merely talking out loud to himself, or at least to another eminent colleague, rather than to a nonscientific layman struggling to understand him. Brilliant he obviously was; a great communicator of science, he was not.

Murrow and Friendly despaired: was everyone at the Institute so incomprehensible? Interviews with several other Institute faculty proved little better. It looked as though the great idea of doing a show about the world's sanctuary for geniuses was turning into a monumental dud. Maybe people such as Einstein, Bohr, and the others simply operated on too lofty a level for the average citizen to understand. Maybe there was a good reason they were removed, or had removed themselves, from society to settle at the Institute: they truly couldn't function or live among the rest of us. They existed on an Olympian plane from which meaningful communication with mere mortals was essentially impossible. Murrow remembered, "I was becoming very discouraged when I went in and sat down with Professor Oppenheimer."[5]

Although perhaps neither man realized it, that moment had been coming for some time, with various threads of circumstance conspiring to bring them together. The lives of Oppenheimer and Murrow shared some striking parallels. They were almost the same age, their birth dates separated by only three days and four years, although Murrow had been born into poverty in rural North Carolina and Oppenheimer into the privileged and comfortable world of New York City's Upper West Side. Each found his own personal defining moment in the midst of World War II, each one carving out a unique place for himself in a role that he literally invented as he went along: Oppenheimer the leader of history's largest concentrated scientific effort, Murrow the radio correspondent who brought the terrors of war directly into the homes of millions. Each man had, in his own way, wrestled with the darkest questions of the twentieth century, and each had dealt with the troubling aftermath of the war in the cold war that followed. Both Oppenheimer and Murrow had faced the specter of McCarthyist paranoia head-on, and both had paid a price for it. They even shared a lifelong addiction to smoking, even if Oppenheimer mostly preferred pipes and Murrow cigarettes. And that particular habit would ultimately kill both men.

Apart from these affinities, their eventual encounter had been fore-shadowed over a year earlier, when Murrow fired his first serious opening shot at Joseph McCarthy by devoting an episode of *See It Now* to the story of Milo Radulovich, a perfectly average Air Force Reserve officer from Detroit who was facing summary expulsion from the service because of his close association with supposed "Communist sympathizers"—namely, his sister and father. Like Oppenheimer, Radulovich had been condemned on the basis of secret "evidence" that he wasn't allowed to see, and like Oppenheimer, he had been judged loyal yet also a security risk. The parallels with Oppenheimer's later trial by fire could hardly escape a man with as finely tuned a sense of justice as Murrow, particularly after he devoted his June 1, 1954, CBS radio broadcast to the final AEC decision on Oppenheimer.

Another thread of fate drawing the two men together came only days before the beginning of Oppenheimer's security hearing. As part of his rambling rebuttal to Murrow's attack on him the previous month, McCarthy charged that America's hydrogen bomb program had suffered a delay of eighteen months. Because of "traitors in our government," he proclaimed darkly, "our nation may well die." Like the rest of the nation, Murrow wouldn't know it until the story of the Oppenheimer hearing broke a week later, but McCarthy was making a veiled reference to Oppenheimer and the charges that he had obstructed the H-bomb program. Although veiled in innuendo and anonymity, Oppenheimer's ordeal had in effect been revealed to the public before *The New York Times* officially published the story—convincing Oppenheimer and his lawyers to give *New York Times* reporter James Reston permission to release the details before McCarthy or Lewis Strauss beat them to it.

Oppenheimer's and Murrow's mutual concerns, interests, and experiences would all be in evidence in their lengthy and wide-ranging conversation. The Oppenheimer "erudition and charm" that had so mesmerized Friendly were in full flower as Murrow interviewed Oppenheimer, in almost comical contrast to Bohr's rambling, obtuse performance. For almost three hours, with two cameras filming the entire encounter, Oppenheimer and Murrow chatted about matters small and large, from the work of the Institute faculty and Oppenheimer's basic duties as their leader; to politics, including the immigration laws that

hindered foreign scientists visiting and working in the United States; to some elementary quantum mechanics, with Oppenheimer explaining some equations on a blackboard as Murrow watched; to Oppenheimer's childhood; to the threat of atomic fallout and the possibility of human extinction.

The easy rapport and respect each man had for the other was clear, even if the air in Oppenheimer's office wasn't. The one topic they *didn't* address directly was Oppenheimer's security hearing and loss of government clearance. As much as the ubiquitous smoke from Oppenheimer's pipe and Murrow's never-ending chain of Camel cigarettes, the subject was a permeative, evanescent presence in the room in which the two men conversed, even if, like the smoke, it was never openly acknowledged.

Murrow and Friendly left the Institute with hours of footage and no idea how they were going to turn it all into a compelling television program. "On the way back from Princeton, Ed spoke very little until we reached the Lincoln Tunnel," Friendly remembered. "And then he said what both of us had been thinking for fifty miles: 'There isn't one foot of usable film in all that stuff we did with Bohr and all the others, but the Oppenheimer interview is quite a hunk of film. Let's run it for a half hour.' "[6] As Murrow biographer Joseph E. Persico writes, "He felt that he could have run virtually all the [Oppenheimer] film uncut and have produced gripping television."[7] That, of course, was out of the question; *See It Now* had half an hour of airtime each week and no more. In fact, Murrow had even less time to work with, since that half hour of airtime also had to accommodate the commercial messages of his sponsor, the aluminum company Alcoa. Cutting down an almost three-hour interview to a mere twenty-five minutes for broadcast "was one of the toughest editing jobs we ever had," said Friendly. "We did it by stages, first to seventy minutes that simply couldn't be cut, then agonizingly down to fifty minutes. . . . we left out almost as much good material as we were able to include."[8]

But the technical and aesthetic ordeal of editing was only one of the obstacles Murrow and Friendly faced in getting Oppenheimer on national television. CBS hadn't escaped the attention of the McCarthyist blacklisters, and even before Murrow's open attack on McCarthy, it was considered in some circles "the Red network." Bending to the pressure,

the network, in the words of Bob Edwards, "skipped the middleman and did its own Red-hunting, assigning company attorney Daniel O'Shea as in-house 'clearer' of present and prospective employees."[9] O'Shea instituted "loyalty oaths" for all CBS personnel and became the network's de facto security chief, tasked with cleansing the company of any Communist or "pinko" taint.

In the introduction to his McCarthy program, Murrow himself had admitted that his subject matter was "by definition controversial." Now, almost a year after Murrow and Friendly had used CBS as a weapon to directly assault Senator Joseph McCarthy, they were proposing to give airtime to J. Robert Oppenheimer, another person who was "by definition controversial," and who had officially been found to be a security risk and had admitted close Communist ties in his past. What, O'Shea demanded, were Murrow and Friendly trying to do to the network?

O'Shea's protests were derailed by the unusually close friendship that Murrow enjoyed with the CBS chairman of the board and network founder, William S. Paley. Although Paley didn't always agree with Murrow's opinions or his methods, and as often as not chose to avoid the controversy caused by Murrow rather than to embrace it, everyone at CBS knew that if Murrow really wanted something, he usually got his way, thanks to his direct pipeline to the chairman. And Murrow really wanted to do the Oppenheimer broadcast. Murrow's former colleague Alexander Kendrick points out that Murrow and Friendly "could easily have forgotten the whole thing, and substituted another program. But Murrow felt that it had to be shown, not only in justice to Oppenheimer as a teacher and human being, but for its own values, as a thought-provoking contribution of the kind that television had too few of."[10] The concerns of CBS's resident anti-Communist hatchet man were not going to stop Murrow.

O'Shea did have one consolation, however. Just as the network had refused to pay for advertising for certain other controversial *See It Now* programs, notably the McCarthy edition, the CBS bean counters denied Murrow and Friendly any advertising money for the Oppenheimer show. And just as they had responded before, Murrow and Friendly again laid out their own money, $1,500 each, to place large ads in *The New York Times* to promote the episode. The ad itself was studiously neutral: a photo of a quizzical-looking Oppenheimer before his equation-filled blackboard,

and the words "A Conversation with Dr. J. Robert Oppenheimer, Director, Institute for Advanced Study, Princeton, N.J." Nothing sensationalistic about the "Disgraced A-bomb Pioneer J. Robert Oppenheimer" or "Security Risk J. Robert Oppenheimer" or even, as some would no doubt have preferred, "Communist Traitor J. Robert Oppenheimer." Just the facts, and the time and date of the show. The rest would be left for the audience to decide for themselves.

Assuming, of course, that there was a show at all. Even as Murrow and Friendly struggled to edit the show down to manageable length while fending off O'Shea and the other nervous naysayers at the network, another complication threatened to undo all their hard work. Oppenheimer himself was now trying to stop the broadcast.

His reasoning was disarmingly simple. He had originally agreed to a television show not about himself, but about the Institute for Advanced Study, of which he was only a part. Whether or not the other members of the Institute such as Einstein had agreed to participate, Oppenheimer knew full well that he was leading a collection not only of the world's greatest intellects but also of the world's greatest egos, many of whom, in all fairness, were more accomplished in their fields than even himself. Presenting a program that purported to be about the Institute while focusing only on Oppenheimer as its biggest star and sole personification was bound to annoy a few people. Aside from the interpersonal and political friction at the Institute and the personal embarrassment Oppenheimer knew such a portrayal would cause, he simply thought it unfair to his Institute colleagues. No one was more acutely aware that many of them were Nobel Prize winners, while he was merely a publicly disgraced scientist whose advice had been rejected by his own government. Surely he had no right to be placed above men such as Albert Einstein, Kurt Gödel, John von Neumann, Niels Bohr, and many others, as the face of the Institute, whether he was its director or not.

As soon as he learned that Murrow had decided to use nothing but his own interview for the entire show, Oppenheimer protested that the original concept of the episode, a portrait of the Institute, was being discarded in favor of a new idea to which he hadn't agreed, a portrait of one man. For both Oppenheimer and his wife, there was also the simple practical human consideration that they had to live with the people at

the Institute. Aside from work, there were the cocktail parties and other social occasions hosted by the director, the friends who dropped in for informal visits and dinners, the collegial atmosphere of a great institution of learning.

Oppenheimer had already been cast out of one life that had been important to him, the Washington elite of which he had once been such an important member. All he had left was the respect, admiration, and friendship of his scientific and intellectual colleagues, and it was with them at the Institute that he had found refuge and acceptance after his fall from governmental grace. What if he was to be ostracized yet again, banished from the very world that had provided him with his only remaining solace, simply because some television reporter decided to make him seem important? Would he have to spend the rest of his life explaining that the TV show wasn't supposed to be about him, that he tried and failed to step out of the spotlight that Murrow and Friendly forced upon him? That would be too much to bear. He resolved that he could not allow it to happen, even if it meant disappointing Edward R. Murrow.

The Oppenheimer *See It Now* was scheduled for January 4, 1955, and as Friendly and his staff labored to put the show together in time, they were fighting a rearguard action with Oppenheimer, with lawyers from both sides arguing and negotiating, and Friendly and Murrow both in direct contact with the reluctant Oppenheimer. "In the three days prior to the program we talked to Princeton ten times, made two trips, saw lawyers and mutual friends at the Institute, and prepared to run an alternate program," Friendly recalled. Aside from the protests of Oppenheimer and O'Shea, Friendly knew he was in a "precarious situation." "The Oppenheimers didn't want us to do the show, the sponsor would be happy if we dropped it, and CBS had no wish to put on another controversial program. The archliberals would castigate us for doing a half-hour about Oppenheimer without condemning his 'persecutors'; the extreme right wing would castigate us for 'defending the Red Professor' by not even mentioning that he was a security risk."[11] Once again, Murrow and Friendly found themselves up to their necks in rapidly rising water. But they were used to that by now, and had almost grown to like it.

Only days before the broadcast, Murrow and Friendly visited Oppenheimer again in Princeton to argue their case. Oppenheimer seemed to be finally weakening; afterward he wrote to Murrow, "I have from the

first been most grateful for your interest in undertaking a story about the Institute, knowing you both as a great craftsman, and a man of great courage and spirit. It is thus natural that I should readily defer to your own judgment, and understand your decision to present an account of the Institute almost wholly through the conversation that you and I had about it. . . . Had you, a month ago, offered to devote one of your programs to a sketch of one Robert Oppenheimer, even my great respect for you would not have overcome my own certainty. I would have refused. I thus take courage to ask you again to make the program that you are planning for next week as much as it can be a story about the Institute for Advanced Study, and as little as it need be a portrait of one man."[12]

Two days before the broadcast, Friendly sent Oppenheimer a transcript of the interview, telling him that "Ed received your letter and is most anxious for you to be assured that the purpose of the program remains what it always has been. You would have heard from him personally but for the fact that he is deeply involved in the annual year-end correspondents' report which is being broadcast this afternoon. . . . No material not indicated by this script will be used on Tuesday night's program, although there is some editing which will have to be done before this is ready for air."[13]

But Oppenheimer had apparently not quite "overcome his own certainty." That same evening, Murrow was busy hosting a party for CBS foreign correspondents at his home, but instead of tending to his guests, he ended up spending almost the whole time on the phone with a still-hesitant Oppenheimer. In the showdown between two men of such legendary powers of argument and persuasion, perhaps it was only Murrow, who had enthralled the free world with his wartime broadcasts and helped to convince a nation of the dangers of a renegade senator, who could have bested Oppenheimer. And by now, his patience was exhausted. You haven't seen the film of your interview, Murrow told Oppenheimer; Fred and I have. We know how good it is, and that it will do nothing but reflect the greatest credit on the Institute and yourself. "Dr. Oppenheimer, we are going to run the interview as we see fit," Murrow insisted. "If you don't like it you can say so publicly, but I venture to predict that after it is over you will call me up to tell me that it had value for the Institute and for Dr. Oppenheimer."[14]

Murrow and Friendly were still worried about Oppenheimer's ultimate reaction to the show. A displeased interview subject would do neither the show nor the network any good, and removed from government or not, Oppenheimer could still make headlines if he chose. But it was too late now. The show was going ahead, one way or another. *The New York Times* made it official on December 31: "Dr. J. Robert Oppenheimer, the atomic scientist, will discuss his background, philosophy and interests in a filmed conversation to be presented over the Columbia Broadcasting System television network on Tuesday from 10:30 to 11 P.M.," announced a short article, which also noted that "the program would not devote itself to the 'Oppenheimer case.' "[15]

Murrow and his producer got a last-minute dose of reassurance on the morning of the broadcast, when they showed the nearly finished edit to Paley. They still had about two minutes to cut, but they were so proud of what they had that they wanted somebody else to see it before the night's broadcast. Much to their surprise, Paley was delighted by the show. Paley used to complain that Murrow's shows always gave him "stomach aches," but this particular program, for once, didn't cause him any gastrointestinal distress. Instead of dressing down Murrow and Friendly with dire predictions of sponsor trouble and political heat, Paley all but insisted that they leave the show untouched, even if it ran over its allotted half hour. It was just too good to cut, Paley said. Friendly later wrote, "I explained that we all felt that way but that the network lines were automatically pulled by the telephone company thirty seconds before eleven o'clock, so Dr. Oppenheimer would be interrupted in mid-sentence unless we shortened the film." Some hard facts of the television business were beyond the influence of even a network chairman.[16]

The show would go on. How the public, the government, and the man himself would react to this "questionable" person being brought into the comfortable bosom of millions of American living rooms was still an open question.

* * *

On a pleasant morning some months earlier, April 12, 1954, in Washington, D.C., Robert Oppenheimer had begun the most excruciating, humiliating, profound, and surreal three weeks of his entire life. Leading a group of several men

and one woman, he approached the rear door of the nondescript Temporary Building III near the Washington Monument. Passing by a row of parked cars, the group was joined by a uniformed guard who escorted them deeper into the structure. Dressed in dark, impeccably tailored suits, they could have been business executives, salespeople, advertising people, any of the varieties of interchangeable organization types of the 1950s. The lone woman was moving slowly on crutches, having broken her leg several days before.

Oppenheimer, as usual, stood out from the others, because of both his dignified, almost aristocratic demeanor and the distinctive porkpie hat that crowned his tall, thin frame. To any casual observer of the group, it would be the hat, more than anything else, that would have transformed him from an anonymous suit into an instantly recognizable celebrity. Several years earlier, in fact, a picture of just the hat on the cover of a magazine was all that was needed to tell everyone who was featured inside.

The stray passerby would probably have assumed that he was there on some crucial government business, perhaps to chair a high-level meeting of scientists and military officials or to brief a coffee klatch of congressional staffers, obviously on something to do with the nation's atomic energy program and defenses. The men accompanying Oppenheimer were no doubt scientists or congressmen or some other high government officials. As for the woman, well, she was probably a stenographer or secretary, who would record the august deliberations of Oppenheimer's group for posterity.

That idle observer would have been astonished to discover just how wrong his assumptions were. The men with Oppenheimer were his lawyers, and the woman on crutches was his wife, Katherine "Kitty" Oppenheimer. They had accompanied him to this building to stand with him before a secret Atomic Energy Commission hearing. At issue was the suspension of his top-secret security clearance. Dr. J. Robert Oppenheimer, a man who hobnobbed with presidents and kings, a national figure some even credited with winning World War II as "the father of the atomic bomb" and who had been advising his government at the highest levels ever since, was now accused of being unable to keep secrets, of being disloyal to the United States and possibly even a Soviet spy.

For the next three weeks, in room 2022 of this building, every detail of Oppenheimer's life, both public and personal, would be subjected to the most painful scrutiny. Oppenheimer himself would spend hours in a witness chair being grilled as ruthlessly as a murder suspect, despite the insistence of the hearing's chairman that the process was "an inquiry, and not in the nature of a trial."

The chairman was right. In a trial, Oppenheimer would have been allowed to examine and question the evidence and witnesses against him. Instead, during the hearing, Oppenheimer and his attorneys were deprived of vital documents freely available to the other side, denied the names of hostile witnesses, and forced to refute anonymous and hearsay evidence. In the name of national security, the internationally renowned and respected Oppenheimer was deprived of the basic rights enjoyed by the lowliest criminal in open court. According to one witness, former AEC director David Lilienthal, "There hadn't been a proceeding like this since the Spanish Inquisition."

CONFIDENTIAL

FEDERAL BUREAU OF INVESTIGATION

FD-72
0-16-60

FORM NO. 1
THIS CASE ORIGINATED AT — SAN FRANCISCO FILE NO.

REPORT MADE AT	DATE WHEN MADE	PERIOD FOR WHICH MADE	REPORT MADE BY
NEW YORK	10/20/54	9/14, 15; 10/5, 5,8,11/54	FREDERICK E. SMITH mo

TITLE	CHARACTER OF CASE
DR. J. ROBERT OPPENHEIMER	INTERNAL SECURITY-R

SYNOPSIS OF FACTS:

LEE MORTIMER, Columnist for the New York "Daily Mirror", wrote on 8/27/54 that a "controversial atomic scientist" had been approached by MVD agents during a recent visit to the Virgin Islands. MORTIMER indicated he had received this information from HOWARD RUSHMORE, NY "Journal American" columnist who declined upon interview to reveal the source of this information. Subject interviewed upon arrival at Idlewild Airport, 6:20 p.m., 6/29/54, and denied contact by MVD agents. Subject scheduled to speak over CBS radio on arts and sciences, 12/26/54.

- P -

DETAILS:

ALLEGED APPROACH BY MVD AGENTS IN
VIRGIN ISLANDS

LEE MORTIMER'S column "New York Confidential" New York "Daily Mirror", dated August 27, 1954, read in part as follows:

business): "Daily Worker please copy (if you're still in business):

DO NOT WRITE IN THESE SPACES

100-17828-1 20 82

RECORDED - 14

6 - Bureau (100-17828) (RM)
1 - Newark (100-31936) (Info) (RM)
3 - San Francisco (100-3132) (RM) OCT 22 1954
1 - Washington Field (100-12258) (RM) (Info)
2 - New York (100-9066)

INDEXED - 14

OCT 28 1954
/24 COPIES DESTROYED

2

The Sage of Princeton

The January 4, 1955, edition of *See It Now* begins not with a shot of Robert Oppenheimer, but with a view of the Institute for Advanced Study's famous digital computer, designed and built by John von Neumann. "This is the computing machine at the Institute for Advanced Study, Princeton, New Jersey," says Murrow's voice-over. "It is virtually the only piece of scientific equipment at this Institute." Over shots of the Institute grounds, mostly of the Christmas-wreath-bedecked main building, Fuld Hall, Murrow continues: "There is no student body here . . . just chalk and blackboard and books and scholars. . . . The men of this Institute probe far beyond the existing frontier of man's knowledge. This is a brief report on the work and purpose of the Institute as seen through the eyes and mind of one man—its director, Dr. J. Robert Oppenheimer, a physicist." That, Murrow hoped, would satisfy Oppenheimer that nobody was attempting to glorify him above his colleagues.

A two-minute ad for *See It Now*'s sole sponsor, Alcoa, follows, extolling the virtues of aluminum truck bodies, and then the show begins in earnest, continuing with no further commercial interruptions. A sharp cut from a title card reading "Institute for Advanced Study" reveals both men seated at a table in Oppenheimer's book-lined office, a gray-suited Oppenheimer leaning over the table to light the inevitable cigarette of his fellow smoker, the two already establishing a rapport through their affinity for tobacco. With Oppenheimer sitting back

puffing his pipe, Murrow asks him to talk a little about the Institute in general, noting, "I have heard you describe it as a 'decompression chamber.'" Oppenheimer smiles and responds, "Well, it is for many people. There are no telephones ringing, and you don't have to go to committee meetings, and you don't have to meet classes. Especially for the people who are here for life, the first years are quite remarkable, because most people depend on being interrupted in order to live. . . . they're used to having to attend to other people's business. When they get here, there is nothing of that, and they can't run away. It's to help men who are creative and deep and active and struggling scientists and scholars to get the job done that it is their destiny to do."

At Murrow's prompting, Oppenheimer goes on to talk about some of the members of the faculty and to explain what they are working on. "Some are pure mathematicians. There's Hassler Whitney, an extraordinarily imaginative and creative man, whose field"—a quick smile—"it won't mean much—whose field is essentially topology."

"What exactly is that?" Murrow asks.

"Well, it is a study of those relationships which do not have to do with measure and size but with shape and arrangement. Let me digress. . . ." Oppenheimer mentions the psychologist Jean Piaget, who had visited the Institute earlier in the year and whose specialty was studying "the way children learn to think." Tying child psychology together with higher mathematics, Oppenheimer explains that Piaget "found out those things which in normal mathematical instructions are the most highbrow, are the things children know first. Children know first whether objects are inside each other or separate—whether they can be deformed into each other, and these are the notions that topology deals with." Numbers, measurement, calculations, all that comes later, but children seem to first learn about "the things that have to do with relatedness," for example, "the fact that a doughnut can't be turned into a sphere without tearing it . . . this kind of thing the child knows, and these logical notions . . . are the basis of topology."

Pretty heady stuff for a mass television audience, to be sure, yet Oppenheimer makes it sound simple and understandable, without a hint of arrogance or talking down to Murrow or the television viewers. After a brief discussion on some of the other Institute members, Murrow asks about the most famous resident.

"And Professor Einstein is still here too, isn't he?"

Oppenheimer's face crinkles up in a big smile. "Oh, indeed he is. Indeed he is." He pauses thoughtfully for a moment, as if searching for the perfect description. "He's one of the most lovable of men."

"Does he ever call you up on the telephone?" Murrow inquires.

"Hmm, sometimes," says Oppenheimer. "I think he calls me when he reads in the newspapers something about me that he doesn't like and he calls me up and says: 'That's all right. That's just right.'"

Murrow asks about the younger generation of scientists and their training. Are they getting the support and opportunities they need? "I don't know," Oppenheimer admits. "I am very bad about it, because I work in my own life with rather few people as students. I always have." He adds wryly, "They wouldn't let me at undergraduates because they are afraid I'll confuse them." Murrow joins in Oppenheimer's self-deprecating laugh. Turning serious, Oppenheimer continues, "We're just beginning to realize that if we want people to do very hard things, we've got to provide money in some way to see them through their training; if we want them to go into a profession which will never be very remunerative, we won't be successful unless we provide scholarships and that kind of thing. One great man of learning changes a country." Alluding to Bohr, he says, "Denmark has one enormous figure in physics, and the whole country is changed by that."

Oppenheimer's enthusiastic recounting of the Institute's members and their fields, from pure mathematics to art history to political science, provided an effective impression of the varied and advanced work of the Institute and its reason for being. But just as striking as what he was saying was how Oppenheimer said it, as Joseph Persico describes: "Tall, ascetic, remotely mystical, his pepper and salt hair resembling a monk's skull cap, Oppenheimer spoke with a modest, almost hesitant manner."[1] Oppenheimer paused frequently, not out of nervousness or hesitation, but because he was carefully considering the question, marshaling his thoughts, searching for just the word or phrase that would make his point, his warm eyes gazing off into the middle distance. Here, obviously, was a man who thought deeply about questions large and small, who knew much and had done much, yet had somehow escaped the grip of the arrogance or self-satisfaction a lesser individual might have displayed.

Until that Tuesday evening, most Americans had known J. Robert Oppenheimer only through photos on the front page of newspapers, or the occasional brief newsreel shot. Never before had they been exposed to the full force of the Oppenheimer magnetism, the self-deprecating charm, the intellectual passion, the gift for explication, the downright charisma that had made him a legendary teacher from his early days as a Berkeley professor. For many of those watching him that night, it would prove to have a powerful and overwhelming effect.

Murrow decides it's time to turn the conversation to somewhat more touchy matters. Quite aware of the backlash in the scientific community against the AEC and other government agencies because of Oppenheimer's humiliation, he knows that addressing that issue is a way to skirt around the 800-pound gorilla of the security case without actually mentioning it. "Tell me, is there a very widespread reluctance of scientists in this country to work for the government?"

"No, I don't think so," says Oppenheimer, his manner sober. "This also gets very much distorted when it's talked about in sloganistic terms. See, if you take a scientist who's excited by and interested in new discovery, he may have a problem as to whether he wants to do applied science—and for the government, that's what he would be doing—and that's a, that's a legitimate doubt, and if all the scientists in the country did applied science, it would be terrible for us. I think that scientists like to be called in and asked to advise on how to make the Voice of America a better thing. They like to be called in and asked for their counsel. Everybody likes to be treated as though he knew something."

Murrow doesn't prompt Oppenheimer further. He doesn't need to. Oppenheimer chooses his words carefully, yet his eyes betray the personal pain behind them. He continues evenly, "I suppose that when the government behaves badly in a field you are working close to, and when decisions that look cowardly or vindictive or shortsighted or mean are made, and that's very close to your area, then you get discouraged." A thin smile. "And you may recite George Herbert's poem—'I Will Abroad.' But I think that's human rather than scientific."

Leave it to Oppenheimer to turn a touchy political question into an obscure poetical reference. It is another quintessentially Oppenheimer moment. Herbert was a seventeenth-century English poet and contem-

porary of John Milton, and Oppenheimer was referring to a 1633 work
entitled "The Collar":

> *I struck the board, and cry'd, No more;*
> *I will abroad.*
> *What? Shall I ever sigh and pine?*
> *My lines and life are free; free as the rode;*
> *Loose as the winde, as large as store.*
> *Shall I be still in suit?*
> *Have I no harvest but a thorn*
> *To let me bloud, and not restore*
> *What I have lost with cordiall fruit?*
> *Sure there was wine,*
> *Before my sighs did drie it: there was corn*
> *Before my tears did drown it.*
> *Is the yeare onely lost to me?*
> *Have I no bayes to crown it?*
> *No flowers, no garlands gay? All blasted?*
> *All wasted?*
> *Not so, my heart; but there is fruit,*
> *And thou hast hands.*
> *Recover all thy sigh-blown age*
> *On double pleasures: leave thy cold dispute*
> *Of what is fit, and not. Forsake thy cage,*
> *Thy rope of sands,*
> *Which pettie thoughts have made, and made to thee,*
> *Good cable, to enforce and draw,*
> *And be thy law,*
> *While thou didst wink and wouldst not see,*
> *Away; take heed:*
> *I will abroad.*
> *Call in thy deaths head there: tie up thy fears.*
> *He that forbears*
> *To suit and serve his need,*
> *Deserves his load.*
> *But as I rav'd and grew more fierce and wilde,*
> *At every word,*

Methought I heard one calling, "Childe":
And I reply'd, "My Lord."

For Robert Oppenheimer, the scientist with the soul of a poet, there could be no better or more fitting epitaph to the "cold dispute" of the year just past than Herbert's poem, for a man whose biggest challenge was to "Forsake thy cage, / Thy rope of sands, / Which pettie thoughts have made," to "Recover [his] sigh-blown age." The poem is a classic picture of a soul resigning itself to an undeserved fate with grace and dignity—in Oppenheimer's case, the "collar" of his public disgrace and banishment. Oppenheimer doesn't deign to quote the poem; he knows the reference will be lost on most of his listeners, particularly those eager for some admission of guilt or regret, or for a juicy jeremiad addressed to his tormentors. Yet in his characteristically obscure way, he makes his point and reveals the depths of his pain to the sympathetic cognoscenti among his audience, while denying his enemies the satisfaction of seeing him still bleeding. He doesn't have to mention the name of Lewis Strauss, the Gray Board, or the AEC when he speaks of "decisions that look cowardly or vindictive or shortsighted or mean." Herbert's words say all that is necessary.

Murrow, of course, was never one to avoid controversy, and for those watching who were becoming bored with quiet talk about topology and poetry, his next question was bound to perk up their ears. "Dr. Oppenheimer, are you worried about all the impediments placed in the way of free intercourse, travel and exchange among scientists?"

The gentle scholar suddenly turns fiery, sitting up as if the question had evoked a physical response. "Very much."

Murrow continues, "I think this is true, that had the McCarran Act been enforced, neither Fermi nor Szilard would ever have been permitted to enter the country, which would have been a rather expensive loss." He is referring to the Immigration and Nationality Act of 1952, also known as the McCarran-Walter Act, which had clamped tight restrictions on the immigration and visitations of foreign citizens to the United States and provided for the deportation of immigrants or naturalized citizens who were found to be "subversive." The law had prevented many eminent foreign scientists from teaching and attending scientific conferences and congresses in America.

Oppenheimer responds with an acidic smile. "Perhaps not even Einstein." The smile evaporates. "This is terrible. This is just terrible, and seems a wholly fantastic and grotesque way to meet the threat of espionage. Just an enormous apparatus, surely not well designed, for that, and terrible for those of us who live with it. We are rightly ashamed by the contempt that the Europeans have for us, and we are rightly embarrassed that we can't hold congresses in this country—that we can't—often don't let people go to congresses where they're most wanted. Year after year, we've met in Rochester to discuss the kind of basic physics that . . . There is one man who's the world's greatest in this, and very, very good. Oh well, he sends his deputies and his representatives, but *he* doesn't *come,* and that's not one situation. It's over and over again. This is a scandal."

Murrow deftly switches gears before the show devolves into a political discourse. "Well, sir, apart from running the Institute, what do you do here?"

Oppenheimer could change the subject just as smoothly, in perfect concert with Murrow. "I do two kinds of things. One is to write about what I think I know, hoping that it will be understandable in general, and one is to try to understand physics and talk and work with the physicists and sometimes . . . try to have an idea that may be helpful." He proceeds to treat Murrow to a brief scientific lecture. "The part I really get excited about is just what is called particle physics or atomic physics in its modern sense," Oppenheimer confesses, rising quickly to a blackboard next to the table, which is covered with mathematical symbols. "About why are things the way they are." Animated now, smiling, he begins explaining the "scheme" he had drawn on the board, falling effortlessly into the role of teacher. Suddenly, he is now speaking both to Murrow and to the camera, as if to a class of Berkeley grad students, while a fascinated Murrow looks on. The cameraman obliges with a few close-ups of the board, trying to follow Oppenheimer's gestures as he points to the symbols with an obvious, endearing excitement.

Murrow senses Oppenheimer's enthusiasm and, before things get too obscure, gently interrupts the scientific discourse with a philosophical query. "Tell me, Dr. Oppenheimer, do you ever become frightened at what you are finding out here in this area that can't be measured in either time or space?"

Still standing at the board, Oppenheimer leans on the table, intrigued.

"I—you see, that's a real point. I only get frightened when—and it happens very rarely, I think—I have an idea. That is, what people *find* isn't frightening, but the *understanding* of it sometimes has this quality. I remember a man who was my teacher in Göttingen, who is in Chicago now, James Franck. He says, 'The only way I can tell whether my thoughts are—really have some weight to them is the sense of terror when I think of something new.' Well, so the kind of order that will come out of this"—a nod to the blackboard—"*that* is frightening. But the fact that, this is like walking through the woods and seeing that there are different kinds of flowers and it's all very amusing, and so it is when you try to see why there is necessity to it—why it is this way and no other way. Because all you can do here is guess in the night and correct in the daytime." Oppenheimer sits back down finally. "And you have to try to find the mistakes."

Now Murrow poses the question that he knew would be the first that most people living in the cold war would want to ask an atomic scientist. "Is it true that humans have already discovered a method of destroying humanity?"

Another man might be thrown by the question, but not Oppenheimer. "Well, I suppose that really has always been true," he muses lightly. "You could always beat everybody to death. You mean to do it by inadvertence?"

Murrow nods. "Yes."

Oppenheimer considers, his face turning dark, his voice dropping to a gentle murmur, his manner somber. "Not quite. Not quite." And in case anyone has been comforted by that answer, he adds, in a tone that is no less chilling for its matter-of-factness, "You can certainly destroy enough of humanity so that only the greatest act of faith can persuade you that what's left will be human."

Another long pause. Off Murrow's quizzical look, Oppenheimer continues: "This is a matter on which much, much, much, much more should be known. There's every reason for us to say what we know, and above all, what we *don't* know. The genetic problems, the problems of what might happen in the future to the human species as a result of having radioactivity in the body or having radiation outside—the geneticists don't know enough to be sure of that. We do know what happens if you're near a bomb explosion. We know it from experience and

common sense. The things we know ought to be in the public domain so people are fearful only in the measure in which fear is justified and rational. The things that aren't known should be talked about because one of the ways to get things found out is to have it clear that we don't know the answers. And also one of the ways to give people the kind of responsibility and humanity which we would like or think we have is that they recognize when they don't know something and take their very ignorance into account in their planning."

Oppenheimer apologizes for giving such a long answer, but Murrow waves this off and asks, "In this era that is more threatened and dominated than any previous one by scientists, their decisions, their discoveries—what about the poor uninformed civilian?"

"It isn't the layman that's ignorant," Oppenheimer responds firmly, stating what he considered an obvious fact. "It's *everybody* that's ignorant. The scientist may know a little patch of something, and if he's a humane and intelligent and curious guy, he'll know a few spots from other people's work. He may even be able to read a book. But his condition is a condition of everyone, which is that almost everything that's known to man he doesn't know anything about it at all, or knows it only in a very sketchy way. And that's because it's gotten a bit complicated. The problem of a coherent civilization is the problem of living with ignorance and not being frustrated by it, so that occasionally a man knows two things, and that intersection may be a great event in the history of ideas. Occasionally, a man may think that something is relevant or exciting which no one before thought concerned him professionally. That may change the history of the world. And these are the connections, these virtual connections, these casual and occasional connections which make the only kind of coherence we have. That and affection—that and respect—that and, I suppose, a kind of humanity." Consciously or not, his words echo a speech he had given at Columbia University, broadcast on CBS radio the previous week.

Oppenheimer returns to the difficulties of science interacting with government: "It's possibly not really science. It's pretty much practical application because no one in the government of the United States needs to worry about whether the isotopic spin or the strangeness number are the real invariants of this subatomic work. They need to know sometimes things that are very hard to answer. Can a ballistic rocket

enter the Earth's atmosphere if it's gone a few thousand miles and have a skin that isn't burned up? And so on. They need to know, is there any limit to the size of explosions you can make? They need to know all kinds of technical things. And these are not, in the narrow sense, the frontier of science, but they are technical and complicated. Some will understand one another in one area, some in another, and you get a kind of lacework of coherence. And that requires"—he pauses—"I used the word 'affection' before. For the government, it might be better to say 'trust.' Though I think even for the government, 'affection' wouldn't be a hopeless word."

He smiles. "Take the government itself, which consists of laymen. Take the president or his secretary of state or his secretary of defense. All he can do is be sure that in one way or another, the advice he's being given is subject to criticism. If he gets a statement of how it is—this will cost so many dollars and take so many years, this is impossible—that anyone who has a different view and the professional qualifications that make it interesting, can get to him. And I think that isn't too bad in the parts of the government I have been close to. . . . I think people have been able to tell their stories and that folly has been corrected."

For those working outside of the government, however, freedom of communication and information is even more crucial. "There is really a point that I feel most deeply, and I think I speak really now the voice of my profession, and that is the integrity of communication. The trouble with secrecy isn't that it inhibits science—it could—but in this country it's hardly been used that way. Technical things are really quite widely known and those at the growing tip of any science are so far from prac- tice that the people talk quite freely about them, and should. The trouble with secrecy isn't that it doesn't give the public a sense of participation. The trouble with secrecy is that it denies to the govern- ment itself the wisdom and resources of the whole community, of the whole country, and the only way you can do this is to let almost anyone say what he thinks—to try to give the best synopses, the best popular- izations, the best mediations of technical things that you can, and to let men deny what they think is false, argue what they think is false, you have to have a free and uncorrupted communication.

"This is so the heart of living in a complicated technological world," Oppenheimer goes on. "It is so the heart of freedom that that is why we

are all the time saying, 'Does this really have to be secret?' 'Couldn't you say more about that?' 'Are we really acting in a wise way?' Not because we enjoy chattering, not because we are not aware of the dangers of the world we live in. But because these dangers cannot be met in any other way."

After such an impassioned statement, Murrow can do nothing more but say, "I think you were speaking there not only for your profession but for mine." But he is intrigued by Oppenheimer's assertion that few things are ultimately secret.

"There aren't secrets about the world of nature," Oppenheimer explains, glancing back to the equations on the blackboard. His gaze turns back to Murrow. "There are secrets about the thoughts and intentions of men. Sometimes they are secret because a man doesn't like to know what he's up to if he can avoid it." He joins in Murrow's laugh.

What about another issue that was troubling many good people, nuclear testing? "If enough nations get messing about with hydrogen bombs, is there any danger of contaminating the atmosphere—of the fallout being so heavy that we may damage ourselves without meaning to?"

Oppenheimer can provide only provisional assurances. "I'm not unworried about it," he says, although "I tend still to worry about war rather than peace. I think the scale of things in these experimental undertakings is so vastly smaller and their location so much more secure than what you'd expect if the battle were joined . . . we would do well to worry about the latter before the former."

With that, the televised half hour came to an end. If the broadcast had been allowed to run a bit later, as Paley had wished, viewers would have heard Oppenheimer talk about what he wanted to be when he grew up. "When I was a kid I had three professions in mind. One was science, about which I didn't know much. One was architecture. And one was poetry. I still don't know." He proceeds to comment on the relationship between science and poetry, remarking that there really are no similarities, at least in the sense of what each communicates. He tells an anecdote about his physicist colleague, Paul Dirac, from their student days in Göttingen. "He took me to task one day. . . . he said, 'I don't understand you. You do science. You do physics and you do poetry. I

don't understand that at all. In physics we try to say things that nobody ever knew before in a way that everybody can understand, whereas in poetry . . .' So I think from the denotative side there is no similarity at all. The kind of unity, the kind of evocation, the kind of ambiguity, and the kind of subjectivity which you have to have in poetry are just the things you try to exorcise from science, which should be communicable, unambiguous and all the rest of it."

But Oppenheimer, the scientist-poet, isn't going to stop there. "From the point of view of the human spirit, of the troubles and sorrows and exultations of creation, of course there is a similarity. Poets and scientists understand each other as creators, though the scientist may not like the poetry and the poet will in general regard the science as dull and trivial."

Unfortunately, the unalterable exigencies of television meant that this particular episode of *See It Now* ends with Oppenheimer's dark comparison of rapid human extinction through war with its slow extinction through fallout, rather than his thoughts on science versus poetry. The camera cuts back to Murrow in the studio for his customary closing. He notes that what viewers have just seen has been only "a brief glimpse of a two-and-a-half-hour conversation," adding a remark that once more casts the focus away from Oppenheimer and back on the Institute: "One thing that impressed this reporter at that Institute was that he never heard so many people say—'I don't know.' These men recognize mystery. They welcome it and they wrestle with it." Then, as usual, the signature Murrow sign-off: "Good night and good luck."

One last Alcoa ad, this one on the superiority of aluminum snow shovels, and then, fade out. Except for one final announcement, unusual for the show, that "a one-hour version of this conversation with Dr. Oppenheimer will be made available to any college or university requesting it by the Fund for the Republic." No one realized it yet, but that innocuous statement heralded trouble ahead.

For now, it didn't matter. The show was over. Murrow sat in the darkened studio and allowed himself a deep breath, relaxing for just a moment.

As he and Friendly had so many times before, he wondered about the reaction. Particularly from one tall, thin man back in Princeton.

It finally came in a telegram that arrived a little less than an hour later. "You were right as often. Robert."

* * *

The hearing began calmly enough. The AEC Personnel Security Board consisted of three distinguished men: chairman Gordon Gray, president of the University of North Carolina, and a former secretary of the Army and special assistant to President Truman; Thomas Morgan, businessman, investment banker, and former chairman of Sperry Rand Corporation; and Ward V. Evans, a chemistry professor and prominent conservative. Oppenheimer and his chief counsel, Lloyd K. Garrison, accepted Gray's opening assurances that the proceedings were not adversarial in nature, but would be a fair and balanced inquiry into the truth of the charges facing Oppenheimer. It did not take long before they realized their naïveté.

After Gray read the AEC charges and Oppenheimer's response into the record, Oppenheimer took the stand and spent the first two days recounting his career and general background under Garrison's gentle questioning. Oppenheimer was perfectly composed, the same man who had mesmerized congressional committees, reporters, and the public with his infinite charm, self-assurance, and erudite humor.

By the second day, the story had broken in the national press, causing a predictable uproar. Most of Oppenheimer's friends and colleagues were convinced not only of the foolishness of the entire affair and that he would soon be cleared, but that he would come through the ordeal unscathed. Syndicated newspaper columnists Joseph and Stewart Alsop confidently asserted that "although Dr. Oppenheimer may have been foolish about politics in the 30's and 40's, he is anything but a fool. He is a brilliant and eloquent man, and when he has his day in court he can be expected to hold his own."[2]

Everyone who had ever seen Oppenheimer charm reporters, diplomats, and even the notorious House Un-American Activities Committee would certainly have agreed with the Alsops. But Oppenheimer had never faced an inquisitor quite like the man Strauss had picked to represent the AEC's case. Oppenheimer's true ordeal began with his cross-examination by the chief AEC counsel, Roger Robb, on the third day.

SAC, New York (100-9066)

(Orig. & 1)

January 10, 1955

Director, FBI (100-17828)

RECORDED - 3 100-17828-2130 APR#90-2608

DR. J. ROBERT OPPENHEIMER
INTERNAL SECURITY - R

ALL INFORMATION CONTAINED
HEREIN IS UNCLASSIFIED
DATE 6-17-99

EX-125

 Assistant Attorney General William F. Tompkins, Internal Security Division, Department of Justice has pointed out that following Edward R. Murrow's interview of Dr. Oppenheimer on January 4, 1955, on Murrow's television program, "See It Now," an announcement was made to the effect that copies of the dialogue would be available to universities and other similar institutions by contacting the Fund For The Republic. Assistant Attorney General Tompkins requested the Bureau to obtain a copy of the interview.

 New York is requested to attempt to obtain a copy of the dialogue through its unlisted post office mailing box or through an established reliable source without revealing the identity of the Bureau and without revealing that the Bureau is interested in obtaining a copy of the dialogue.

 This matter must be afforded immediate and expeditious handling..

cc - 1 - Newark (100-31936) (For Information)

cc - 1 - San Francisco (100-3132) (For Information)

cc - 1 - Washington Field (100-12253) (For Information)

NOTE: Fund For The Republic established in 1952 by Ford Foundation and presently headed by Dr. Robert Hutchins, former President of the University of Chicago, who in 1953 publicly remarked, "We are cursed today by a tremendous glorification of the FBI." In December, 1954, Fund For The Republic granted $100,000 to Association of Bar of City of New York to study Federal Loyalty - Security Program. Fund previously authorized a study of Federal, Industrial, and other security cases which study is still pending. Latter study headed by Adam Yarmolinsky, D. C. Attorney with a pro-Communist history. Purpose of study is to evaluate effectiveness of Government Loyalty - Security Program. Not believed desirable to make any direct contact with Fund For The Republic to obtain dialogue. Believed more desirable for New York to discreetly obtain copy as directed in body of letter. (100-391697)

MAILED 8
JAN 1 1955

Tolson
Boardman
Nichols
Belmont
Harbo
Mohr
Parsons
Rosen
Tamm
Sizoo
Winterrowd
Tele. Room
Holloman
Gandy

JEM:jaa:dlt
(7)

J JAN 17 1955

3

The Price of Celebrity

The initial reaction to the Oppenheimer show wasn't quite the Noachian flood that previous *See It Now* programs had generated. The switchboards were duly staffed and ready for the onslaught, but only about eighty calls came into CBS that night, most of them favorable. The real response began a day or so later. It seemed that America's people and press needed a bit of time to digest and contemplate what they had just seen, before offering their thoughts.

When they did, Murrow and Friendly were "amazed," as Friendly later wrote. "All of Oppenheimer's fragile, sensitive quality had been transmitted over the television tube. In the scientific community, it was as though a stuck window had been opened. As someone said, too optimistically, 'Egghead is no longer a dirty word.' "[1]

That was one viewpoint. Another was that CBS had provided thirty minutes of national television airtime to a man that most of the country didn't trust, at best, or thought was the closest thing to an outright traitor, at worst. "Millions of Americans never knew the difference between a 'security risk' and a 'loyalty risk,' if indeed there was intended to be a difference," notes Murrow biographer Alexander Kendrick. Oppenheimer "was still 'controversial,' indeed to many 'that traitor.' And Murrow, as he had been the man who 'attacked' McCarthy, had now become the man who 'defended' Oppenheimer."[2]

The earliest press reaction zeroed in not on Oppenheimer's proud

recounting of the Institute's accomplishments or his philosophical musings, but on his politics. "Alien Act Scored by Oppenheimer: He Charges McCarran Law Is 'Fantastic Way' to Meet the Threat of Espionage," read a *New York Times* headline the next day. Oppenheimer "was caustic in his attack on the McCarran Act procedures . . . the scientist pressed strongly for free communication between men instead of barriers that barred exchanges of knowledge," said *The Times,* going on to sum up the major points Oppenheimer had raised the previous evening.[3] With *The Times* devoting more than half of the article to Oppenheimer's McCarran criticisms, anyone who hadn't been watching CBS the night before might have missed the fact that those comments had filled only a couple of minutes of the actual broadcast. As might be expected, European newspapers also emphasized Oppenheimer's comments on the McCarran Act and the restrictions the United States placed on foreign scientists.

A day or so later, more thoughtful reviews of the Murrow show began to appear. *The New Yorker*'s take was characteristically literary and eloquent. "When it was all over, I must confess, I was overwhelmed by the beauty and candor of the principal speaker, and by the courage of Mr. Murrow in pushing ahead with his project and seeing it through," wrote Philip Hamburger. "Mr. Murrow seems to have more courage—or, to use the midtown term, guts—than many of his brethren, and that alone may be the explanation of why he interviewed Dr. Oppenheimer before anyone else did. In any event, the half hour was thoroughly engrossing—even hypnotic—and it will be a long time before I forget it."

For Hamburger, Oppenheimer came across as "a true study, I should think, in genius—tense, dedicated, deeper than deep, somewhat haunted, uncertain, calm, confident, and full, full, full of knowledge, not only of particles and things but of men and motives, and of the basic humanity that may be the only savior we have in this strange world he and his colleagues have discovered." Hamburger went on to quote Oppenheimer at length, illuminating the poetic and literary grace of his words, and concluded: "And there were a great many other notable things said by Dr. Oppenheimer, who is, incidentally, a security risk."[4]

One of the most interesting aspects of the response to the Murrow broadcast is that to a large extent, it involved a subset of journalists

who until then had never had an opportunity to deal with or comment on matters Oppenheimer: television critics. Throughout most of the comings and goings of Oppenheimer's public life, his pronouncements and the controversies that followed him had been the exclusive province of the hard-news journalists and political columnists. Now, writers who rarely had a chance to ruminate on anything more weighty than *Father Knows Best* had been given a subject far more profound, a new television personality far from Milton Berle, a real and legitimate poet of science rather than a Percy Dovetonsils. Most of them seemed awestruck by the experience, yet their professional sensibilities as media critics allowed them to appreciate the stylistic subtleties of the Oppenheimer broadcast in ways that other commentators were ill-equipped to comprehend.

"I've waited several days for the impact of last Tuesday's 'See It Now' program to fade. It hasn't faded," noted *The Washington Post*'s TV critic, Lawrence Laurent. "Dr. Oppenheimer, no matter how you feel about his politics, possesses a wonderfully expressive face and a fine manner for TV. He came across to this viewer as a man of great humility and wisdom. . . . many of us had the same general reaction to the telecast: That in spite of mighty achievements and conquests of nature, the creature that walks this sphere and calls himself Man is a puny thing."[5]

John Crosby of the *Chicago Sun-Times* observed, "It is possible that the impact of J. Robert Oppenheimer's philosophy may be far greater since he became a security case than it was before. Certainly very powerful forces have come to his defense. I doubt that Edward R. Murrow would have devoted 28 minutes on a national network to Oppenheimer if the security question had not blown him into the headlines again. There are certainly advantages to being controversial." Be that as it may, Crosby agreed that the interview "showed the mind, personality and philosophy of a remarkable man. It demonstrated . . . that a guy who is brilliant at physics is likely to be pretty bright in all other departments, and I guess all of us were greatly impressed by his gift for a phrase, his insight into humanity and his great simplicity. . . . what we got was a portrait of a man who persistently spoke of his scientific colleagues as philosophers and statesmen, who often used the words affection and trust and humanity—and who exemplified all those things."[6]

One TV critic that Murrow and Friendly always followed closely was

Jack Gould of *The New York Times*, who had been an enthusiastic supporter of Murrow's McCarthy broadcasts and other controversial efforts. He didn't disappoint them this time, although his remarks were more balanced than those of some other critics. After noting that "the broadcast represented the first time that the controversial physicist . . . had been afforded a coast-to-coast television hearing," Gould pointed out that "not so many months ago such a telecast would have been certain to raise quite a storm. Not so last Tuesday. The Columbia Broadcasting System had the switchboards manned in the event of an avalanche but after the program only about eighty telephone calls—sixty favorable and twenty unfavorable—were received. By TV's standards that is a negligible response." When he wrote that line, Gould had no way of knowing how premature a judgment that would prove to be.

"Before the cameras Dr. Oppenheimer is unquestionably an absorbing figure," Gould observed, echoing his colleagues. "His lean, almost ascetic face and his frequent poetic turn of phrase arrested the viewer's attention. . . . fully as interesting as what Dr. Oppenheimer said was the way he said it. The pauses as he groped for the desired phrase, the look in his eye or his pensive reflection were a TV cameo of a mind at work."

As usual, Gould had zeroed in precisely on the heart of the matter, the core truth of the show's impact. It wasn't anything Oppenheimer said, or any of the controversies it may have caused, that resulted in the telecast's great effectiveness. It was the elegant, perfectly calibrated, fully realized match of the peculiar qualities of the still-new medium of television and Oppenheimer's own personal quirks of expression, appearance, and interpersonal nuance.

In 1955, the very nature of contemporary TV technology, with its inevitably huge cameras, bulky sound equipment, and hot, blinding lights, none of which were easily portable, dictated that the show would be little more than two men sitting in a room, talking. There could be no following Oppenheimer around from place to place for a "day in the life"–style cinema verité portrait. Viewers would see and hear only the two men, the tone and inflections of their voices, the subtle movements of their faces as they smiled or frowned, their gestures as they lit a pipe or pointed to a blackboard. The Oppenheimer show was slow and stately in its flow, without jarring commercial in-

terruptions to diminish its mood and thoughtful atmosphere. By the standards of twenty-first-century TV, it was the most boring half hour of television imaginable.

But to the 1955 audience, television was still a new and fascinating thing. And this enigmatic man, Oppenheimer, in close-up, with his preternatural gifts of communication that had enthralled coeds and congressmen, quietly speaking about philosophy and fallout between puffs on a pipe, was wholly in his element. Murrow's cameras focused all of Oppenheimer's powers of connection, the steady gaze, the soft but powerful voice, the precisely measured gestures, the subtle facial expressions of his mind at work, into a laser beam of personality that made nearly every person watching that Tuesday night feel that he was speaking to, lecturing to, confiding in not Edward Murrow, but him or her personally.

That was the singular power of the television medium, worked on an audience to which it was still completely new and awe-inspiring. The "unblinking eye" of television, as a reporter once called it, revealed all and hid nothing. In the case of the Oppenheimer-Murrow interview, it was the perfect marriage of style and content: the intimacy of the TV frame and the Oppenheimer charisma.

Even *Life* magazine paid tribute to the sheer power of Oppenheimer's face on the screen: in its "World's Week" news section, it presented five shots of Oppenheimer's face in various expressions, with the corresponding quotes underneath. His face, his words: no more was needed.[7]

Oppenheimer was always a man who knew how to perform when necessary, with an instinctive flair for the right words and gestures at the right time to the right audience. Perhaps he sensed again that here was another opportunity, and somehow subconsciously realized that television would be the ideal conduit, the stage best suited to his communicative gifts.

One wonders whether the occasions on which those gifts failed him spectacularly, most notably at his security hearing, would have turned out quite differently if he'd had an audience to play to. After his performance on the Murrow show, it's tempting to speculate that, had his hearing been televised, the press and public reaction to his suspension and perhaps even the outcome of the case would have been much more

favorable to him. Just as witnessing on the TV screen the extent of Joseph McCarthy's vile methods and heedless cruelty made the public realize his flaws and the danger he presented, perhaps seeing Oppenheimer's sensitivity and humanity as exposed during his security hearing would have evoked wider sympathy and understanding on his behalf.

Whatever speculations of this sort one might wish to entertain, the Murrow interview did prove one undeniable truth: long before the concept became common coin, Oppenheimer was a natural on the television tube.

But his powerful impact through the TV screen worked both ways. For some, it simply reinforced their own negative opinions. The very directness of Oppenheimer's television persona allowed viewers to see what they wanted to see. The gentle, thoughtful pauses, the slow consideration of his words before speaking, could also readily be interpreted as evasive and mealymouthed, if one were so inclined. Even his frequently shifting gaze, no doubt partly due to the distracting movements of Murrow's crew outside of the frame, could be characterized as "shifty-eyed" and thus suspicious. Even if one didn't choose to view Oppenheimer's on-camera demeanor in such a negative light, the lack of any acknowledgment of his "security-risk" status was in itself an admission of guilt and nefarious intent for some viewers.

"Don't look now, but a concerted campaign is under way to apply a coat of whitewash to Dr. J. Robert Oppenheimer and clean up his appearance to the public eye," declared right-wing columnist Fulton Lewis Jr.,* a man Joseph Alsop once called "Joe McCarthy's chief journalistic incense swinger." Lewis continued, "Murrow once again abandoned his carefully-nurtured facade of impartiality by devoting his entire half-hour to interviewing Oppenheimer and trying to portray him as an unvindictive, benign and benevolent scientist-scholar."[8]

For Lewis and other right-wing commentators, the mere fact that Murrow had put Oppenheimer on national television was offensive enough. Even without any overt remarks intended to defend or redeem himself, Oppenheimer's sheer presence on television gave him what

* Lewis's personal legal counsel was none other than Roger Robb, the AEC chief lawyer at Oppenheimer's hearing.

some considered an undeserved legitimacy and authority, something that should obviously be denied anyone who was a proven "security risk."

Oppenheimer consciously avoided public comment on the frays that the broadcast had generated in the press, but he wasn't able to escape the heavy downpour of letters and telegrams that inundated him in Princeton. Some, of course, were from friends, colleagues, and professional acquaintances. Lloyd Garrison, the lead attorney in his security case (and who had since become Oppenheimer's official buffer for all inquiries on the case and related matters since then) wrote, "I sat in on your television appearance and was moved and touched by it. I'm glad that you spoke out against the McCarran Act, and what you said about scientists and the government seemed to me just right. Indeed, the whole performance was right and true and nobly spoken. I have met literally countless people who watched and listened to you, and each in his own way expressed to me something of the emotion which I have tried to express above."

Representative Chet Holifield from the Joint Committee on Atomic Energy assured Oppenheimer, "Someday, this whole system of 'security' evaluation will be changed, and a man will be judged by that which he does, rather than that by which he might believe or those with whom he might choose to associate. I hope to take part in the process of restoring, once again, the individual liberties and freedoms which I believe to have been denied during the past few years of hysteria."

Another friend observed, "The personality of the 'whole man' carried conviction with it as it came over the air waves. And the total lack of venom, the high restraint of any bitter feeling after the soul-trying experience you have been through was, I thought, beyond praise."

There were also letters from people that Oppenheimer didn't know at all, some from individuals or organizations requesting transcripts or film or audiotape copies of the broadcast (which Oppenheimer's secretaries duly referred to CBS or the Fund for the Republic), and some from ordinary citizens who had been profoundly moved and impressed by the man that Edward R. Murrow had brought into their homes, and felt the need to express their feelings and thoughts to that man.

From a Wisconsin housewife: "In confused times like these, it is indeed an inspiration to be able to hear quiet, free speech from a very

great man. The very fact that there are still such big, humane people in the world capable of rising above pettiness is a very quieting thing. . . . we all went to bed feeling the world was a better place than we had given it credit for being."

A woman from Colorado: "Civilization will survive and go on to the betterment of humankind so long as there are scholars, men of clear thinking, integrity—and humor, such as you. . . . Thank you so very, very much for taking time from your private life to come out among us, and give us encouragement and new incentive; and confidence in the future, in ourselves, and in the eventual sanity and peace man must grow into."

From a New York man: "Unfortunately most people visualize a physicist as a cold blooded scientist—your humility on Tuesday night's program proved otherwise. While listening to you I thought—'I am really listening to a beautiful sermon.'"

Oppenheimer received hundreds and hundreds of such adulatory and effusive letters from all over the United States. But while the vast majority of the correspondence was positive, there was also the disgruntled minority of naysayers. One postcard read: "Sir: After seeing you on Mr. Murrow's show. It only proves what you said to Mr. Murrow. People like you know very little about the outside. As little as you know you put your two cents in for your leftist feelings. The only faith you have is in socialism. Godless people like yourself caused European countries to turn against us. You should be in a cage not a university."[9] There were also the misguided missives of correspondents who felt compelled to enlighten Oppenheimer on their personal theories of ultimate salvation, absolute scientific truths that had naturally been "ignored" or "suppressed" by nameless evil forces, or merely incomprehensible ravings, of the sort that every famous individual inevitably receives.

Among the many noteworthy public figures who took a special interest in Oppenheimer's appearance on See It Now was none other than Lewis Strauss, who considered requesting the opportunity to appear on See It Now himself as a sort of counterbalance to Oppenheimer, and was also none too pleased with the idea of the Fund for the Republic distributing the film of the show all over the country. Strauss had already been scheduled to appear a little over a week after the Oppenheimer

program on Murrow's other television show, *Person to Person,* which featured interviews with various celebrities, movie stars, and other public figures, but after the Oppenheimer broadcast he requested a month's postponement.

As Murrow later told Fund for the Republic director Paul G. Hoffman, he hadn't bothered to offer Strauss a chance to "rebut" Oppenheimer directly, because he thought Oppenheimer hadn't said anything that called for any such response from Strauss, but still, he was happy to bring Strauss onto *See It Now* if the aggrieved admiral really thought it was necessary. Strauss apparently reconsidered, and made his originally scheduled *Person to Person* appearance later, without any "rebuttals" to Oppenheimer.[10]

Murrow and Friendly stayed in touch with Oppenheimer after the show, keeping him apprised of the response, which, Jack Gould's early reports notwithstanding, continued to be massive. Friendly told Oppenheimer's secretary in a phone call that "to date they have tabulated some 2500 letters, of which about 35 were anti, and these mostly crank. The usual proportion of mail response to a See It Now show is 8 or 9 pro—one anti."

Although he had, of course, seen the original broadcast, Oppenheimer had yet to see the longer edit that was to be distributed by the Fund for the Republic, and Murrow and Friendly invited Oppenheimer to come to lunch in New York not only so that he could see the show, but so that they could also "tell him some of the interesting things they have heard from Washington, which they think [he] will find very heartening."[11]

Oppenheimer took them up on their offer at the end of January. Murrow's friend, the poet Carl Sandburg, happened to be in town. As Friendly recalled, Sandburg "insisted on meeting the physicist, whom he greatly admired, and viewing the film with him. Afterward we took the professor and the poet across the city for a special luncheon with Bill Paley. I think each of us found it a fascinating experience—no one more so than the chairman."[12]

For both Oppenheimer and Murrow, the luncheon was a fittingly distinguished coda to a rewarding and remarkable episode in both their lives. But nothing ended neatly or peacefully for Robert Oppenheimer anymore. As the controversy over the *See It Now* interview stubbornly

continued, his professional standing and integrity were about to be challenged on a new and unexpected front.

<p style="text-align:center">* * *</p>

An assistant U.S. attorney who had litigated twenty-three murder cases, Robb was a wily and experienced courtroom gladiator who relished the battle. And he had another decided advantage: an emergency "Q" security clearance granted by the AEC. Robb enjoyed access to the vast store of classified documents, reports, and other material that had been compiled on Oppenheimer over years of surveillance. Although Garrison had applied for clearance over two weeks before the hearing, the AEC turned him down, saying there was no time to conduct the requisite investigation. Yet Robb had earlier been investigated and cleared in only eight days. Without clearance, Garrison not only would be unable to examine vital evidence, but would actually be forced to leave the hearing room whenever classified material was being discussed—leaving his own client unrepresented. Oppenheimer was not even able to review his own official papers, since they had been removed from his office at the Institute for Advanced Study in Princeton as soon as his clearance had been revoked.

Not only did Robb enjoy this unfettered access to classified material—including up-to-date FBI surveillance reports and bugging transcripts that kept him fully apprised of every legal move his opponents were considering—so did the Gray Board. And they had been thoroughly briefed on it all by Robb personally for an entire week before the hearing, in sessions that Garrison was barred from attending. As the members of the board sat at their table listening to testimony, each had before him a large black dossier filled with classified documents that were to be used as evidence against Oppenheimer. Even before one word of testimony had been heard, they had been immersed in a sea of secret FBI reports, anonymous witness statements, surveillance reports, internal AEC memos, and various other material, all assembled with a view toward discrediting Oppenheimer. The Gray Board began the hearing not as impartial, objective judges who would be encountering evidence fresh and without prejudice or preconceptions, but as men whose minds had already been persuasively tilted against the subject of their inquiry by a ruthless prosecutor.

Robb was acutely aware of his privileged position, and he wasted no time in taking advantage of it. He began by tripping up Oppenheimer on various dates, the wording of casual statements made a decade earlier, and precise sequences of

events, forcing Oppenheimer into a series of self-contradictions as the scientist struggled to answer questions strictly on memory while Robb had the facts at his fingertips. A favorite tactic that Robb used repeatedly was pinning a witness down to a specific date or statement through dogged questioning, then producing or quoting from a document—often one the witness had never seen——a fact that directly contradicted the witness, thus turning a shaky memory into an implication of dishonesty. He used this trick most effectively when questioning Oppenheimer on perhaps the most damaging single episode of Oppenheimer's career: the "Chevalier incident."

FEDERAL BUREAU OF INVESTIGATION

FORM No. 1
THIS CASE ORIGINATED AT SAN FRANCISCO

SJ 105-2819

T-4 and T-5 advised that they noted no unusual or suspicious activities on the part of the subject or his wife.

T-6, of known reliability, advised SA ROBERT L. ZIMMERMANN on March 4, 1955, that the subject and his wife arrived in St. Croix, Virgin Islands, on February 19, 1955, aboard the chartered boat "Windsholm." According to T-6, the "Windsholm" had sailed from St. John, Virgin Islands, on February 18, 1955, and made a stop at Peter Island, British Virgin Islands, enroute to St. Croix.

T-6 stated the OPPENHEIMERS stayed at the Commanche Hotel, Christiansted, St. Croix, Virgin Islands, from February 19, 1955, to February 22, 1955, when they departed for San Juan, Puerto Rico, via Caribbean Atlantic Airlines.

According to T-6, the OPPENHEIMERS were interested in purchasing some property in St. Croix but were experiencing difficulty in obtaining what they wanted. He advised that they were ultimately considering purchasing property on Peter Island.

T-6 advised that while in St. Croix the OPPENHEIMERS remained at the hotel. He stated that Mrs. OPPENHEIMER was drinking heavily and other guests at the hotel were horrified at her conduct. He stated that on one occasion she was so intoxicated that she fell into the hotel swimming pool. He advised that the subject conducted himself soberly and at times had his hands full keeping Mrs. OPPENHEIMER in check. He advised that neither Mr. nor Mrs. OPPENHEIMER looked good physically.

T-6 stated that the OPPENHEIMERS indicated they intended to return to St. Croix during the summer for approximately six weeks and that they would bring their children. In this respect he advised that they made inquiries concerning chartering the yacht "Commanche" for a cruise during part of that time.

T-6 advised that as far as he knew, the OPPENHEIMERS avoided any discussion relating to the subject's security status.

- R U C -

- 3 -

4

The Bleak Face of Unhumanity

Not long after that genial luncheon in New York, Oppenheimer and his wife left Princeton for temporary refuge in the Virgin Islands, which had become a favorite Oppenheimer retreat in the previous several years. If a decisive escape from the past year's tribulations and his unique exile wasn't possible, a brief periodic respite from it all was still a mercy that the world afforded Oppenheimer— even if he was not completely free from his keepers. He would return to Princeton to find himself in the eye of several intersecting new storms that would keep his name in the papers and his life in an uproar.

Judging from the flood of requests for the hour-long version of the Oppenheimer-Murrow interview the Fund for the Republic received from schools, universities, community groups, and even commercial theaters after the CBS broadcast, it appeared that his being a security risk hadn't diminished the public's curiosity, if not sympathy, regarding Robert Oppenheimer. The sample of the Oppenheimer charm they had witnessed on the Murrow show hadn't been enough; people wanted to hear more of his words and soak up more of his wisdom. They wanted to see the long version of the interview, which, most notably, included more comments by Oppenheimer on his Institute colleagues and their work; his unedited minilecture on particle physics, much more compre-hensible in its full glory than the severely chopped version in the final broadcast; and his admission that for relaxation, he liked to "talk, ride,

and sail. . . . I have in the past done a little painting and I like the sea and the desert and the mountains." Oppenheimer the teacher was being writ large, no longer confined to a single classroom or lecture hall, but being brought to more venues and more eager students than he could possibly have encountered face-to-face. The film that Murrow and Friendly had put together made the rounds for Oppenheimer, touring the country as his proxy, as if he were an intellectual rock star.

In fact, his infamy as an official object of distrust only served to increase public interest and involvement all across the country, particularly in those communities where outraged patriots protested and tried to ban showings of the film. The stalwarts who considered Oppenheimer a traitor, a subject unfit for public display and acclaim, damaging to the health of the Republic, might not have been able to stop Murrow's broadcast, but they could certainly keep the film of this Commie sympathizer from poisoning the minds and hearts of their hometowns and their children.

The first notable skirmish came in March, in Pleasantville, just north of New York City. The local Americans for Democratic Action chapter organized a showing of the Oppenheimer film in the local high school, a plan that mightily offended Pleasantville's American Legion chapter, which filed indignant protests with the board of education requesting it to block the screening. But the school board allowed the screening to proceed as scheduled to an audience of about two hundred people, without incident and without the fall of the nation, or at least Westchester County, to Communist forces.[1]

Similar protests arose in other communities, but the curiosity of the local citizens to see Oppenheimer on film tended to overcome them. The response to the hour-long version of the interview was at least as enthusiastic as the reaction to the original broadcast version, if not more so. The American Legion continued its campaign to block the film wherever possible, with a notable lack of success. The screenings of the film went on throughout the spring and into the summer across the country.

Oppenheimer may have provided another cause célèbre for the pundits and patriots to scrap over, but the impact of the film failed to be blunted or diminished. Requests for it continued through 1955 and well beyond. Apparently, the Oppenheimer mystique trumped the best

intentions of those dedicated souls trying to prevent the scientist from reemerging from the shadows.

The uproar over the Murrow show may have been distracting or disturbing for Oppenheimer, but in a practical sense, it didn't affect him directly. He was still free to sail in the Virgin Islands or work quietly in his Institute office while the newspaper pundits debated the motives of the Fund for the Republic or the subversive qualities of the broadcast. But upon his return from the islands, he found a more personal threat to his career and livelihood waiting on his desk. It was, as he called it, a "sad little letter" from a friend, Dr. Edwin A. Uehling of the University of Washington Department of Physics.

Some months earlier, Uehling had extended a formal invitation for Oppenheimer to deliver a series of physics lectures at the university. Abruptly, those plans had been canceled by the university president, Dr. Henry Schmitz. "President Schmitz refuses to approve of the good arrangements which you and I have discussed," wrote Uehling. "The basis of his refusal is a vague fear that some elements of the public would react unfavorably. . . . You can probably guess that I and others are greatly disillusioned. Until now we thought that we were members of a university. Now we are not so sure. We look like a university, but in some respects at least we behave like a trade school."[2]

In explanation, Schmitz would say only that "bringing [Oppenheimer] here at this time would not be in the best interests of the university." He refused to explain further, but the implications were all too clear. Oppenheimer was trouble. He was controversial. Why invite embarrassing publicity and charges of harboring a "security risk"?

It had been bad enough that Oppenheimer had been ousted from his position as a government adviser. But now, for the first time, he was being barred from his life's work, the teaching and practice of physics. Was he to be cast out of the only remaining realm of respect and admiration that remained for him?

If Schmitz believed that disinviting Oppenheimer would preserve the peace and sanctity of his campus, his students and faculty soon proved him wrong. Schmitz's decision caused an immediate and resounding surge of protest and condemnation that rippled from the halls of the University of Washington to eventually engulf the entire American scientific

community. A local television station declining to broadcast the hour-long version of the Murrow-Oppenheimer interview could be dismissed as simply gutless and weasely; but preventing one of the world's top scientists from speaking, not on politics but simply on the subject of his own expertise, science, was nothing less than an infringement of the students' rights and a direct attack on academic freedom.

Adding to the unpleasantness was the inevitable publicity. Anything involving more controversy about Robert Oppenheimer was press catnip. "Oppenheimer Barred," intoned *The New York Times,* although in small type, as if to imply that such a thing was becoming so routine that it was hardly worthy of great notice.

Initially, Schmitz didn't deign to give a direct reason for his decision, other than the "best interests of the university" excuse. But, quoted in a sympathetic editorial in the *Seattle Post-Intelligencer* soon after the announcement, he explained that he had resolved to reject Oppenheimer after reading the transcript of the security hearing.

Or at least part of it. Schmitz described reading the transcript up to the point where Oppenheimer had admitted lying to security officers because he had been an "idiot." Apparently, that was enough for Schmitz, who didn't go on to read the remaining eight hundred–plus pages of the hearing. Schmitz, said the *Post-Intelligencer,* had "found immediately that Dr. Oppenheimer is an admitted liar on a security matter. . . . Dr. Schmitz did not continue his investigation beyond this point."[3] Perhaps Schmitz simply didn't feel like finishing what is admittedly a very long and difficult book.

Uproar among the students followed. Two hundred of them from the university's mathematics, physics, and chemistry departments signed a letter to Oppenheimer: "We wish to express our deepest disappointment and regrets that, due to the unfortunate decision of the University's administration, we will be deprived of the honor and privilege of your presence this spring. We are very sorry to lose the opportunity to have such a distinguished and highly accomplished guest, and further hope that our school has not been the source of any personal embarrassment to you."[4]

Meanwhile, the university's student newspaper echoed the sentiment. "Oppenheimer was engaged to come to Washington and talk physics—not sociology, not geopolitics, not ideologies. No federal board, no other

agency, no man has challenged his eminence in his professional field. Dr. Schmitz has made a grave—perhaps a dangerous—error. His decision should be reviewed at once by the University's Board of Regents."[5]

The board of regents did in fact review the decision, and upheld it, despite the official protests of several student organizations and the unofficial protests of the students themselves, some of whom even hanged Schmitz in effigy on the campus quadrangle. A delegation of students marched on the state capitol in Olympia, where Governor Arthur Langlie agreed to meet with a small group to hear their grievances. Langlie told them that he was neutral in the matter and it was up to Schmitz, but he couldn't help scolding them for "being divisive when they should be uniting against Communism."[6]

The press and student reaction, however, proved to be only the first rumblings of the earthquake. More serious for the university and the academic and scientific communities in general were the reactions of faculty and scientists, both in Washington State and elsewhere. Some of Oppenheimer's onetime Los Alamos colleagues had settled at the University of Washington after the war, and they were among the first to oppose Schmitz. In a statement he had submitted to the local papers but which they had refused to publish, physicist Seth Neddermeyer asked: "Do we have a University, whose aims are the seeking and teaching of universal knowledge, or a medieval school which is more concerned with preserving existing prejudice than with discovering the truth? . . . It is difficult for me to believe that a university which condemns any man because he has held unpopular opinions can be an effective vehicle for truth and reason."[7] Other University of Washington faculty members, including Uehling and John Manley, another friend and Los Alamos colleague, made their displeasure publicly known.

For the University of Washington, the bad publicity and indignation of its own faculty and students were bad enough. Then it got worse. An academic boycott of the university began to coalesce, beginning with a few scattered, independent scholars refusing to follow through with scheduled appearances, then threatening to escalate into outright censure of the institution. By March the university found prestigious scientific conferences it planned to host beginning to fall apart. Seven scientists who were to lead a planned biochemistry symposium banded

together to boycott the university, telling Schmitz in a joint letter that "it seems to us that you have clearly placed the University of Washington outside the community of scholars."[8] Their protest and the subsequent collapse of the symposium made national headlines.

The Oppenheimer ban also made the *Congressional Record* that month. Senator Richard Neuberger of Oregon took the floor to commend his state's educational authorities for not bowing to pressure to cancel Oppenheimer's upcoming Oregon lecture tour and offering some thoughts on academic freedom. "When pressure can bring about cancellation of the lecture of an eminent scientist, then every American has lost a little bit of his freedom," Neuberger declared, before reading into the record a selection of the newspaper editorials condemning Schmitz's action.[9]

On March 18, faculty member Dr. Stanley Bennett wrote a lengthy letter to the university vice president, H. P. Everest, warning that "if the boycott and other adverse external influences be sufficiently protracted and sufficiently intense, we can expect an alarming decline in our University, perhaps even approaching a disintegration."[10] But Schmitz and the board of regents still refused to change their minds, although a special committee was set up to review the university's policies and procedures of inviting guest lecturers.

And then, anticlimactically, the waves of indignation and outrage petered out and exhausted themselves. The entire uproar faded away as rapidly as it had arisen. President Schmitz survived being burned in effigy and continued as president until his retirement in 1958.

A major reason for the fizzling out of the controversy was no doubt Oppenheimer's refusal to be drawn into it personally. His only public comment on the matter was that "it seems to me that the University has embarrassed itself." Privately, however, especially to his friends who happened to work at the university, he was rather less flippant. "If in any way I can help to undo the damage, any appropriate way, you know you can count on me," he wrote to John Manley. "If I had had any notion at all that we were headed for a flap, and a public, noisy and rather disagreeable one at that, I would certainly have tried to stop it." He added, "Outfits like the ADA and ACLU have been pestering me to come [to Seattle] both before and after Schmitz' decision; but this is not my dish."[11]

Oppenheimer had been perfectly content to remain on the sidelines,

watching the burning controversies stoked by his name and reputation from a discreet distance, without making any serious effort to either fan the flames or quench them. He was weary of the struggle, and knew that whatever he might do would only make such matters even more bitter and destructive. And in any event, he had other concerns, such as preparing to visit the many places where his name was still honored and his presence still welcomed. He left on April 17 for a West Coast trip to Oregon and then California on a flight that, ironically enough, took him through Seattle for a change of planes the following morning. During the layover at the Seattle airport, he was joined for coffee by several University of Washington physics faculty (and the wife of Edwin Uehling, who couldn't make the coffee klatch himself due to an early class that morning).

Inevitably, Oppenheimer attracted some reporters, who wanted to know if he would still be willing to visit the University of Washington if he were invited again sometime. "Certainly I would come," he said. "No one is interested in a repetition of the events in the past four months." Then the reporters had some shocking news for Oppenheimer: Albert Einstein had just died. Shaken, Oppenheimer managed to find words for the press. "For all scientists and most men, this is a day of mourning. Einstein was one of the greats of all ages."[12]

Einstein and Oppenheimer, in fact, had never been close, and there had always been some fundamental differences in their respective outlooks on philosophy, politics, and even physics. But there was no denying Einstein's stature, or the depth of his loss to both science and the world at large. Earlier in the year, Enrico Fermi had also passed away, and Oppenheimer didn't fail to note the devastating impact of the dual loss on his own field. "Physics," he observed sadly, "isn't getting any easier."

Later in the spring, theater critic Brooks Atkinson picked up on a peculiar darkness in the zeitgeist. "There seems to be something in the spiritual climate today that makes loneliness a universal theme," he wrote. "It underlies a good deal of the writing for the stage—*Cat on a Hot Tin Roof, Bus Stop, Tea and Sympathy.*" Atkinson cited Robert Oppenheimer as an avatar and a prophet of this new mood of loneliness. "In his speech at Columbia University last winter, Dr. J. Robert

Oppenheimer consciously discussed the theme of loneliness in the lives of nuclear physicists who work in an intellectual world they cannot share with the layman. For one reason or another, individuals everywhere seem to have an increasing sensation of not participating in the life of the community. The great forces that are controlling their lives and that have already set the course of history are alien to most individuals and largely unknown. In the mystique of today, loneliness is a relevant subject."[13]

Still weathering his first year of exile, Oppenheimer was facing that loneliness on several different fronts. Persona non grata to his own government, the object of almost mystical adulation and fascination, as well as self-righteous contempt, from the public and press, he could still find solace in the Institute, the life of the mind, the alternate world of academia with its own standards of value and respect that had nothing to do with security criteria.

Although he tended to keep close to himself his own thoughts and feelings about his new status and his new life of exalted exile, hints of a new awareness and perhaps a sober, hard-won wisdom occasionally emerged, not just in his carefully worded public pronouncements but, less guardedly, in his more personal communications. When several students from Amherst College wrote to him for help on an American studies project dealing with the government security program, Oppenheimer, as was his usual practice, demurred: "I have avoided, quite purposefully, any discussion with strangers about any aspects of my security case, and I think I should not make an exception even for you, who are students."

And yet, he felt compelled to add one observation in his return letter. Among other things, the students had asked about men in responsible positions conforming themselves to public expectations. Perhaps because he was struggling so closely at the time with the question of the public's expectations and perceptions of himself, Oppenheimer couldn't help answering. "It may not be the obligation of a man in a position of responsibility to conform his actions, and his words about his actions, to what the public desires; but if he wishes to play an effective part in politics, it is clear that he must either conform himself to what the public desires, or persuade the public to accept what he is."[14]

It was an intriguing statement coming from Oppenheimer, perhaps

an insight into his state of mind concerning not only the Murrow show and the reaction to it, but also something that had recently occurred in Washington concerning a colleague, John von Neumann, the brilliant mathematician and Institute for Advanced Study faculty member. As Oppenheimer's influence in the Washington power circles had been stripped away from him, von Neumann's star had been steadily rising.

After the conclusion of the Oppenheimer case in mid-1954, several of Lewis Strauss's fellow AEC commissioners resigned (one, the dissenting Henry DeWolf Smyth, directly because of his disgust over the matter), and Strauss was faced with the need to find replacements. One of the men he recommended to Eisenhower was von Neumann, who had close ties to both Oppenheimer and Strauss. No one doubted his qualifications for the job. He already had a top-secret clearance as a member of the AEC's General Advisory Committee and had worked on the hydrogen bomb program, using his computer at the Institute to make the intricate calculations needed to build the bomb. A quick and easy confirmation by the Senate seemed likely.

But there were two slight problems. First, von Neumann had connections with Oppenheimer, a declared security risk, so there was again that pesky problem of association with "questionable" elements. Also, back in 1946, von Neumann had written a letter of support for a former student accused of conspiracy in espionage. "No one inside the establishment seemed concerned about von Neumann's personal integrity, much less his loyalty, but the potential for a second Oppenheimer case was frightening," wrote Richard G. Hewlett and Jack M. Holl in their history of the AEC.[15]

Strauss found himself in an ironic quandary. Here was someone he fully supported and wanted on his team who was being questioned for the same reasons that Strauss had used to remove Oppenheimer from the government only months earlier. He pointed out that not only had von Neumann's former student been found innocent in that espionage case, but von Neumann had also been cleared by the government for many years, and no new derogatory information had surfaced since his clearance to taint his file further. Strauss seemed oblivious of the fact that precisely the same objections had been offered in defense of J. Robert Oppenheimer, and he had summarily rejected them. But perhaps he didn't find in von Neumann the same "fundamental defects of

character" that he found so objectionable in Oppenheimer. And, perhaps more significantly, far from opposing the hydrogen bomb in any way, von Neumann had helped to create it.

After some delays, the Joint Congressional Committee on Atomic Energy finally confirmed von Neumann unanimously in March 1955. The scientist told the committee members everything they wanted to hear, just in the way they wanted to hear it. Although he didn't agree that J. Robert Oppenheimer was a security risk, he also believed that reopening the case wouldn't be in the public interest, and told the Committee that he was "satisfied with the final verdict by honest, intelligent men" that had been "properly reached."[16] Von Neumann would continue with the AEC until his death in 1957. Perhaps Oppenheimer hadn't found it possible to "conform himself to public desires" or persuade the public to "accept what he is," but John von Neumann had succeeded brilliantly on both counts.

If the Institute for Advanced Study was a refuge, a sanctuary, then it was also an Elba, an island of exile. J. Robert Oppenheimer found himself glumly facing the prospect of spending the rest of his life watching past and present colleagues and contemporaries advising, and receiving the accolades of, the high and mighty, wondering whether he would ever rejoin that elite group himself.

* * *

Sometime early in 1943 during a social evening at the Oppenheimers' house in Berkeley, Haakon Chevalier, a French professor and a close friend, casually remarked to Oppenheimer that a mutual acquaintance, British chemical engineer George Eltenton, had suggested giving technical information to the Russians through the Soviet consulate. Shocked, Oppenheimer immediately responded that such an act would be treason and that he would have no part of it. Chevalier agreed wholeheartedly, saying that he simply wanted to make Oppenheimer aware of the matter. Oppenheimer hesitated to report the matter for fear of subjecting his trusted friend to the merciless ordeal of a security investigation. But in the summer of 1943, when Manhattan Project security officers began investigating a suspected spy ring in Berkeley, Oppenheimer decided he could no longer ignore the incident and reported it. Unfortunately, in an attempt to deflect attention from Chevalier, Oppenheimer inexplicably embroidered the simple facts of

the innocent conversation. Eltenton, he said, had approached three *Berkeley scientists through a faculty member whom Oppenheimer refused to name because "it would involve people who ought not to be involved in this." In subsequent security interviews, Oppenheimer continued to hedge, until finally ordered to reveal Chevalier's name by the head of the Manhattan Project, General Leslie R. Groves. Oppenheimer admitted to Groves that his previous statements had been "a cock and bull story" but had no explanation for needlessly complicating the incident, except a desire to protect his friend.*

Now, under Robb's relentless questioning, Oppenheimer faced the fallout of his mistake.

"Did you tell Pash {Lieutenant Colonel Boris Pash, Manhattan Project security officer} the truth about this thing?" Robb inquired.

"No," Oppenheimer admitted.

"You lied to him?"

"Yes."

Robb moved to the specifics of Oppenheimer's false story and to Chevalier's involvement, armed with an intimate knowledge of the tapes of Oppenheimer's interview with Pash.

"Did you discuss with or disclose to Pash the identity of Chevalier?" Robb asked.

"No," said Oppenheimer.

"Let us refer, then, for the time being, to Chevalier as X. . . . did you tell Pash that X had approached three persons on the project?"

Oppenheimer hesitated: "I am not clear whether I said there were 3 X's or that X approached 3 people."

Robb pressed forward. "Didn't you say that X approached 3 people?"

"Probably," Oppenheimer allowed.

"Why did you do that, Doctor?"

"Because I was an idiot," Oppenheimer said.

Roger Robb later recalled that he went home that night and told his wife, "I've just seen a man destroy himself."

Some historians, notably Kai Bird and Martin Sherwin, have argued that this moment has been misportrayed ever since the hearing transcript was made public, claiming that Robb's description of Oppenheimer "wringing his hands, white as a sheet," reduced to utter humiliation as he whispered the "idiot" line is "nonsense, self-serving publicity designed to promote Robb's courtroom image, and his humanity." Bird and Sherwin maintain that, instead, Oppenheimer's

"idiot" statement was made in a more off-the-cuff, wryly self-critical manner. "He was using a colloquial phrase in a self-deprecating attempt to disarm his interrogator," they write.[17]

Whatever the truth, it was still a pivotal moment. Robb had forced Oppenheimer to admit himself a liar, at least in this one instance. As Oppenheimer himself later acknowledged, he had displayed poor judgment in his handling of the "Chevalier incident." To those sitting in judgment of him, however, it was only one example of a dangerous indiscretion and disregard of the requirements of security at best—and at worst, evidence of divided loyalties.

A RUGGED TIME

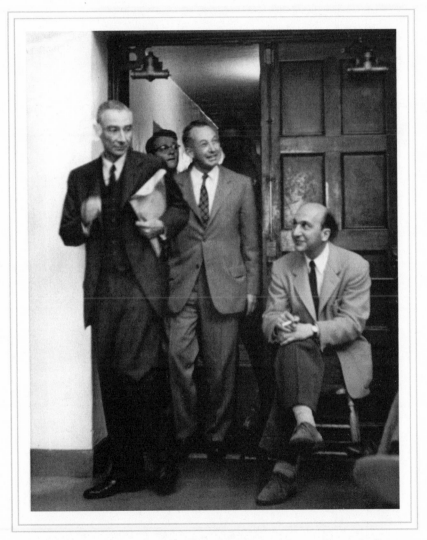

Banished from government, Oppenheimer takes solace in the scientific
community: with colleagues at a conference, 1955.

I believe that we are now deeply injured by the simplifications of this time.

—J. ROBERT OPPENHEIMER, "AN INWARD LOOK," *FOREIGN AFFAIRS*, JANUARY 1958

SECRET

July 20, 1955

BY COURIER SERVICE

RECORDED 87/00 - 17825 - 2198

EX-104

Honorable Lewis L. Strauss (Original)
Chairman
Atomic Energy Commission
19th and Constitution Avenue, Northwest
Washington 25, D. C.

Dear Admiral:

On July 14, 1955, Assistant Attorney General
William F. Tompkins advised that after consideration
of the Dr. J. Robert Oppenheimer case, it has been
determined that prosecutive action could not be
successfully concluded without additional evidence. (W)

The above is submitted for your information.

Sincerely yours,

J. Edgar Hoover

cc - 1 - Captain John A. Waters BY COURIER SERVICE
Director of Security
Atomic Energy Commission
Room 2314, T-5 Building
16th and Constitution Avenue, N. W.
Washington 25, D. C.

WTW:ss
(6) NOTE: Office of origin and auxiliary offices
being advised by separate cover.

Tolson
Boardman
Nichols
Belmont
Harbo
Mohr
Parsons
Rosen
Tamm
Sizoo
Winterrowd
Tele.
Holloman
Gandy

5

A Great Open Windy World

About a month after the day he would have delivered the first of his now-canceled lectures at the University of Washington, Oppenheimer strode into the lobby of a hotel roughly two hundred miles south, in Eugene, Oregon. Instantly recognizable in his trademark well-worn porkpie hat, stained with the sweat and dirt of the years at Los Alamos, he was met not by protesters but by reporters, who noted that along with the hat and the slightly rumpled suit draped over his thin frame, he was sporting a copy of *The Wall Street Journal* tucked under his arm.

"I read too many newspapers, probably," he admitted to the newsmen. He gamely answered a few random questions, tossing in some commentary about a report in that morning's *Journal* regarding the harnessing of atomic energy for peaceful purposes, and remarking that he was dubious about the prospects for near-term success. One newshound was curious whether Oppenheimer's current theoretical-physics work might open the door to even greater power for humankind. "Don't you think we have unleashed enough energy?" Oppie retorted flippantly.[1]

Then he and Kitty retreated to the sanctuary of their hotel room, where Oppie could settle in and prepare himself for the purpose of his visit: delivering the Condon lecture series at Oregon's major centers of learning, namely the University of Oregon in Eugene, Oregon

State in Corvallis, and Portland State College. Oppenheimer would not be speaking of bombs, fallout, McCarthyism, or his previous year's security ordeal, only the innocuously invisible realm of hyperons, K-mesons, charge symmetry, and broken parity. He was touring Oregon's academic strongholds not as a philosopher or celebrity, but merely as an eminent physicist talking about the subjects nearest and dearest to his heart. There would be no lofty pronouncements on the arts and their relation to the human heart, or the role of science in government, or even the restrictive immigration policies regarding foreign-born scientists against which he'd railed on the Murrow show.

Not that it mattered. Oppenheimer being Oppenheimer, there was simply no way that his brief Northwest tour could be a routine, unheralded lecture series by a respected scientist. A year had passed since Oppenheimer had become a private citizen once more, and officially speaking, his case was long closed. But for those obsessed with sinister Red infiltrators hiding under America's beds, the sticky black tar of the "security-risk" brush didn't wash off so easily—nor was the purple martyr's shroud, draped over Oppenheimer's shoulders by those who would dub him a sacrificial lamb to McCarthyism, so easily shed. It seemed that neutrality was nearly impossible when Oppenheimer was involved. The mere mention of the name demanded a reaction, an adoption of some sort of position. Your initial reaction might be that he was a "Red," a "Commie sympathizer," even a "traitor." Conversely, you might think of him as a "victim of the times," a "martyr," a champion of freedom and scientific openness. Or you might find yourself taking a less-polarized viewpoint, believing Oppenheimer to be a brilliant but perhaps somewhat politically naïve scientist who had upset the wrong people and suffered for it. Or, if your interest in and involvement with current events and culture were limited to Uncle Miltie and the size of the tailfins on next year's Chevys, you might not know too much about Oppenheimer, except that he had something to do with atomic bombs, he had been in some kind of trouble, and there was something not quite right about him, some undefined shadow on his name, some lingering suspicion, and so he was a topic better left alone.

No matter the form such reactions might take, his name, his actions, his words, demanded attention and comment. After the Murrow broadcast and the University of Washington uproar, quite irrelevant to his own intentions or desires, Oppenheimer was beginning to find himself cast in an altogether new role: not only as a lightning rod for controversy and comment, but that of a political litmus test. The manner in which an individual, an institution, a newspaper, reacted to and regarded the man and his doings proved an inescapable barometer of one's political, ethical, even moralistic leanings. It didn't even matter whether Oppenheimer was saying or doing anything that could be considered vaguely political—something that he was scrupulously attempting to avoid in any case—or whether he was merely going about his normal business of being a theoretical physicist and addressing audiences on K-mesons, as he would do in Oregon (and would have done in Washington).

Although they may not have been completely conscious of such a phenomenon at the time, the Oregon State Board of Higher Education, the entity that sponsored Oppenheimer's lecture series, couldn't help but notice the contrast between the paranoid, craven behavior of the University of Washington's leaders who had banned Oppie and their own much more enlightened handling of the entire situation. Nor were they or the press so obtuse as to believe that the enthusiastic response Oppenheimer enjoyed across the state had anything to do with a sudden, passionate interest in nuclear physics among the Oregonian populace. Oppenheimer's appearances in Eugene, Portland, and Corvallis attracted crowds well beyond the capacities of the humble university auditoriums to hold them. At Oregon State, the Oppenheimer talks had to be moved from the home economics auditorium to the university coliseum. It may have been the first time in the history of the schools that hordes of willing students and members of the public sat through a series of lectures that were so obviously beyond them. Oppenheimer certainly couldn't be accused of false advertising: "I'll talk about some things that the audiences won't understand, and that's too bad because I don't either," he joked to a university newspaper. And he freely admitted that while his lectures were probably too technical for a

general audience, they would definitely be too basic for a trained physicist.[2]

His presentation entitled "The Constitution of Matter" was in two parts, each delivered on a separate evening, broken up to increase suspense like an old-time movie serial. Oppenheimer covered what he termed "the subatomic zoo" of particles that mid-twentieth-century physicists had corralled and identified in their cosmic ray detectors and particle accelerators. The presentation was simplicity itself: Oppie, a lectern, and a blackboard. Speaking in his quietly precise, erudite, vaguely self-deprecating manner, covering the blackboard with equations and Greek symbols, Oppenheimer managed to enthrall each of his audiences, including the overflow members who couldn't score a seat or a space on the floor in the main hall and had to sit in hallways, lounges, and coffee shops, into which the lectures were piped over the public address system.

"While most of his language was technical, Oppenheimer's asides were not, and the listeners were alert for each lapse into sidewalk English," noted *The Eugene Register-Guard,* citing attendance of over 2,500, "the largest crowd in the history of the Student Union building." In an editorial, the paper mused on the question of "Why Did They Go Hear Oppenheimer?"

The first and most obvious answer was simple curiosity. "Many just wanted to see what this guy looked like. They'd heard about him and read about him." Some, no doubt, "wanted to see for themselves whether or not this guy has horns. They found none." Apart from curiosity, people showed up "because they recognized in him one of the greatest minds of our time" and wanted to be able to "tell their children and grandchildren some day that they had heard J. Robert Oppenheimer."

Still, such theories didn't explain why anyone would hang around more than the first five minutes. Why wasn't there a mass exodus as soon as Oppenheimer scrawled his first equation on the blackboard? Sheer force of personality, according to the *Register-Guard* editors. Oppenheimer's shy, self-effacing demeanor was both appealing and endearing. "They liked the way he scratched a spot behind his ear as he worked on complicated formulae on the blackboard. They liked the

way he was concerned lest somebody in the back be unable to hear him." When all was said and done, said the editors, "the great nuclear physicist turned out to be a very appealing, human guy," whose enthusiasm and love for his topic also came through loud and clear as he spoke of the beauty of the hydrogen atom. The editors gave the last word to a music professor, who compared Oppenheimer's performance to "listening to a fine concert. Even if you can't understand the music . . . you can still sit back and enjoy it."[3]

The record attendance, audience enrapturement, and press response followed Oppenheimer as he proceeded to Oregon State in Corvallis and finally to Portland State at the end of the month. Most impressive to both interested and disinterested observers was the persistent dichotomy between the esoteric difficulty of Oppenheimer's lecture topics and the size and fervor of the crowds, most of whom "didn't know a meson from a melon," as one paper put it. It was decidedly not the sort of attention that scientists were known for stirring up, at least not in their routine occupations of teaching and lecturing.

Oppenheimer seemed to take it all in stride. Some thought his quiet, almost nervous demeanor at the lectern to be a manifestation of shyness or stage fright, but in fact Oppenheimer was in his element: explaining science, communicating his passion for it to others. If he was at times overwhelmed by the thousands who might show up for his lectures, he didn't let that stop him; he proceeded just as he would have if he were back in Berkeley leading a handful of graduate students through a seminar. He also had no illusions regarding the comprehension level of such general audiences. He knew perfectly well that very few of them, if indeed any, would truly understand the details of what he was saying. Some scientists would be discouraged by lecturing to an uncomprehending audience, or would consider it a waste of time and energy, or even a task far beneath their professional dignity.

Not Oppenheimer. He had the excitement of science, of learning, of finding out something new, to communicate. "Knowledge is fun!" he exclaimed to one student interviewer. And, as he repeatedly assured his audiences, even the scientists still knew very little, and there was so

much more to learn. More than anything else, it was Oppenheimer's obvious humility, almost pious in its intensity, in the face of mystery, that endeared him to his listeners and made them want to at least try to understand, even if they ultimately failed. Oppenheimer was also temperamentally unable to patronize or talk down to his audiences. While that may have made it harder for them to comprehend, it also helped them to feel respected and included. One came away from an Oppenheimer lecture just *feeling* smarter somehow—confusion about mesons and melons notwithstanding.

Oppenheimer's experiences in lecturing to the masses combined to give him a celebrity cachet, something entirely new to this man who used to hobnob with presidents and generals. Some saw it as a less than positive development. "It must be a bit disturbing as well as flattering to a nuclear scientist . . . to learn that he has become a celebrity and possessed of something like the appeal that commands $50,000 a week at the Las Vegas luxury hotels," observed *The Portland Oregonian*. "The pursuit of learning is a grand and glorious thing, but let's hope it does not hold for the great scientists the fate of mob adulation. That should be reserved for such as Liberace and Johnny Ray."[4]

But not everyone saw the prospect of a superstar celebrity scientist as a necessarily bad thing. "I should like to know just what damage would result if we 'mobs' were really to transfer our loyalty from Liberace to the top scientists," wrote one disgruntled reader. "Even the poorly educated are intensely interested in the thing which may either benefit or destroy us" (i.e., atomic energy). Affirmed another *Oregonian* correspondent: "I consider it a favorable sign for our society that there are those who prefer adulation of a scientist with a conscience to more common objects of public adulation."[5]

Although the "public adulation" didn't go to Oppenheimer's head and convince him to begin charging a Liberace-level $50,000 for lecture appearances, the Oregon interlude was a welcome turnaround from the University of Washington flap, not to mention the negative reactions to the Murrow show and his other posthearing public appearances. "There was a feeling of friendliness here that I have not experienced in many parts of the country," he told an Oregon newspaper with characteristic restraint.[6]

On his way back home to Princeton from the West Coast, Oppenheimer stopped off for several days at Iowa State College in Ames, where he gave another lecture in honor of a physicist colleague who had died the previous year. Again, Oppenheimer packed them in, with an estimated twelve hundred bodies jammed into the college's nine-hundred-seat Memorial Union and still more listening by PA in the union basement.

After a brief period back in Princeton at the Institute, Oppenheimer and his family departed in mid-June for what was becoming their regular summer getaway in the Caribbean, after their shorter idyll in the Virgin Islands earlier in the year. They spent the next two months sailing, snorkeling, exploring, and simply soaking up the sun. Back in Princeton, Oppenheimer's faithful and long-suffering secretary, Verna Hobson, attended to his always-voluminous correspondence and routine business, keeping in touch with the boss as often as the mail service to the faraway Caribbean permitted.

This time at least, when he returned home in mid-August, Oppenheimer found no ticking time bombs of impending controversy waiting on his desk, like the Washington affair six months earlier. Instead, it was business as usual: the affairs of running the Institute (including matters dealing with the void left by Einstein's passing), punctuated by an occasional visit to the private George School in Newtown, Pennsylvania, where son Peter was enrolled.

The new intellectual rock star proceeded to fulfill some more public commitments in 1955, most notably a visiting fellowship at the prestigious Phillips Exeter Academy in New Hampshire. For some, the prospect of Oppenheimer exerting his baleful influence on the cream of American youth simply could not be overlooked. "Dr. J. Robert Oppenheimer's visit to Phillips Exeter Academy is revolting," complained the *Manchester Union Leader,* "an instance of glaring arrogance and utter disregard of proprieties, patriotic and otherwise."[7] No serious moves materialized to ban his appearance, but controversy over the "propriety" of his visit to Exeter raged on for weeks after his departure. But the Phillips Exeter boys "couldn't have shown any more enthusiasm for Marilyn Monroe," one teacher told a Boston newspaper, quite a statement regarding the student body of an

all-male school. Oppenheimer himself left New Hampshire feeling "rewarded and exhausted."[8]

Despite the cloud that still hung over his name, the year 1955 had provided Oppenheimer with ample evidence that in some quarters at least, he was not only accepted but welcomed wholeheartedly. Perhaps his counsel was no longer valued and sought by his government, but in the intellectual, scientific, and academic firmaments, his star shone apparently undiminished.

Others were also doing their best to help the Oppenheimer cause in various ways. One of the most direct was lawyer Charles P. Curtis, who published a book over the summer entitled *The Oppenheimer Case: The Trial of a Security System*. Curtis dissected the lengthy hearing transcript in exhaustive, merciless detail, pointing out improprieties in the Gray Board's procedures and rulings, the viciously inappropriate tactics of AEC chief counsel Roger Robb, and the illogic and inconsistencies throughout the Gray Board verdict and the subsequent AEC decision.

Meanwhile, German-Swiss foreign correspondent Robert Jungk had been trying to write a novel about the atomic scientists, but after some months of work, he abandoned his fictional treatment and instead began to think about doing a nonfiction account of the scientists who had discovered and developed atomic energy, from their early halcyon days in 1920s Europe through Los Alamos and beyond.

Jungk wouldn't be the first to write such a book—for one, there was William L. Laurence, the *New York Times* science reporter who had been officially assigned by the government to cover the Manhattan Project, had been the only journalist present at the Trinity test, and had even accompanied the atomic bombing mission to Nagasaki. But Jungk proposed a more in-depth and, perhaps, personal effort, "not one more book about the working and problems of atom-physics, but the story of a prominent and important group of intellectuals," and began doing preliminary research. In September 1955, convinced of the feasibility of his project, he wrote to his editor, Joseph Barnes, at Simon & Schuster (coincidentally, also the publisher of Oppenheimer's 1954 collection of speeches, *Science and the Common Understanding*) and, aside from inquiring whether Barnes might be interested, asked for an introduction to Oppenheimer in hopes that he might be willing to assist in the project.[9]

Barnes replied with definite interest in Jungk's ideas and a decided reluctance to put the author in touch with Oppenheimer. "You are right that we are his publishers. I am also his editor. For reasons that you will appreciate, he has a feeling these days that his personal life has been gone into with considerable care by experts in this line of investigation. Therefore I find him reluctant to aid or abet anyone who seems more interested in his personality than in his ideas." But Barnes offered to forward any specific questions to Oppenheimer and try to get some answers for Jungk.[10]

Jungk, however, was determined to interview Oppenheimer in person. "As you know, person to person talk with the direct exchange of opinions, of queries and answers, is worth one hundred written questions."[11] Planning a research trip from his home in Zurich to the United States in the spring of 1956, Jungk pressed Barnes to broker a personal meeting with Oppenheimer. Barnes gamely made the attempt, asking Oppenheimer whether he wanted to meet the journalist—"Or would you rather I told him a fine story of my own concoction which would leave you in peace?"[12] A gun-shy Oppenheimer wrote back to Barnes, "I do not like the sound of what he is up to, and if you think you can cope with him in my stead I would be most grateful."[13] Oppenheimer in fact did not have much free time during the period of Jungk's U.S. visit, but more than that, he was indulging his general distrust of such endeavors. Barnes eventually did meet with Jungk and told Oppie he was "a pleasant fellow" who "does not seem troublesome."[14] Jungk's book, *Brighter Than a Thousand Suns: A Personal History of the Atomic Scientists,* would eventually be published in Europe the following year, with an English translation following in 1958.

But the most notable publication of 1955 concerning Oppenheimer was his own: another collection of essays (like his previous book, derived from several speeches), entitled *The Open Mind.* The eight lectures in the book were the major ones given by Oppenheimer during the years 1946 to 1954, ending with the Columbia University "Prospects in the Arts and Sciences" address from Christmas 1954. Published to excellent reviews, the book landed on the bestseller lists. Even the FBI, still taking dutiful note of Oppenheimer's doings, reviewed the book internally and noted that it was "of no significance

with regard to our past investigation of Oppenheimer's communist associations."[15]

There would be peace—for a while, and of a sort. Nineteen fifty-six brought more speaking engagements and intellectual touring for Oppenheimer, along with the regular business of running the Institute. He took his "Constitution of Matter" lectures to other universities, to much the same befuddled but bewitched response as in Oregon.

But before long, rumblings of trouble drifted in from the horizon. If Oppenheimer was beginning to feel more at ease, if not fully content, in his quieter and more cerebral public life, and perhaps even allowing himself to believe that displays of contempt and condemnation were surely beginning to ebb and would eventually cease, he would soon discover otherwise. When the next major storm of Oppenheimer outrage broke, there would be no doubt that the mere mention of the Oppenheimer name still had more than enough power to stir political and ethical passions in every quarter of American culture.

* * *

For days, Robb continued to question Oppenheimer on details of his past: his association with left-wing organizations, friends and family members, even a night he spent with an emotionally distraught former Communist girlfriend during a trip to Berkeley during the war—while married to Kitty. None of this was new. Oppenheimer had been thoroughly investigated and cleared before he joined the Manhattan Project, kept under constant surveillance during and after his years on the project through wire and phone taps, opening of his mail, and shadowing by teams of security agents. He was probably watched more closely and for a longer time than almost any other American during the time of his government service, yet this mass of supposedly "derogatory information" had been disregarded and dismissed when he was cleared again by the government upon his appointment as AEC official consultant in 1947.

But the recounting of Oppenheimer's past "sins" served its purpose. If the man was so obviously a liar, dismissive of security requirements, and sympathetic to

anti-American causes, then the reasons for his more recent opposition to official policies were clearly not the result of an honest difference of opinion but must have a more pernicious basis. Maybe Oppenheimer wasn't a traitor or Soviet agent, as some had accused. But could he be trusted with his country's most dangerous secrets?

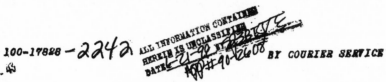

100-17828-*2242* BY COURIER SERVICE

Date: June 26, 1956

To: Director (orig. & 1)
Central Intelligence Agency
2430 E Street, N. W.
Washington, D. C.

APPROPRIATE AGENCIES
AND FIELD OFFICES
ADVISED BY ROUTING
SLIP(S) OF Declassifica-
DATE non 8/1/77

Attention: Deputy Director, Plans

From: John Edgar Hoover, Director,
Federal Bureau of Investigation

Subject: DR. J. ROBERT OPPENHEIMER
INTERNAL SECURITY - R

Reference is made to my memoranda dated
August 11, 1954, and August 26, 1954, in which you
were furnished information indicating that the subject,
while on a trip to Europe during July and August, 1954,
planned to disappear behind the "Iron Curtain." As you
are aware, the subject did not so defect.

This Bureau has been advised that the subject
intends to depart the United States on or about July 1, 1956,
for a two-month visit to France, Denmark, England, and
Switzerland. During this trip, the subject will lecture
at the Summer School of Theoretical Physics at Houches,
Haute-Savoie, France. It is requested that you furnish
any information pertaining to the subject that comes to
your attention while he is abroad.

cc - 1 Legal Attache, Paris

Note for Legal Attache, Paris: Reurlet 6-6-56. Since
Bureau has requested CIA to furnish data pertaining to subject
no active coverage of his activities should be maintained by
you.

- Foreign Service

6

The Climate of Suspicion

n September 1956, Oppenheimer enjoyed a minor bit of personal vindication when he found himself in a place that, not long before, had banned him as a "liar"—the University of Washington. Top-rank physicists from all over the world were brought in to, as Oppenheimer put it, "review the striking and beautiful achievements of the past decade" for an international physics conference. This time, perhaps because President Schmitz and the university were still red-faced over the past year's debacle, partly because this event had more of a cosmopolitan and less of a university flavor, no one caused any trouble regarding Oppenheimer's presence.

When reporters inevitably asked him if he harbored any resentments or "special feelings" about the university after his previous public rejection, he refused to be baited. He simply smiled his enigmatic Oppenheimer smile, the one that always hinted at volumes left unsaid, and told the newsmen: "I am very glad to be at this conference at this place. Period."[1]

After a holiday retreat to the Virgin Islands, Oppenheimer's next major gig was a homecoming of sorts: a visit to Caltech, where, along with the University of California at Berkeley, he had taught physics before being swept up into the Manhattan Project. Sponsored by an

organization no less American and apple pie than the Caltech YMCA, it was another freewheeling few days during which Oppenheimer sat in on classes, spoke to small informal groups of undergraduate and graduate students, and delivered a few formal science lectures.

But Oppenheimer was yet to be permitted to complete fully his metamorphosis from disgraced public figure to America's statesman and philosopher of science, troubled only by the occasional snide *National Review* piece or Fulton Lewis radio commentary. The bitter truth remained that in some quarters he was still considered to be the quintessential American scientific traitor, liar, and general villain of the modern age, no less than Alger Hiss or the Rosenbergs.

What rankled was that unlike them, Oppenheimer had somehow gotten off the hook. Yes, he had been kicked out of government and banned from public service, but he had escaped legal prosecution for his supposed "crimes," and worse yet, he was obviously still held in high regard by some people as some kind of hero. To those who found all this morally intolerable, the idea that Oppenheimer was still welcomed and feted by certain institutions and organizations as an honored guest, and treated as though he were worth listening to, was nothing less than a personal affront. And not all those who held such opinions on Oppenheimer were content to write nasty letters to the editor: a small but influential group of Harvard University alumni was spearheading a zealous campaign to get Oppenheimer's next major public appearance canceled.

Oppenheimer was set to serve as the university's William James guest lecturer in the spring of 1957. As soon as the appointment had been announced back in the fall of 1955, one prominent alumnus, Edwin Ginn, a Boston financier and 1918 Harvard grad, resigned from a fund-raising post in protest, publicly complaining, "Why must Harvard insult a large body of loyal alumni by inviting so dubious a character to lecture? My conscience will not allow me to continue financial support to the college while such an attitude prevails."[2]

By February 1956, a 1921 alumnus named Kenneth D. Robertson had taken up the anti-Oppenheimer flag, beginning by harassing the

university's Board of Overseers with a series of increasingly indignant letters. "As an interested alumnus, I ask you as a member of the Board of Overseers . . . whether or not you now approve of the Oppenheimer appointment as William James lecturer," Robertson demanded of his correspondents. "I would like a yes or no answer to that question regardless how you voted at the Board meeting which 'approved' the appointment . . . and I would like your answer to include your views as to Dr. Oppenheimer's moral qualifications to lecture on the subject of ethics and philosophy to the young students at Harvard. . . . If this letter makes you angry by speaking too plainly, please don't take it out on me. After all, I didn't have a Communist as an intimate 'girl friend,' didn't contribute money to the Communist Party, didn't associate with Communists and employ them in secret government work or fail to pass security tests. Nor have I lied about the foregoing when questioned thereon. Finally, don't blame me for appointing him."[3]

The thirty-member Harvard Board of Overseers to whom the utterly blameless Robertson addressed his missive was an impressive group by any standards, including Undersecretary of State Christian A. Herter, American ambassador to Russia Charles E. Bohlen, and various other congressmen, industrialists, journalists, and dignitaries (some years previously, Oppenheimer himself had served on the board). The chairman of the board, Charles E. Wyzanski (Harvard, '27), responded to Robertson with a note inquiring whether or not "the urbanity of temperament, the courtesy of manners . . . beyond even tolerance . . . a spirit of neighborliness and charity of spirit" were not "among the outstanding merits of the traditional conservatives." In other words, perhaps Harvard students had a right and an obligation to hear from a variety of viewpoints, even from one such as Oppenheimer whose "moral qualifications" were supposedly questionable.

Robertson and a number of fellow alumni, including Edwin Ginn, Brooks Harlow, and even Colonel Archibald B. Roosevelt (decorated war-hero son of former president Theodore Roosevelt), put together a self-styled, formal group called the Harvard "Veritas" Committee

(named after the university motto, "veritas," or "truth"), dedicated to the express goal of stopping the Oppenheimer appointment and finding out just how it had happened—implying that perhaps less-than-savory maneuvering or behind-the-scenes manipulation had taken place. Who was responsible for this shady Oppenheimer character being named to such a prestigious post? The "Veritas" Committee decided there had to be a conspiracy. "How did this extraordinary choice happen to be made? Some individuals, or groups, must have been responsible for forwarding this strange selection to the members of the Board. Members of the 'Veritas' Committee feel constrained to find out who and why." The committee urged the overseers and alumni to make a closer review: "We think that if the Overseers, as individuals, had an opportunity to study all the pertinent facts, they would not approve of Dr. Oppenheimer's appointment."[4]

In all their righteous indignation, however, the eight members of the "Veritas" Committee seemed to overlook the simple truth that none of the terrible facts against Oppenheimer they felt needed to be brought into the light were new. All of it—Oppenheimer's past leftist associations, his admitted lying to security officers, his opposition to the H-bomb crash program—was old hat, part of the public record not only in the published transcript hearing but in the reams of press coverage generated by the entire case. To claim that the Board of Overseers or most Harvard alumni were unaware of it and needed to have it all brought to their attention was patently absurd.

And to some, it was more than absurd—it was insulting, and the suggestion that it should be used as a pretext to stop Oppenheimer's appointment was contrary to the principles upon which the university was founded. Judge Learned Hand, famed juror and Harvard alumnus, informed the "Veritas" Committee that he "could not more completely disagree with your effort, or think it more to the disadvantage of the University." As to Oppenheimer's moral status, "I need say no more than that I am wholly satisfied that Dr. Oppenheimer is qualified morally, as he certainly is professionally, for the position for which he has been chosen."[5]

Before the matter went too far, the university officially confirmed that Oppenheimer's appointment would proceed as scheduled. As to the supposed "mystery" of his selection, he had been nominated for the James appointment jointly by Harvard's psychology and philosophy departments, and the appointment had been duly approved by the dean of the arts and sciences faculty and the Harvard Corporation, and finally by the Board of Overseers. It had all been quite proper and routine, with no influence from shady and subversive quarters.

Oppenheimer would deliver a series of eight lectures entitled "The Hope of Order," the first on April 8 and the last on May 10. This "dubious character" would thus join a long list of distinguished former William James lecturers including John Dewey, Bertrand Russell, and B. F. Skinner.

While failing to get Oppenheimer banned from the hallowed ground of Harvard, the "Veritas" Committee did succeed in one objective: creating a national press uproar. As might be expected, the "Veritas" Committee crusaders had their supporters. "We wish this enterprise every success, and hope it may inspire similar crusades among the alumni of numerous American colleges and universities," declared the New York *Daily News.* "Too many of these, we think, have long been extending far too much hospitality to people who hate the Capitalist system off which they live, and are determined to use our educational institutions toward its destruction. If 'academic freedom' obligates Americans to tolerate such a conspiracy as that, then we'd better revise our definition of academic freedom."[6]

The *National Review,* predictably enough, supported the "Veritas" Committee as well, praising the "indefatigable" Robertson and printing what the editors considered "the wisest statement on the Oppenheimer appointment," authored by an unidentified Harvard alumnus (their copy was "censored," claimed the *Review*). This anonymous analyst offered the interesting theory that Harvard "has been mouse-trapped into a general maneuver at rebuilding Oppenheimer's damaged reputation. . . . to protect Oppenheimer as a scientist is not enough for

his friends. They want him made into a great administrative educator, and at Princeton they have succeeded in making him so. They want him also elevated into a seer on human ethics and morals, and are using Harvard as the pawn." Instead of retreating gracefully into "decent obscurity," then, Oppenheimer was refusing to go away, allowing this undefined "them" to help him retool and reinvent himself as a great thinker and educator. "If Oppenheimer and his friends were endowed with as much taste as wilfulness, they and he would never have subjected Harvard—whose loyalty he tapped abundantly as an Overseer—to this repugnant dilemma," said the writer, apparently forgetting the fact that Oppenheimer hadn't invited himself to Harvard or any of the other institutions that repeatedly welcomed him for visits.[7]

Others, however, ridiculed the notion that Oppenheimer was somehow not qualified to deliver the James lectures because he was both "immoral" and also not a professional philosopher but a scientist. On the contrary: "By participation in and leadership of the actual development of the thermonuclear forces which have so overpowering an influence on our civilization today and by a demonstrated inclination to analyze their impact on human beings and human problems, he has proved himself a uniquely qualified philosopher of this atomic age," said *The Toledo Blade*. And even if "there may be room to question the wisdom of some of Dr. Oppenheimer's individual acts in the past," the same could be said of most other people—and "there are very few among us who have had our loyalty and our morality examined by two quasi-judicial groups in Government who have specifically endorsed our loyalty even as they withheld security clearance. On this ground alone, Dr. Oppenheimer is uniquely qualified to discuss the philosophic problems of our times."[8]

Learned Hand was far from the only illustrious recipient of the "Veritas" Committee form letter who had responded with indignation, as the student newspaper, *The Harvard Crimson*, reported. "It is the dirty and discredited banner of McCarthyism which you are trying to raise anew, clothed in the honored respectability of the Harvard University

motto," Walter Raushenbush, '50, wrote to the committee. "What you are doing seems to me bad for Harvard and for our country. I don't like it, gentlemen. Count me out." Wrote John G. Conley, '38: "You are entitled to your opinions, but I do not share them at all. As one who has read Oppenheimer and heard him on the celebrated Edward R. Murrow interview, I must say I envy the opportunity that the students of Harvard will have to hear this extraordinarily thoughtful and stimulating American. I only wish I could be present to hear him myself!"

Eleven students of Harvard's Divinity School wrote to *The Crimson:* "We oppose the anxious attempts of 'righteous moralists' to undercut Harvard's responsibility for providing the opportunity and the risk proper to higher education." Another alumnus mused about the "Veritas" Committee: "I can't help but feel that such a parochial few would cause William James to 'roll over in his grave.'" On the other hand, wrote another alumnus, "Wouldn't [Harvard] expel a student found guilty of the very misconduct confessed by Oppenheimer, whom she has honored by asking him to teach ethics to her students?"[9]

Settling in for his month in Cambridge, Oppenheimer kept his usual lofty distance above it all, concentrating on writing and delivering the James lectures. The overheated editorial writers who feared that Oppenheimer would use his appointment as a bully pulpit to destroy the capitalist system or at least corrupt the morals and ethics of America's youth had nothing to fear. Instead, in the eight talks that made up "The Hope of Order," Oppenheimer spoke of open knowledge and science in his characteristically eloquent, sometimes opaque, often inspiring manner.

Rather than advocating anything "subversive," he criticized the restrictions of knowledge and learning in the Communist world: "This is an open world in which it is not wrong for anyone to know anything— the Communist world is an exception to this. . . . governments and societies must be judged by the learning offered to their citizens. . . . knowledge is not the property of a small class of people." The free

world, said Oppenheimer, faced "an enemy who doesn't share our notion of liberty and development and destroys them when he can."[10] Even the "Veritas" Committee, which was notably silent when the lecture series finally began, must have been impressed.

No picketing or other protests were recorded at any of Oppenheimer's talks, just the usual enthusiastic overflow crowds. Quoting Harvard president Nathan M. Pusey's introduction of Oppenheimer as a "distinguished son of Harvard" and his assertion that "the security of the country depends largely on a few highly educated people—Mr. Oppenheimer is a member of this group," *The Providence Journal* noted, "The president's words, ringing through the open gates of Harvard, cast defiance upon those who would ostracize the nonconformer, the unorthodox, the lonely who see the world as few are granted the gift to see it. Harvard again has shed a gleam of light in a dark world."[11]

The rest of Oppenheimer's lectures ranged widely over physics, the limits of knowledge, the challenges faced by scientists, and the duty of all to "learn as much as we can." He explained later to an interviewer that while he didn't expect everyone to understand everything he'd said, "explaining atomic physics to the layman is both impossible—and necessary. I hope lectures like this will give an impression of how the technical fellow looks at his job. They can also remind people how very far they are from these things—and encourage them to do something about it. Everybody is pretty much uninformed about everything—that's the starting point for us all."[12]

While in Massachusetts, Oppenheimer also cautiously consented to a brief television appearance on Boston's WGBH station in which he was interviewed by the curator of Harvard's Nieman Fellowships, Dr. Louis M. Lyons. The two kept the conversation along the same lines as Oppenheimer's speeches, with some nods to science issues in the recent press such as the dangers of nuclear fallout from bomb testing (about which Oppenheimer was equivocal); the prospects for disarmament ("No disarmament will ever put the nuclei back in their box"); and the popularization of science by means such as Op-

penheimer's public lectures ("I believe in the popularization of science. I don't think I do it terribly well. But we must know that it is as impossible as it is essential. It has those two inescapable sides, I think").[13]

With the end of Oppenheimer's Harvard appointment, he returned to the Institute, the "Veritas" Committee disbanded, and Oppenheimer's coterie of critics settled back down into their usual low level of peeved muttering. As Oppenheimer made summer plans to visit Europe, along with the family's usual idyll in the Virgin Islands, he may have caught an article published in the May 1957 *Atlantic Monthly* entitled "Dissension in the AEC." The piece, by *Washington Post* reporter Warren Unna, described the growing rivalry between AEC chairman Lewis Strauss and AEC commissioner Thomas Murray. Strauss and Murray, of course, had both voted against restoring Oppenheimer's security clearance, but since 1954, as Unna detailed, that was about the only issue on which the two men had agreed. Even though Murray's term as an AEC commissioner was about to expire, the political and personal conflicts between the two men were destined to have repercussions that would range far beyond the immediate concerns of the AEC, engulfing others who were no longer involved with the organization—including Robert Oppenheimer.

And, quite unexpectedly, Strauss's increasing political turmoils would soon combine with a sea change in the American cultural climate that would offer new promise for Oppenheimer's ultimate vindication and triumph. But as was always the case where Oppenheimer was concerned, the struggle would not be without casualties.

* * *

Having established Oppenheimer's untrustworthiness in the eyes of the Gray Board, Robb smoothly moved on to the main issue of the hearing: Oppenheimer's advice on the H-bomb.

Robb grilled Oppenheimer on the 1949 meeting of the General Advisory

Committee considering the H-bomb question. At the time, the hydrogen bomb was only a theory, and no one had any idea whether it was practical or even possible. As the AEC's chief scientific advisory panel, the GAC advised against a crash H-bomb program with what GAC chairman Oppenheimer described as "surprising unanimity," citing both the technical uncertainties and the ethical questions raised by such a "superweapon." The committee's final report stated that "we are all agreed that it would be wrong at the present moment to commit ourselves to an all-out effort toward its development." An appendix to the formal report was even more definitive: "We believe a super bomb should never be produced. Mankind would be far better off not to have a demonstration of the feasibility of such a weapon until the present climate of world opinion changes."

The decision had not been quite so unanimous, however. One member of the GAC, Glenn Seaborg, was absent from the meeting but had expressed rather ambiguous support for the H-bomb effort in a earlier letter to Oppenheimer.

Robb sprang his favorite trap again. After Oppenheimer testified that he and the GAC were unaware of Seaborg's position at the meeting, Robb produced a copy of Seaborg's letter. Embarrassed, Oppenheimer admitted that he did not remember the letter, and pointed out that Seaborg declined to state his position on the H-bomb at the next GAC meeting. It proved a fatal lapse of memory, which Robb managed to characterize as a deliberate attempt at deception.

As Robb portrayed it, the GAC report was only the beginning of a concerted effort on Oppenheimer's part to stop the H-bomb by any means. After President Truman ordered the development of the bomb in January 1950, Oppenheimer declined to return to Los Alamos to aid the effort. Some scientists working on the project resented that, as they saw it, Oppenheimer wasn't using his considerable influence to persuade his colleagues to help. The enthusiastic H-bomb proponent Edward Teller felt that Oppenheimer was even actively trying to dissuade others from joining the project. Robb demanded explanations: What if you had done more to aid the project? Wouldn't we have had the H-bomb sooner? For a man of your influence, isn't lack of enthusiasm the same as outright opposition? Why did you have moral scruples about the H-bomb but not the atomic bomb? Oppenheimer's attempts to clarify his position were repeatedly challenged by Robb's lacerating questions.

Oppenheimer had never faced such an assault before. And it was beginning to take its toll. Old friends were startled and shocked as Oppenheimer seemed to be visibly aging as the hearing ground on relentlessly.

And, so far, it had been only a week.

Mr. A. H. Belmont

September 13, 1957

Mr. R. R. Roach

THOMAS A. MORGAN
NEW YORK INDUSTRIALIST

On September 12, 1957, Liaison Agent Bates saw Mr. Morgan at the swearing in ceremonies at the Atomic Energy Commission for the new commissioner, Mr. John Graham. Mr. Morgan was one of the three board members who heard the J. Robert Oppenheimer case at the Atomic Energy Commission (AEC) several years ago. Mr. Morgan advised Bates that he had never had an opportunity to express his thanks to the FBI for the outstanding job done on the Oppenheimer case. He said he was amazed to see the thoroughness with which the Bureau handled the Oppenheimer case and was also appreciative of the many requests made by the Board which the FBI handled most expeditiously. He commented that he always had felt that the FBI was good but his first association with the work of the Bureau in the Oppenheimer case convinced him that the FBI was not only good but was even better than that.

Mr. Morgan, who is a friend of Mr. Graham's had been invited by Mr. Graham to attend the swearing-in ceremony. Mr. Morgan ended by stating that if he could ever be of service to the FBI he would certainly appreciate being called on.

ACTION:

For information.

100-17828-

NOT RECORDED
140 SEP 20 1957

CWB:bjt
(5)

1 - Mr. Belmont
1 - Mr. Branigan
1 - Liaison Section
1 - Mr. Bates
1 - Main File on J. Robert Oppenheimer

INITIALS ON ORIGINAL

67 SEP 24 1957

7

A Sense of Panic

In the middle of 1957, not long after the upheavals of the Harvard appointment had subsided and his name had once more quietly slipped from the front pages of America's newspapers, freeing him to retreat to the tranquillity of Princeton and the Virgin Islands that he so valued, Robert Oppenheimer did something quite unexpected. He put himself right back on the front pages.

This time, it wasn't another crew of outraged patriots protesting another planned Oppenheimer appearance, or a snide right-wing commentator mounting another of the attacks on the scientist that were de rigueur in conservative circles, or a new accusation from a long-lost and disgruntled Berkeley ex-Communist regarding Oppie's ancient Red ties. This time Oppenheimer was the initiating force, the prime mover. Instead of gamely fielding the questions of reporters who gathered around him at public events, this time Oppenheimer actually sought out one of their number, not to respond to queries or accusations or controversy, but to speak openly for himself and about himself.

Oppenheimer granted an interview to Victor Cohn of the Minneapolis *Sunday Tribune*. Nothing so unusual there; although Oppenheimer was known to grant such access only sporadically and only on his terms, he also wasn't completely incommunicado to the press. But for once, Oppenheimer was changing the ground rules. Aside from close friends and family, the only person with whom he had ever discussed his

security-case ordeal in any detail had been author John Mason Brown, for Brown's 1956 book *Through These Men*.

Brown's insights into the case had been enhanced by the cooperation of Oppenheimer, who agreed to discuss the experience with Brown. This enabled some of Brown's most eloquent and telling observations: "The hearing abides in the Oppenheimer home as a permanent resident. In Kitty's blood it continues to boil, an understandable source of indignation. Oppenheimer has tried to put it behind him, explaining, in a phrase large in spirit and Biblical in phrasing, 'I cannot sit with anger.' But the hurt is there and always will be, and the scars are deeper than the deep ones which show."[1]

Otherwise, the topic had been strictly taboo, studiously avoided by gentleman's agreement during the Murrow interview, deftly fended off or simply ignored by Oppenheimer if reporters dared to bring it up, perhaps acknowledged only indirectly by a trademark Oppenheimer enigmatic quip or facial expression.

But now Oppenheimer was willing to talk about the case and how it had affected him, and he wanted to do so with Cohn. Why he chose this particular journalist and this particular newspaper is something only Oppenheimer knew. Perhaps it was simply a classic case of good timing: Cohn happened along just at the most opportune moment, when Oppie felt like talking. Perhaps the recent Harvard contretemps had exhausted Oppenheimer's patience, made it obvious how misunderstood he was by many decent citizens, brought home how many misconceptions and plain wrong assumptions were still clinging to his name. Perhaps Oppenheimer felt that the time was right to take a bit of an offensive tack, rather than always defending himself against the detractors or trying to ignore them. He was certainly experienced enough to realize that, despite the old chestnut dispensed by mothers around the world, bullies sometimes *don't* "just go away" when you ignore them.

So it was time to speak up a bit, give his own side, and to do it in his own words rather than through sympathetic proxies. And perhaps more than anything else, Oppenheimer wanted to show the world that despite everything, despite all the talk about how he had been "destroyed" and "ruined," despite the critics and persistent personal enemies who would be perfectly happy to see him fade into permanent obscurity or

simply crawl back under a slimy rock, he had survived. He was still alive, still around, and he was going to stay.

He said as much in the very first line of Cohn's story: "I have tried to prove that a security risk can survive." Noting that "this lean and lined man" didn't discuss the case with any eagerness, and that the article which followed would not attempt to retry or rejudge it, Cohn said: "But the plain news about Oppenheimer today is that he has survived it."

Cohn recounts the basic facts of the Oppenheimer case for any who might have been unaware of them by now, and notes that after the AEC decision to not restore his clearance, many thought that Oppenheimer's career was completely destroyed, including his tenure as director of the Institute for Advanced Study. "It seemed to me that I couldn't accept that," Oppenheimer tells Cohn. "I had two alternatives. One was to seek ways to appeal the decision. I didn't think we'd buy ourselves anything by that." Mindful of all the hopeful talk during the past three years about finding some way to restore his clearance, he adds, "Perhaps I was wrong."

No matter. His other alternative was "to prove that, in spite of some incredible words the commission wrote about me, these words would not necessarily be believed by all people. In other words, I had to establish by other means that what was put out as a final judgment about me wasn't *the* final judgment. And the only way to do this was by surviving."

For anyone trying to tease out the inner motivations and feelings of this extraordinarily complex man over the past three years, these simple sentences provide all the explanation necessary. Maintaining, he knew instinctively, would be enough, at least for a while. Another battle, and maybe vindication, could wait until later, perhaps when the political and social climate had changed enough to permit it. In the meantime, Oppenheimer felt, merely making it clear to all, both supporters and enemies, that he was bloodied but not bowed, down but not out, defeated but not completely beaten, was all he could ask for and all that was necessary.

And to do so meant to move on in every respect, and not allow himself to be dragged down into endless tunnels of self-deprecation and second-guessing, as would happen if he allowed the security case to

define and shape the entire remainder of his life and career. Which meant, with only a few and extremely carefully chosen exceptions, that he would avoid discussing the case and would instead let the record speak for itself. "He determined to avoid self-pity," wrote Cohn, "and one part of this was a determination to avoid commenting again and again on the case."

Instead of allowing himself to become a professional martyr to Mc-Carthyism, then, Oppenheimer would combine his experience as a policymaker and adviser with his scientific genius to forge a new role for himself: "He seems to be accepted more and more as America's outstanding scientific spokesman and interpreter."

"For 12 years I had been acting as an adviser to the government," Oppenheimer tells Cohn. "That is a role no sane man would choose for pleasure—but that career has been destroyed." Oppenheimer gives no hint to Cohn as to whether he welcomes or regrets the loss of that particular career. That life is decidedly over, and he now has a new part to play.

"As we spoke, he was simple in manner, if sometimes intricate in his thought," Cohn remarks of Oppenheimer. "And he was full of humor—but never the gay, light-hearted variety." Cohn makes it a point to mention Oppenheimer's continual pipe smoking, exactly as had been in evidence during the Murrow television show. In the 1950s, of course, smoking was as ubiquitous as hats on men and tailfins on automobiles, but the mention of Oppenheimer's pipe, or on occasion his cigarettes, was as inevitable in any description of Oppenheimer during this period as was a remark regarding his "thin" or "birdlike" features.

Cohn regards a "decisive point" in Oppenheimer's posthearing survival to be the decision of the Institute for Advanced Study to keep him as director. "It seems very likely that if he had been thrown out of this job, everything afterward would have been very different." Although it could be argued that no man with Oppenheimer's credentials would have stayed unemployed for long—most likely another university or institute would have snapped him up, either in the United States or elsewhere—there is no question that the Institute was a vital factor in Oppenheimer's "survival." It provided a refuge, a retreat, a home base where, despite the unique problems and challenges of dealing with the egos and personalities of such brilliant individuals (and despite the fact

that he was not always universally loved and respected by everyone at the Institute), Oppenheimer could feel secure, accepted, and needed, and where, even with his administrative responsibilities, he was still free to do science.

Oppenheimer certainly appreciates both the goodwill of the Institute and the trust it displayed in him: "I owe very much to the faculty and board of trustees of this Institute." He also lauds the "several prominent and spirited writers" who have defended him in the press and public forum, along with "the prevailing—although not unanimous—weight of scientists against the decision." And in a larger sense, Oppenheimer is grateful for "the good sense and good courage of many Americans," including all those citizens who hasten to defend him in the editorial pages and letters columns and who refuse to believe the many inaccuracies and untruths regarding him peddled by various demagogues and rabble-rousers.

What about his family? How did Oppenheimer's ordeal affect them? Here, as always when such personal matters came up with the press, Oppenheimer is tight-lipped, but regarding the children, Peter, then sixteen, and Katherine ("Toni"), then thirteen, he offers: "It has not affected their lives. Everyone has treated them very well." Unfortunately, although no one, including Oppenheimer, fully realized it at the time, the lives of both Peter and Toni would in fact be profoundly affected by their father's difficulties, even if those effects would not be manifested until much later.

As to the larger effects of his security case? "I know the incident had a disturbing effect on a lot of young people, both in their attitude toward government service and toward the pursuit of science," says Oppenheimer. "I believe it may have discouraged some scientists from speaking on the disturbing aspects of United States weapons and military planning."

Despite its candor, Cohn's encounter with Oppenheimer was definitely not a tell-all interview. Oppenheimer had offered his most candid words to date on the security case and its consequences, but he had still refrained from any detailed commentary. He had avoided, in the stock McCarthyist phrase, to "name names" or comment specifically on Strauss or any of the other men who had maneuvered behind the scenes to get his clearance suspended and then put him through the ordeal of

the hearing. He had made no counteraccusations and offered no mea culpas. He had, in fact, merely allowed one reporter to take him back for a more or less objective retrospective view on the events that had altered the course of his life three years previously. Cohn's piece held no huge revelations or big scoops apart from the fact that Oppenheimer was deigning to allow himself to make direct statements regarding the security case, and even that was a quiet sort of story.

The rest of the Cohn feature is little more than a series of Oppenheimer profundities taken from a selection of his recent speeches, artfully arranged to create a portrait of the state of Oppenheimer's big-picture thoughts, attempting to highlight the contrasts between Oppenheimer's gentle words and his own personal experiences. "This man who has aroused great enmity still speaks of love," Cohn writes, before quoting the final lines of Oppenheimer's Columbia speech. Cohn provides other excerpts from Oppenheimer's talks, prefaced by brief introductions: "This man who found trouble partly because he was 'different' writes. . . . This man scarred by the atom is no defeatist. . . . This man scarred by our changing world says. . . . This man scarred also by speech on controversial issues . . ."

The effect is to enhance the image of Oppenheimer as a thoughtful philosopher who holds no rancor, a deep and elegant thinker who has risen above the pettiness of so many of his fellows. But a feeling of uneasiness remains from Cohn's piece. Yes, Oppenheimer has moved on, has overcome the demons, or at least reached an accommodation with them, without letting them destroy him. He's still an honored and respected scientist and thinker. And yet it's clear that unfinished business remains. The shadows still cling to the man, and the light that will banish them for good is nowhere to be found. Oppenheimer may have survived, but in a real sense, compared to his previous lifetime when he walked with giants, he has still been somehow diminished, in power and influence if not in individual human dignity.

Perhaps the most inadvertently revealing part of the entire Cohn article is its brief sidebar about Oppenheimer's brother, Frank, noting how Frank's former Communist Party membership ultimately cost him his position at the University of Minnesota: "Unemployed since as a physicist, Frank and his family have been living ever since on a Colorado ranch, raising cattle." Unspoken but all too clear is the implication

that, but for a few twists of fate, Robert also could have been exiled from his lifetime pursuit of science to a career in animal husbandry, instead of managing to hold on to one of the most prestigious postings in the academic world.

"This is a picture of Robert Oppenheimer today," concludes Cohn. "Think what you like of him, it is a picture of a man who will make other people think all of his life."[2]

No one could deny that Robert Oppenheimer had survived, and he would continue to do so and continue to be heard from. But he had not prospered, and he had not been fully exonerated, either legally or philosophically. Lauded he might be by some, but his government still considered him unfit to serve. Three years after that cruel judgment, that fact was no closer to being altered. And no one knew that better than Oppenheimer himself.

The Cohn article was picked up by other newspapers and distributed nationally, but attracted only some mild attention. For the pro-Oppie contingent, it was nothing they didn't already know and believe; for the Oppie bashers, it was merely another example of dissembling and distortions from the mealymouthed Oppenheimer.

At least Oppenheimer could rest in the knowledge that he had said his piece. He had expected nothing more. The hopes and efforts of friends and supporters notwithstanding, Oppenheimer knew that his unquestioned, unopposed, and complete absolution, if it ever came, was still a hazy prospect far in some unknowable future.

And then a 187-pound metal sphere came hurtling out of the steppes of Kazakhstan to change everything.

Practically no one, except perhaps inside the scientific circles where nationalist concerns and cold war scorekeeping were of little concern, expected what happened on Friday, October 4, 1957, to, well, actually *happen*.

Since the beginning of the cold war, the Soviet Union had been playing catch-up with the United States. First it took the Soviets four years to achieve our great war-ending technological miracle, the atomic bomb, and that in itself shocked many of the experts, some of whom had believed that the Russians wouldn't get the bomb for another ten or even twenty years. The fact that, as we soon learned, the gestation

period was cut down considerably because the Russians cheated by spying on us didn't make their A-bomb any easier to live with.

As bad as that was, we still had a way to stay ahead, and after a fair amount of arguing, posturing, and hand-wringing, we forged ahead at the order of the man who had dropped the atomic bomb, Harry Truman, and built the hydrogen bomb. We did it over the objections and advice of people like Robert Oppenheimer, who argued that not only would the hydrogen bomb steal valuable resources from our well-established A-bomb program, but it wasn't even necessary: we still had plenty of atomic bombs, many more than the Russians, and we could still wipe them out whenever we chose to, hydrogen bomb or no hydrogen bomb.

Oppenheimer and his allies really annoyed people when they also pointed out that aside from the questionable tactical and technical objections, there were moral considerations. A case could be made that the atomic bomb was chiefly a military weapon. One could effectively A-bomb air bases and troop formations and submarine pens. But the H-bomb was too big: it was good for nothing but the wholesale slaughter of civilian populations.

All such concerns were swept aside in the all-important rush to stay ahead of the Russians. America got its hydrogen bomb in November 1952 and rejoiced in its restored technological and military superiority. But the honeymoon seemed even shorter this time. Less than a year later, the Soviets claimed to have developed their own H-bomb, and to add insult to injury, one capable of being delivered by an airplane—unlike our own H-bomb, which had been less a bomb than a small industrial plant. Later we learned that the Soviets had been considerably exaggerating their achievement, but the fear that the Russians had bested us right out of the H-bomb gate was nothing if not galling.

With every passing year, the competition grew more intense and ruthless, expanding to every realm with the slightest possible strategic or military application: supersonic aircraft, atomic submarines, electronics, radar, and, of course, rockets and missiles. Work was progressing steadily on America's first intercontinental ballistic missile, the Atlas, along with ever smaller and more sophisticated atomic weapons for it to carry aloft. But it wasn't easy, and sometimes it seemed that inventing the atomic bomb had been a simpler task than to construct a

missile that could travel five thousand miles from one point on the Earth to another and hit a target with any accuracy. The Russians already claimed to have a working ICBM. So far, it was only talk, but it kept the engineers and designers in America's defense companies working late into the night.

Even so, no one seriously expected that America was about to lose the technological race to the Soviets. When the time came to launch a rocket into space, all the way and not just to the tentative sixty or seventy miles of altitude that both sides had been probing, obviously that rocket would be sporting stars and stripes, not a hammer and sickle. And that applied whether that spaceship was an ICBM or a peaceful scientific shot.

Beginning in July 1957, countries all over the world engaged in the International Geophysical Year, a coordinated campaign of research and exploration aimed at achieving a better understanding of Earth, from deep inside the planet to the outer reaches of its atmosphere and beyond. The IGY was led by the United States and the Soviet Union in a stellar display of peaceful scientific cooperation and felicity. As part of the effort, both countries were planning to send aloft satellites to circle the Earth and make scientific observations. Everyone knew, of course, that the United States would be launching the first satellite, the data from which would graciously be shared with the Soviet Union and all the other countries participating in the IGY. The United States would be first because, as everyone knew, it was the foremost scientific and technological force in the entire world.

Everyone knew and believed that until that evening of October 4, 1957, when the Soviet Union launched *Sputnik,* humanity's first artificial satellite, into orbit. It was probably the biggest, nastiest shock to American self-confidence and complacency since Pearl Harbor, and had nearly the same impact as an attack from out of the blue, even though not one shot had been fired except for the Russian R-7 rocket that had hurled *Sputnik* into space. To make it worse, this was a demonstration of Russian dominance that Americans could see for themselves from their own backyards as it passed overhead emitting its mocking radio beeps.

The immediate question on the lips of everyone from outraged congressmen to learned news commentators to the average bewildered citizen was, how did it happen? How did a supposedly technologically

backward nation, one whose refrigerators and cars and appliances were punch lines to jokes, suddenly best the United States in a feat of science and technology?

Obviously, somebody had been sleeping on the job. Worse, somebody had not been *doing* his job. We had allowed ourselves to grow soft and lazy and careless, smug in the certainty of our superiority, and while we had been taking our time and not paying attention, Russia had come out from behind on the clubhouse turn to take the commanding lead.

"For all its simplicity, small size, and inability to do more than orbit the Earth and transmit meaningless radio blips, Sputnik's impact on America and the world was enormous and totally unanticipated," writes Paul Dickson in *Sputnik: The Shock of the Century*.[3] The satellite evoked anger, fear, and a primal sort of panic that *something had to be done,* and fast. Not only did we have somehow to match and surpass the Soviet achievement, but we had to figure out how and why we'd been beaten to the punch in the first place, and then do whatever was necessary to correct the situation.

Some blamed an American culture drunk on fancy automobiles, television, and rock and roll, but others had a more serious diagnosis. "It is time to ask ourselves whether preoccupation with our 'scientific secrets' instead of with science itself has not resulted in impairing the real source of our strength and in loss of the supremacy we once could claim," declared *The Washington Post* a week after *Sputnik's* launch. "In sober truth, we have driven out of our laboratories a great many preeminent men of science; J. Robert Oppenheimer and Edward U. Condon are among them. . . . We have let scientists become targets of suspicion and abuse. . . . in the name of security, we have sacrificed security."[4]

For an aroused nation suddenly made keenly aware of science and its importance to national security and prestige, scientists had become the frontline soldiers in the cold war struggle against the Soviets. Where were all the great scientists when we needed them, while Russia was busy getting ahead of us? Why, they were all being investigated by security boards, getting denied clearances, being kicked out of government laboratories, and being banished to the ivory towers of academia.

Overnight, J. Robert Oppenheimer became the poster boy for America's neglected scientific elite, the face of our collective folly that had

caused us to sabotage ourselves by keeping our most brilliant minds out of public service. Having become arguably the nation's foremost spokesman for science and scientists, and the first name anyone thought of in American science, Oppenheimer was now held up as the chief victim of America's own shortsightedness.

A week after *Sputnik,* Dr. John P. Hagen, the head of America's official satellite program, Project Vanguard (the one that was supposed to be first), was asked by a reporter: "If we want to keep in first place scientifically, can we afford to waste an Oppenheimer?" Hagen didn't hesitate. "Whether we want to stay in first place or last place, we can't afford it," he replied.[5]

In a television interview, physicist Edward Condon mentioned Oppenheimer as someone whose expertise had been lost to the government because of security concerns. Because "it has become fashionable in Washington to attack the integrity of the nation's leading scientists," he said, "many of them have gone into political exile."[6]

If the Russians had beaten us fair and square, as obviously they had, then part of the reason was that we had weakened ourselves by lobotomizing American science through anti-Communist witch hunts and loyalty checks. The point was driven home more strongly at the beginning of November, when the Soviets launched *Sputnik II,* a much bigger craft with a living passenger, a dog named Laika. We couldn't comfort ourselves by chalking up the first *Sputnik* as a stunt or a lucky shot. This couldn't be dismissed. Not only had the Russians done it again, they'd done it better, indicating a sophisticated and organized effort.

As if to rub it in and to underscore the point that at least some nations aside from the Russians actually did value scientists came the news that France had given Robert Oppenheimer its highest civilian award, the Legion of Honor, only a week before *Sputnik* took flight, at the end of September in a champagne reception at the French Cultural Service in New York. "The award was made because of the esteem and admiration of the French government for a great American scientist," said Edouard Morot-Sir, cultural counselor of the French embassy. "His soul is very close to that of the French philosophers." In a short speech at the ceremony, Morot-Sir spoke of Oppenheimer's "extraordinary contribution" to the "philosophy of science."

Although the award was made on September 25, the news didn't hit

the papers until a month after *Sputnik*. Morot-Sir denied that the delay had anything to do with an attempt to sneak the medal to Oppenheimer "under the table" because of the scientist's persona non grata status with his own government. "I issued a press release but it did not appear in the newspapers," he said. He explained that all such decorations and awards were given in the same manner at the New York cultural office. "The decoration of the Legion of Honor is given to many Americans, it was said, and announcements are not regularly made," pointed out *The New York Times*. Even Oppenheimer himself wryly noted, "A number of my colleagues have received such honors and I've heard about it only when I read their obituaries."[7]

The point that an American scientist was now being honored by a foreign government after such a resounding defeat for American science wasn't lost on the press. "In making Dr. J. Robert Oppenheimer an officer of the Legion of Honor recently, the French Government demonstrated anew the force of St. Matthew's observation that 'a prophet is not without honor, save in his own country, and in his own house.' . . . Does it contribute to the security of the United States that the genius of such men should, for whatever reason, go unemployed by the Government in this time of crisis?" asked *The Washington Post*.[8]

"The announcement comes at a time when the air seems full of sputniks," drily noted Raleigh, North Carolina's *News and Observer*. "It is about time that this country realized that it has more to find than to hide. And that it cannot afford to reject and hamper the best brains it has available—the brains it desperately needs. The verdict which held Oppenheimer a loyal American who could not be trusted was contradictory and silly when it was made. It is the basis of a dangerous extravagance in American resources now. And many other, though smaller, Oppenheimers have been hampered when they were not publicly barred from helping America's effort to lead in scientific advance."[9]

"The point is made that the rulers of the Soviet Union remain barbarians, even as they send their Sputniks hurtling into outer space to the amazement and chagrin of more civilized nations," observed *The Trenton Evening Times*. "It is not out of order to ask if the United States is consistently appreciative of and grateful for distinguished and unselfish service. Take, as an example, the men who produced the scientific

miracle of the atomic bomb—Einstein, Fermi, Compton, Urey, Chadwick, Bohr, and yes, Oppenheimer. How have they fared at the hands of the government they served?"[10]

No one had to ask how J. Robert Oppenheimer had fared at the hands of his government. But the tectonic shift in attitudes and political will brought about by the shock of *Sputnik* was soon to provide his first real possibility for reinstatement.

* * *

Aside from arousing the ire of H-bomb advocates in the early 1950s for what was later termed "a failure to enthuse," Oppenheimer had run afoul of the military establishment. As a participant in various defense policy studies, he soon adopted the view that more resources should be directed toward strengthening United States air defenses, particularly early-warning radar networks and antiaircraft capabilities. But this rankled Air Force generals hungry for vast fleets of offensive bombers since they were wedded to a strategy of massive retaliation and saw Oppenheimer's emphasis on defensive measures as a threat to their position. Robb spent considerable time questioning Oppenheimer and other witnesses on this issue, at times all but implying that Oppenheimer had conspired to weaken the Air Force.

Garrison repeatedly objected to Robb's adversarial tactics, particularly his fondness for ambushing Oppenheimer with classified documents. He pointed out the absurdity of withholding such documents from Oppenheimer's own counsel while Robb proceeded to quote them at length in open court for all to hear. But to no avail. The mild-mannered Garrison was no match for the aggressive Robb, and found most of his objections shot down by Robb's responses or the board's rulings.

Office Memorandum · UNITED STATES GOVERNMENT

TO : A. H. Belmont

DATE: 11/12/57

FROM : P. R. Bibler

SUBJECT: DR. ROBERT OPPENHEIMER;
~~_____~~ INFORMANT
INTERNAL SECURITY - R

Tolson ____
Nichols ____
Boardman ____
Belmont ____
Mason ____
Mohr ____
Parsons ____
Rosen ____
Tamm ____
Nease ____
Winterrowd ____
Tele. Room ____
Holloman ____

Massachusetts, telephoned at 7:20 p.m., 11/11/57. He desired
to speak to the Director, and was referred to SA P. R. Bibler in
Mr. Belmont's Office.

_____ said he was a "little drunk." He wanted to
speak for Dr. Robert Oppenheimer, not acting as his agent, but
as a friend. He says Oppenheimer is being wasted, that he was
"dying" to get into some big project, but for some reason the
Government would not use him. He described him as the best
brain in the country, going to waste at the Institute of Advanced
Study at

Memorandum · UNITED STATES G

~~... furnished no factual~~ information, just wanted to
urge that Oppenheimer be used, if we could do anything about it.

The Atomic Energy Commission published a decision,
6/29/54, denying Oppenheimer access to classified data.

Indices check on _____ negative.

ACTION:

For information.

100-17828
PRB:smk
(4)

1 - Mr. Holloman
1 - Mr. Belmont
1 - Mr. Bibler

RECORDED - 23 10 17735 2288

11 NOV 14 1957

INDEXED - 23

5 2 NOV 19 1957

8

Rumblings of Redemption

Where was Oppenheimer during all this furor? As usual, quietly going about his routine business. For part of the month of October, he was at Columbia University, participating in an event called the American Assembly. The assembly had been instituted by Dwight D. Eisenhower while he was serving as president of Columbia and was designed to bring together top thinkers from business, science, labor, politics, and academia, among other fields. The idea was that the various pundits would address "issues of national concern" and make recommendations.

The October 1957 session, "Atoms for Power," focused on civilian applications of atomic energy, and Oppenheimer was a natural choice to participate. His overview on civilian reactor programs, "The environs of atomic power," was published in the assembly's final report. Fortunately, since the mandate of the "Atoms for Power" conference was completely nonmilitary and unclassified, no one could question the participation of a supposedly untrustworthy expert such as Oppenheimer.

At the end of October, Oppenheimer was in Washington, D.C., watching Niels Bohr accept the AEC's first "Atoms for Peace" award. In between, he tended to the usual Institute business and took his daughter to a series of dentist appointments.

So, even with all the talk on the editorial pages about how Oppenheimer was an example of how the country treated its scientists

badly and thus had fallen behind the Russians, and how a proper response to the challenge of *Sputnik* might somehow involve correcting the great injustice done to Oppenheimer, the *Sputnik*s didn't make that much difference to him personally. But as the repercussions from the second *Sputnik* were still reverberating and America scrambled to respond by launching its own satellite, any satellite, some signs began to appear on the horizon that, maybe, restoring Oppenheimer's clearance might be an idea whose time had finally come.

One clear, if indirect, sign was Eisenhower's decision to bring a scientist into the White House on a full-time basis, when he appointed MIT president Dr. James R. Killian as his special assistant for science and technology. It was not a cabinet-level position, but Killian's appointment was an unmistakable indication that Eisenhower's administration, under fierce attack from all sides for being asleep at the scientific-progress switch, was now taking science and technology seriously.

And for those who felt, as did the *St. Louis Post-Dispatch,* that "the Administration must face the fact that its relations with the scientific community have been estranged ever since Dr. J. Robert Oppenheimer was dismissed in 1954 as a security risk," the Killian appointment was seen as partial vindication. After all, Killian and Oppenheimer were well-known friends and allies, and Killian had testified on Oppenheimer's behalf at the security hearing. "By turning to Dr. Killian, the Eisenhower Administration is in effect appealing for the confidence of the scientific community which was so grievously alienated three years ago," said the *Post-Dispatch.* But it wasn't enough. "To restore the confidence of the best scientists, can the Administration afford to leave unrighted the wrong done to Dr. Oppenheimer—if it was a wrong? President Eisenhower . . . ought to order a review of the Oppenheimer findings by a board of the very highest standing, in order to satisfy the country and the scientific community that injustice has not been done."[1]

Calls for action from newspaper editors and columnists were one thing, and all too easy for the administration to ignore in the torrent of post-*Sputnik* criticism already overwhelming it. But when a former member of that same administration joined the chorus, the song became louder and more insistent. On November 17, Trevor Gardner, former Air Force assistant secretary for research and development, told

reporters that the White House should consider bringing Oppenheimer back into the fold. The president's new science adviser, said Gardner, should consider the question personally, and then reconvene a board to review Oppenheimer's clearance.

Gardner was the man who had led the Air Force's entire aerospace research and development effort, and his resignation in February 1956 had been public and noisy, complete with a thorough lambasting of the Eisenhower administration and dire warnings that the Soviet Union had moved ahead in rocket technology—warnings that were dismissed as alarmist at the time, but whose accuracy was now painfully clear to all. (It was not the first time that Gardner and Oppenheimer had been linked. In 1954, Gardner's confirmation as assistant secretary had been held up for several months in the Senate because Gardner had supposedly attempted to influence a Gray Board member in Oppenheimer's favor during the security hearing. The matter blew over and Gardner was ultimately confirmed when his supposed attempt to illegally "intercede" on Oppenheimer's behalf was revealed to be nothing more than some innocent pro-Oppie remarks made to friends at a Washington luncheon.)

According to Gardner, the United States was at least two years behind Russia in the missile and satellite sweepstakes, and "has a full scale emergency on its hands whether we know it or not." And the Soviet Union "probably" already had its own ICBM, while our rockets were blowing up on the launchpad. Such comments from a man now recognized as having raised the alarm of Soviet superiority long before *Sputnik*—and having been unfairly disregarded—had great impact.[2]

And they inspired others. The next day, as Senate majority leader Lyndon Johnson, chairman of the Preparedness Committee, set up to investigate the reasons why America had been caught so off guard, got ready to open wide-ranging hearings, Democratic senators Henry Jackson and George Smathers announced that they favored reopening the Oppenheimer case, a move they considered "entirely proper" in light of the current crisis. "We must do everything we can to enlist all the brainpower on our side," said Smathers. Senator Clinton Anderson, ranking Democrat and vice chairman of the Joint Congressional Committee on Atomic Energy, joined in support. "Mr. Oppenheimer was

indiscreet in many of the things he said, but you have to take genius the way it exists," he reasoned.[3]

When Johnson's hearings began the following Monday, Oppenheimer's name was bandied about unofficially as a possible witness. But although the hearings dragged on into January as seventy-eight witnesses, among them new scientific superstars such as Wernher von Braun, testified, Oppenheimer was not among them. Some columnists speculated that because Johnson was striving to give the appearance of an impartial, nonpartisan investigation, he deliberately avoided the lightning rod of controversy that was Oppenheimer.

But even if Oppenheimer wasn't called to testify to Congress, he remained a symbol of the government's folly for much of the American public, a man who could have prevented the Russian triumph—if only we'd let him. Observed one letter to *The New York Times,* "This is the same scientist whose services were lost to our Government because it was feared that he was a 'security risk': that he might let some of our secrets leak out to the Russians. The two sputniks seem to indicate that the Russians had no crying need of our secrets."[4]

Unlike other occasions when a brief flurry of pro-Oppenheimer feeling had flared up in the press and popular media, this one was showing no signs of dissipating. In fact, it was only getting started. *Sputnik* had shaken the United States, its government, and its people to their very foundations, heralding a cultural and political change that would leave nothing untouched. Merely by launching two satellites in a month, Russia had changed all the rules. Nothing short of an actual all-out nuclear attack could have been more devastating.

Attitudes, opinions, judgments that had been set in granite and steel, tempered by the pillars of American self-confidence, eternal surety, and McCarthyism had been shown to be obsolete, unworkable, untenable. New ideas, new opinions, new viewpoints, had to be considered, or we were going to be left behind and ground into the dust of history by the Communist juggernaut. Somehow things that once seemed of enormous importance didn't matter much anymore—such as questionable political associations of twenty years past, white lies told in a misguided attempt to shield a friend, or technical judgments that might not agree with the majority opinion.

The bedrock of American society was shifting, and no one was cer-

tain what would be left standing when everything settled down. But everyone could agree that we had to do whatever was necessary to catch up to and get ahead of the Soviets once more. If that meant overlooking some iffy backgrounds and indiscretions, so be it. Perhaps more than anything else since Hiroshima, *Sputnik* made it clear that everything had changed—or more precisely, that *we* had to change if we were going to survive.

Which might even mean that two men who had once been on opposite sides might find common ground. The quest for Oppenheimer's reinstatement took its most bizarre and unexpected turn at the end of November, when former AEC commissioner Thomas E. Murray, a man who just three and a half years earlier had not only concurred with the majority opinion stripping Oppenheimer of clearance, but felt obliged to add his own accusation that Oppenheimer had actually been "disloyal," told an Associated Press reporter that he had "no objection" to reopening the Oppenheimer case and "would not be at all displeased if he [Oppenheimer] were to be reinstated."

Such a statement could have been more startling only if it had been Lewis Strauss himself who voiced the words. Coming from Murray, it was shocking enough. Although Murray was careful not to call specifically for Oppenheimer's reinstatement, recusing himself from such a judgment because he was "out of touch" with the latest technical developments and had been a judge in the original Oppenheimer case, his statement ended up sounding almost like a recantation.

One day after publishing Murray's comments under the headline "Murray Switches on Oppenheimer," *The New York Times* clarified that Murray "had not changed his own judgment. The New York Times yesterday incorrectly implied in a headline that he had reversed his opinion."

Soon after, Murray further clarified his original remarks. He was merely acknowledging that things were different now than they had been in 1954, and that a different judgment on Oppenheimer might now be made. "I have no doubt today that my verdict was justly rendered," he said of his 1954 decision. But that decision had been made "within the context of the exigencies of the moment. Since that time, a new situation of fact has developed in the United States and in the world. . . . Authorities who are competent to judge the exigencies of the

new situation may feel it necessary or useful to recall Dr. Oppenheimer to Government service. It would not be appropriate for me to express displeasure with this decision if it were to be made." It would "simply be a new decision, taken within the context of the national interest, to be judged on its own merits."[5]

By December, it was beginning to seem as if the calls for Oppenheimer's reinstatement were rapidly coalescing into a genuine groundswell of support. Dr. Henry D. Smyth, Murray's former fellow AEC commissioner and the only one to find in Oppenheimer's favor in 1954, said Oppenheimer's clearance should be restored "if he wants to come back." Appearing on television, Republican senator Jacob Javits joined his congressional colleagues in urging Oppenheimer's exoneration. "I would bring him back unless the FBI and the CIA have more information than has been made public," he said, hedging his bets. Interviewed on a New York radio program, two more Eisenhower administration veterans, former secretary of the Air Force Thomas K. Finletter and former undersecretary of the Army Tracy S. Voorhees, hopped onto the Oppenheimer bandwagon. "I think he ought to be brought back," Finletter said of Oppie. "We cannot afford not to have him." Voorhees agreed, adding that Oppenheimer's "ability is pretty good compensation for any indiscretion."[6]

Perhaps most heartening to Oppenheimer personally, if not unexpected, were the words of his friends and former colleagues then serving on Eisenhower's new Science Advisory Committee. Asked by British reporters whether McCarthyism was to blame for America's fall behind the Soviets, committee chairman Isidor I. Rabi said, "It is still too early to judge the long-range effects of McCarthyism, but the exclusion of Professor Oppenheimer, a man who accomplished so much for his country, is indication of the failure of the country and the authorities to value correctly such contributions, both intellectual and substantial, to the welfare of the United States. Only when he is returned to more active Government service will it indicate that a change of heart has occurred. It will be a source of encouragement to the whole scientific community."

The Washington Post's survey of "the President's 17-man Committee" showed that "eight other members endorsed Rabi's statement. None voiced opposition to Oppenheimer's reinstatement." One of them, Bell

Telephone Labs vice president James B. Fisk, called Oppenheimer's loss "a wrong which should be righted now." Hans Bethe said reinstatement would be "a symbol of what this country and our Government stand for." Said *The Post:* "The scientists—all intimately concerned with America's space race against the Russians—believe that (1) 'we can't afford to waste an Oppenheimer' and (2) his return to Government work would stimulate the over-all scientific effort by demonstrating conclusively that the McCarthy era has ended."[7]

Still, noted the *New York Post,* "neither Dr. Rabi nor Dr. Bethe are engaged in any pro-Oppenheimer campaign." And the composition of the Science Advisory Committee, packed as it appeared to be with Oppenheimer supporters, wasn't intended as a sop to Oppenheimer either. "It just happens that most of the good scientists are convinced that Dr. Oppenheimer was right," said Bethe.[8]

And the *New York Post* offered another disturbing thought for anyone who was too encouraged by this outpouring of love for Oppenheimer. "One ticklish aspect of the problem hinges on what might be the attitude of AEC Chairman Strauss who is not considered friendly to Oppenheimer. Some observers feel that Oppenheimer's reinstatement would be interpreted as a slap at Strauss and that the Administration does not seek a showdown with the AEC chairman."[9]

It seemed that the administration itself was offering its own comment on the question later in December, when the *National Review* claimed that Vice President Richard Nixon told editor William F. Buckley that Oppenheimer was still essentially a security risk, and that granting clearance to "men with such a record as Dr. Oppenheimer's would be to 'collapse' our internal security program." An aide to Nixon, however, told *The New York Times* that he could neither confirm nor deny Nixon's statement. A day later, Nixon's office issued a terse "no comment," despite the *National Review's* contention that the words had come "from the Vice President's own mouth."[10]

Imperturbable as always, Oppenheimer was playing it cool. "No comment," he told reporters begging for a response. "The situation is too vague right now." No, he had not been officially approached by anyone in government to discuss his return. The *Washington Post* report about the support of his fellow scientists was "a very nice story, but I have no comment."[11]

If Oppenheimer had no comment, some conservative commentators didn't have the same problem. "Here we have a brilliant but certainly a screwball scientist," sneered columnist John O'Donnell. "In the file of our how-crazy-can-you-get department, this reporter gives top priority to the bewildering but high-pressure drive to get Dr. J. Robert Oppenheimer cleared of security risk charges and given top rank and access to American secrets for defense against our Communist enemies." After the usual rote recitation of the Chevalier incident and other Oppenheimer indiscretions, O'Donnell puzzles over Murray's "verbose and bewildering doubletalk" about reopening the case, and concludes: "If this means anything, it means that there is a group in this capital who seriously believe that it's possible to be a lying security risk in the early stages of a war (and we are at war with Russia, militarily, diplomatically, economically and scientifically) and then some years later come back as a trusted hero. This we can't swallow."[12]

More circumspect was *The Washington Post*'s Warren Unna (who had penned the *Atlantic Monthly* article earlier in the year about the rivalry between Strauss and Murray). Unna noted the great deal of support for Oppenheimer's rehabilitation that had arisen since *Sputnik* began beeping around the Earth, but made it clear that so far, it was nothing but talk. Barring the unlikely event that President Eisenhower himself would deign to intervene, any decisive action would have to come either from Oppenheimer himself or from AEC chairman Lewis Strauss. Neither, Unna observed, seemed likely.

"There have been no indications from Strauss that he is ready to forgive," said Unna. "And there have been no indications from Oppenheimer that he is ready to forget, and come back." In the final analysis, "perhaps . . . the Oppenheimer case resolves itself down to a symbol. . . . If Oppenheimer is invited back to help this Nation expedite its military, scientific, and technological programs, Oppenheimer's personal contribution might be secondary. The big thing would be his return: a symbol to American scientists that the heat of McCarthyism was really off."[13]

But it was no longer McCarthyism that was keeping Oppenheimer out of the restored good graces of his own government and preventing him from serving his country again in another hour of dire need. It was nothing more—or less—than the stubbornness, pettiness, and injured

ego of one Lewis L. Strauss. After having done so much to engineer Oppenheimer's disgrace and removal from government, the AEC chairman was not about to see all his work undone by "the wail of the anti-Communist propagandists about the urgency of restoring their hero, Dr. J. Robert Oppenheimer, to scientific sainthood, so he can mastermind the outer space program," as right-wing pundit (and Strauss friend) Fulton Lewis put it.[14]

Earlier in December, Strauss ran into Gordon Gray, former Gray Board chairman and now director of the Office of Defense Mobilization, at a National Security Council meeting. As might be expected, the conversation turned to matters Oppenheimer, particularly the current furor over restoring the scientist's clearance. Gray told Strauss that Vice President Nixon was concerned about the pressure being brought to bear upon the administration in that regard, and wondered if something should be done. Strauss assured Gray that he would talk to Nixon that very afternoon, and that he had also recommended to Eisenhower that if the Oppenheimer question came up in a press conference, the president should say only that Oppenheimer had received an "impartial and fair hearing" and that anyone had the right to appeal any decision against him if there was new evidence.

According to a report that Strauss duly filed with the FBI, he also told Gray that while he wanted "to leave the AEC and retire to his farm, he may not be able to do so if it would mean that the scientists would get their way as far as Oppenheimer is concerned." Strauss still considered Oppenheimer to be "a risk and a threat."

Strauss also continued to oppose Oppenheimer tirelessly in his capacity as a member of the board of trustees of the Institute for Advanced Study. He attempted to block Oppenheimer's invitation to two Russian physicists to attend the Institute, accusing Oppenheimer of "lying" about the invitation, and intimating that some sinister motives were afoot, despite the fact that, as the FBI later patiently explained to Strauss, both of the Russians were known to Oppenheimer and had attended previous physics conferences in the United States.[15]

Strauss used the line about needing "new evidence" to reopen the Oppenheimer case on the press as well. "I know of no substantial new evidence," he told reporters, adding that he had no plans to reopen the case. "He made it clear that he is in no mood to give in to demands of

Congressmen and scientists that the AEC restore Oppenheimer's clearance for secret atomic information," wrote one reporter.[16]

As Strauss had anticipated, the question came up in an Eisenhower press conference. Asked whether there was "any move within the Administration to bring Dr. Oppenheimer back into the government scientific field," Eisenhower responded, "Not the slightest I have ever heard of . . . Dr. Oppenheimer's case was completely settled and was an issue that was in the past." He added that although he would "certainly have no objections" to reopening the case if "new information" became available, "there is no move that I know of any kind to reopen the issue."[17]

Not everyone was impressed by the Strauss evasion. "Why, in the name of sanity, should it be up to Dr. J. Robert Oppenheimer to offer 'new evidence' in order to obtain a security clearance?" demanded *The Washington Post*. "The country needs his scientific genius—needs it far more, in fact, than he needs any sort of condescending approval from the Atomic Energy Commission and its altogether too secure potentate, Lewis Strauss. It should now be amply clear to everyone, as it was clear to some at the time, that the exaggerated emphasis on secrecy and security and the pillorying of scientists who were considered 'loyal but' was one of the major causes of the scientific lag from which the country is suffering. The President ought, on his own initiative, to order an enlightened review of Dr. Oppenheimer's case. And he ought at the same time to take a good look at the strange spectacle of an atomic energy chieftain presiding over some of the Nation's most important scientific efforts with his mind still firmly glued to the procedures that helped get us into the fix."[18]

Writing to *The New York Times*, Frank Altschul mused about Strauss's need for new evidence: "I wonder whether this is not putting the shoe on the wrong foot. Dr. Oppenheimer rendered the country services of inestimable value over a long period of years. By way of reward he was subjected to a devastating ordeal. . . . In these circumstances he could hardly be expected to reopen the case. It is the decision of the commission, rather than the evidence before it, that seems to call for a somewhat belated review. For this the initiative surely lies with the Atomic Energy Commission and not with Dr. Oppenheimer."[19]

Not long after his letter was published in *The Times*, Altschul heard

from one of the members of the Institute for Advanced Study board of trustees, John F. Fulton, who expressed his support and agreement. Fulton also offered some interesting observations about Strauss's behavior on the board. Although Strauss had "voted enthusiastically" to name Oppenheimer as Institute director, "almost immediately after Oppenheimer's appointment, Strauss began sniping at him on the grounds of his past and present affiliation with leftist thinkers." According to Fulton, Strauss's feelings toward Oppenheimer were so "unreasonable" that Fulton and several other board members questioned whether Strauss could or should continue to serve on the board, an issue they also discussed with Strauss. But, says Fulton, Strauss "stubbornly refused to resign and went on sniping at every possible occasion. Oppie remained silent and treated Strauss with austere politeness and complete dignity." Altschul passed on a copy of Fulton's letter to Oppenheimer.[20]

"I feel a little sad that our country has to forgo the services of one of the finest scientific minds in the world," wrote Eleanor Roosevelt in her syndicated column. "Dr. Oppenheimer was never accused of anything except having felt, as most scientists do, that progress in science should be shared, regardless of nationality. The scientific approach makes this almost inevitable, and I cannot understand the attitude of fear which now has enveloped us. . . . We must cease to be afraid and, instead, rejoice at new discoveries, from wherever they come. And the scientific approach, which holds that any discovery is the result of the work of many people and must be shared for the benefit of mankind, we can ill afford to neglect. . . . Could not our government see the advantage of using one of the brains we need for our scientific development? Dr. Oppenheimer may have made a mistake, but all of us do!"[21]

Hope may have sprung temporarily, but after the initial *Sputnik* excitement began to subside, helped along by America's first successful satellite launching on January 31, 1958, so did any real possibility for a rehearing. Riding on the crest of post-*Sputnik* panic, the optimism and enthusiasm of Oppenheimer's allies finally crashed and broke against the intransigent brick wall of Strauss's iron grip on the AEC.

Oppenheimer expressed his frustrations to his friend and Institute member George Kennan at the end of 1957: "It has been an incredibly noisy autumn, with many hundreds, perhaps a thousand, requests from press and radio and television, and people who want lectures, to almost

every one of which I have managed to say no. The sickly scurrying of this autumn in this country has been a proper match for the sickly smugness that preceded it, and no doubt will close in on us again. There is always a danger that in the discomfort of a loss of confidence, and a disorientation, men will seek simplistic answers; and there are of course many to provide them. There has been very little of nobility in what anyone has audibly said."[22]

And to another friend, Cyrus Eaton, industrialist and philanthropist, who had written to Oppie asking in some desperation for a formula for the United States and Russia to live in peace, Oppenheimer said: "I would like to see far greater courage, and far greater freedom for courage, to look at ourselves and take our measure. Perhaps this is for me the most urgent, the most hopeful, the most desperately needed of all things that may help to keep the peace."[23]

Such thoughts were somber, wistful, and hardly optimistic. For Oppenheimer, all the hysteria over *Sputnik* was a sign not of a new period of American scientific renewal, but an intensification and expansion of the same old fears and the ill-conceived race for bigger and better weapons.

Sputnik may have started the space age, ushered in a new era of history and a new chapter of the cold war, and changed the world in ways that, even in the twenty-first century, are still being felt. But for Robert Oppenheimer at least, when all the hue and cry had passed, nothing had really changed. Like the *Sputnik*s passing mockingly overhead in the American night sky, his chances for redemption and vindication had shone briefly, bright but fleeting, until they faltered and were extinguished as surely and as completely as the two *Sputnik*s burning up as their orbits decayed and they fell back to Earth.

Still, the issue wasn't dead. A certain progress had been made. The idea of Oppenheimer's reinstatement was now firmly established in the collective mind. Even in the midst of the *Sputnik* silly season, some seeds had been planted. They would not sprout for some time; the climate hadn't improved quite enough for that. But when they did, they would bring a new optimism.

* * *

A distinguished series of witnesses appeared to testify on Oppenheimer's behalf. His wartime boss General Groves told the board that he would be "amazed" if Oppenheimer ever committed an act of disloyalty and that he was "completely loyal." Coming from a man who was thoroughly familiar with Oppenheimer's background and had cleared him to work on the country's most secret project, Groves's testimony should have had considerable weight, but Robb managed to get the general to admit that given the stricter standards now in effect, he would not be able to clear Oppenheimer today.

John Lansdale, Groves's security head on the Manhattan Project, also supported Oppenheimer. An experienced lawyer who refused to be bullied by Robb's tactics, he remarked that "the fact that associations in 1940 are regarded with the same seriousness that similar associations would be regarded today is a manifestation of hysteria."[24]

Nobel laureate Isidor Rabi, while agreeing with Robb's assertion that "the board may be in possession of information which is not now available to you," countered by saying that "on the other hand, I am in possession of a long experience with this man, going back to 1929," experience on which he placed "great weight." More than that, Rabi continued, "There is a real, positive record. . . . we have an A-bomb. . . . what more do you want, mermaids?"[25]

More than one witness expressed sentiments similar to those of Vannevar Bush, the distinguished leader of all American scientific research during World War II, who maintained that "no board should ever {decide} whether a man should serve his country or not because he expressed strong opinions. If you want to try that case, you can try me. I have expressed strong opinions many times, and I intend to do so. They have been unpopular opinions at times. When a man is pilloried for doing that, this country is in a severe state."[26]

Most of these witnesses also faced Robb's inquisitorial tactics. Either Robb would pit his documents against a witness's all-too-human memory, as he did with former AEC director David Lilienthal; or he would elicit glowing testimony as to Oppenheimer's character and loyalty, and then attempt to shake the witness's composure by demanding an opinion on some example of Oppenheimer's supposedly dishonest conduct. These are standard techniques of cross-examination, of course, and would certainly be perfectly acceptable in a normal jury trial in open court, when both sides have full access to all of the evidence. But as Chairman Gray had stressed, Oppenheimer was not on trial, and this was merely a hearing. Yet time and time again, he allowed Robb free rein in the most ruthless prosecutorial tactics, while overruling Garrison's objections.

A UNIVERSAL CONFUSION

By the late 1950s, Oppenheimer finds himself an unofficial
international ambassador for science. Passport photo, circa 1958.

It is our duty not least to help create a world in which despair and cynicism are complemented and partly replaced, not by optimism, but by a courage and by hope.

—J. ROBERT OPPENHEIMER,
"THE FUTURE OF CIVILIZATION IN
THE ATOMIC AGE," JAPAN, 1960

THE FOREIGN SERVICE
OF THE
UNITED STATES OF AMERICA
American Embassy
Paris 8, France

Date: February 14, 1958

To: Director, FBI (100-17828)

From: Legat, Paris (105-347)

Subject: DR. J. ROBERT OPPENHEIMER
 INTERNAL SECURITY - R

France Soir, Paris daily, on 2/8/58 reported that
subject, who "was under attack by the famous McCARTHY Committee
(Senator McCARTHY)", will spend two months in France and give
six lectures at the Sorbonne on the subject "The Composition
of Particles and Interaction of Elements." It was indicated
that the first of these lectures will take place on 4/23/58.

As the Bureau is undoubtedly aware, subject was
made a Knight of the Legion of Honor during November 1957
"because he is a great scientist."

It would be appreciated if the Bureau would advise
whether this office should arrange with established French
sources to cover the activities of subject while he is in
France.

Two extra copies of this communication are enclosed
for transmittal to the domestic field.

 P.

ROL:CM
(5)

Let to Paris
3-5-58 - JPW

REC-86

13 FEB 25 1958

2299

REC.D FBI

9

The Answer to Fear

For better or worse, America's intellectuals had to be grateful to the Soviet Union and *Sputnik* for one thing: finally, in the fall of 1957 and spring of 1958, "egghead" was suddenly no longer a term of derision. Now, instead of being ignored or patronized, scientists and engineers and the rest of America's brain trust were being sought out by their government and the people, elevated to a new pedestal of respect and importance.

Suddenly they mattered again. Suddenly people cared about what they thought, what they wanted, what they could do. Their problems and dilemmas became everyone's concern. In *The New York Times Magazine* one spring Sunday, Theodore White addressed the situation in great detail and with a decidedly sympathetic bent. His piece, " 'Where Do We Fit In?' the Scientists Ask," examined the confusion, anxiety, bafflement, and anger of a scientific community trying to find a way through a "bureaucratic labyrinth" of competing military and civilian interests that far too often seemed determined to ignore the very real concerns of the scientists. Who was to determine the course of scientific research? Who would choose where to direct resources? With science and technology such an important factor in the defense of the United States and the future of the free world, who would make the vital decisions that had to be made, and how could science and government work together to each other's benefit?

One of the key problems leading to the present tangle of ennui and inaction, wrote White, was exemplified by the Oppenheimer case. A respected scientist, whose job it was to advise the government on science and related policy issues, had been brought down in an ugly and protracted way because his counsel had clashed with the opinions and judgments of other powerful policymakers in government and the military. Oppenheimer's fate showed the scientists that as far as the government was concerned, they were supposed to be seen and not heard—i.e., do their jobs, build the bombs and radars and superweapons, but keep their mouths shut about what was done with them afterward. "Many scientists insist they learned from the Oppenheimer case only this: To stay carefully within the confines of their mission and sponsoring agency and *not* let their minds range over the totality of the nation's problems," wrote White. Scientists, in a phrase popular at the time, should be "on tap, not on top."

"There is as yet no name for a reorganized partnership of science and government, because there is no name for the new kind of world we live in," White concluded. "But the insistent fact is that a name and an accommodation must be found."[1] In the wake of *Sputnik,* it was obviously time for the American people to start paying more attention to what their scientists had to say.

Even if you had been disgraced and dismissed as an untrustworthy security risk, which was why CBS News went after Oppenheimer to participate in a new special called *Where We Stand* in January. *Where We Stand* aimed to examine just that—America in relationship to the Russians in every area, particularly after the shock of *Sputnik.* "Until the shattering impact of Sputnik, the American public still thought of Russia as a country of black bread and no shoes," observed an internal network outline of the show. "In the view of thoughtful men, this country has been suffering from an over-all cultural lapse at the very time it is being most vigorously challenged. Whether the challenge amounts to a threat of attack is impossible to assess."[2]

But something was wrong, something had to be done, and CBS News and Howard K. Smith were going to tell the nation the unvarnished truth. Featuring interviews with numerous experts, *Where We Stand* would provide some answers.

At first, Oppenheimer refused an interview, but bowing to friendly

pressure from his friends at the network, including Edward R. Murrow, he finally relented and agreed to talk to Smith. For Smith, then still making a name for himself as a newsman, it was a great opportunity—not to mention an intimidating one. He recalled that he was "thrilled to sit down with the brilliant Robert Oppenheimer . . . but the experience nearly destroyed me."

Oppenheimer gave Smith a long and wide-ranging on-camera interview dealing with matters of science and education, and all were delighted with the outcome. Then, while Smith was editing the *Where We Stand* program, he received a call from CBS News vice president Sig Mickelson. "He had orders not to let the interview be aired," Smith remembered.[3]

Apparently, someone in the CBS hierarchy had decided that Oppenheimer's interview was too incendiary to be included in the show. "Shortly before it was to be broadcast, the producer and his special adviser for the program, Mr. Stephen White, told me that there was objection in principle to using what I had done because I was too controversial," Oppenheimer later told Murrow in a letter. Smith considered resigning over the issue, and his colleague and partner on *Where We Stand,* Walter Cronkite, backed him up.

When they showed Oppenheimer a brief edited version of the interview, Oppenheimer decided that the segment wasn't "intelligible enough or good enough to be worth a fight," and "asked them not to press the matter." Looking to avoid another fight that might cost some good reporters their jobs, Oppenheimer was trying to defang the problem by preemptively withdrawing his participation. "He had heard about the dispute and reconsidered," Smith wrote in his memoirs. "He said I was no longer in charge, and neither were the bosses at CBS; he was ordering that the interview not be used and would take legal action if he was not obeyed. I was not happy about it, but could not insist on using an interview to which both CBS and the interviewee were opposed."[4]

But the incident stuck in Oppenheimer's craw, particularly when, at Murrow's urging, Mickelson wrote an explanatory letter to Oppenheimer. Mickelson claimed that the decision to cut the interview was wholly practical and due to "my feeling that there was other material which was more useful to the central theme of the program than your

interview." While this was being discussed, Mickelson said, word came that Oppenheimer had withdrawn his participation.

The producer later put together a half-hour version including excerpts of Oppenheimer's interview that the scientist approved, but this version was never aired. "The whole story has troubled me, and I am not content to let Mickelson's misleading account of it be the only record," Oppenheimer told Murrow.[5] After Oppenheimer's positive treatment by CBS News during his earlier *See It Now* interview with Murrow, such petty maneuverings no doubt felt like a personal betrayal by onetime allies. The incident only served to solidify Oppenheimer's general mistrust of the press, particularly the television variety.

All of these machinations no doubt made Oppenheimer's departure for Europe and Israel in April a welcome relief. Apart from a visiting professorship at the Sorbonne, he was set to speak at the Weizmann Institute of Science in Israel, attend the Solvay Congress in Belgium, and deliver the concluding address at the High Energy Conference in Geneva. Between Belgium and Geneva, he would be visiting Niels Bohr at his Theoretical Physics Institute in Copenhagen. Oppenheimer, Kitty, and Toni arrived in Paris to the sort of hero's welcome that might be expected for a member of the Legion of Honor.

For the next two months, when not lecturing to rapt French physics students, he traveled about Europe, fulfilling his other obligations and doing some sightseeing with Kitty and Toni as well. Son Peter, who had been performing poorly at the tony private George School in Bucks County, Pennsylvania, hadn't been invited along. In a decision that was later to haunt him and contribute to a long rift between father and son, Oppenheimer made Peter stay behind for the summer as punishment for his bad grades. Peter spent the summer out west with his uncle, Frank Oppenheimer, who was still working at ranching rather than the physics for which he'd trained.

It was a grueling, hardworking, and altogether exhilarating period for Oppenheimer. In Europe he was free from the dark associations that dogged him wherever he traveled inside his own country, moving in circles where honor and respect came without question or qualification. At the Weizmann Institute in Israel, he participated in the dedication of the institute's new Nuclear Science Building along with Israeli prime minister David Ben-Gurion and other dignitaries, and no one ques-

tioned the propriety or appropriateness of his presence. Wherever he went, he was received and regarded merely as a distinguished scientist, not a figure of controversy or martyr to McCarthy. The newspaper coverage in the French press and elsewhere was invariably supportive and positive. And although the legal attaché at the American embassy in Paris kept J. Edgar Hoover apprised of Oppenheimer's general comings and goings, no FBI agents tailed Oppenheimer around the Continent or listened in on his phone conversations.

A few American reporters and columnists did keep tabs on Oppie's European peregrinations, however. Dorothy Kilgallen reported, "Scientist Robert Oppenheimer, who has been in Paris lecturing at the Sorbonne, spends most of his free time alone in his hotel room, studying Sanskrit. He tells French interviewers he wants to be able to read the Bhagavad Gita in the original, adding he feels the world sorely needs more philosophers and metaphysicists at this point in history. (For more information on the Bhagavad Gita, call Dizzy Gillespie.)"[6]

Perhaps the most troublesome incident of Oppenheimer's European visit was noted by the International News Service: "Physicist J. Robert Oppenheimer, who doesn't look like an absent-minded professor, went to the airport to fly to London for a brief visit. He was carrying a suitcase but discovered at the airport it was empty."[7]

But Oppenheimer couldn't remain in Europe forever, nor, for that matter, at the family's new retreat in the Virgin Islands, where they repaired shortly after returning from Europe in July. His Institute duties still beckoned, not to mention the usual torrent of requests, invitations, and honors. One of those, at first totally unexpected and flattering, had by now burst into yet another bitter controversy.

At the beginning of February 1958, Oppenheimer received a singularly unusual and yet, for a career scholar, appropriate honor: someone wanted to name a school after him. Louis Souder, secretary of the Bristol Township School Board in Levittown, in suburban Philadelphia, wrote to Oppenheimer informing him that the board was considering naming their about-to-be-constructed $3 million senior high school the J. Robert Oppenheimer High School. It would be "in partial recognition of your contributions not only in the field of science, but also in forwarding democracy and democratic principles."

Souder's letter requested Oppenheimer's permission to name the school, offering to let him examine architect's plans or a scale model. Oppenheimer responded promptly. "It was with great appreciation that I learned from you that you are thinking of naming your senior high school with my name. You have my permission, and my thanks."[8]

Levittown was the largest of the postwar communities that had sprung up to meet the needs of the burgeoning baby boom, and had just opened in 1952, sprawling over what was once rolling farmland and woods in lower Bucks County, Pennsylvania. It was the second of builder William Levitt's planned suburbs, following the one he'd just finished on Long Island, New York, and was a direct response to U.S. Steel's decision to build an enormous new steelworks in nearby Fairless Hills, on the Delaware River. It wouldn't exactly be a factory town, but Levitt knew that all those steelworkers were going to need places to live, and he moved in to fill the void.

With a variety of house models designed by Levitt's architect brother Alfred and laid out in "superblock" subdivisions consisting of winding lanes, drives, and cul-de-sacs, Levittown was the new heart and soul of 1950s America, the place where the men who had fought in World War II and Korea could come home to their own piece of the American dream for no money down, complete with their own backyards, carports, and washing machines. By 1958 the community was growing rapidly, and new schools were desperately needed to accommodate the ever-increasing number of children who kept appearing and would be growing up there. The Oppenheimer School would be the first senior high school in Levittown, a politically amorphous place with no real center that was spread over several townships (including Bristol Township, inside which the new high school would happen to fall) with independent governments.

Souder and the school board members who had picked the Oppenheimer name were quite pleased with their selection and confident that it had been a good decision. In discussing the name selection, they had also considered Albert Einstein, but when someone suggested Oppenheimer, the idea was too good to ignore. Not only was it a more original choice, but Oppenheimer was still alive and active, not to mention American-born and the director of one of the world's foremost academic institutions. Asked for comment, Oppenheimer

told the press he was delighted with the honor, "especially in view of the competition."[9]

Unfortunately, Souder and the school board had ignored one thing: namely, the staunchly middle-class, middle-American nature of the Levittown populace. The people of the area might have been young, but they were also largely conservative, traditional, and fervently patriotic, with many veterans among them, many of whom were active in the American Legion and the Veterans of Foreign Wars. Only two weeks after writing to Oppenheimer to secure his permission, Souder found himself writing to J. Edgar Hoover.

In case the FBI director was wondering about the possible motivations of their decision to christen their school after Oppenheimer, Souder said: "We are well aware of the famed Oppenheimer case and are also aware that Dr. Oppenheimer's personal loyalty to the United States was found to be beyond question although his discretion at times may have left something to be desired." Since the announcement of the naming, however, "certain elements of the community are slanderously spreading word in the area that Dr. Oppenheimer is a traitor, a Communist, or in some way disloyal to the United States."

The upshot of Souder's letter to Hoover is almost touching in its naïveté and blind faith in the good graces of a man who for over a decade had surreptitiously been tailing Oppenheimer, opening his mail, and tapping his phones. "May we have your letter attesting to Dr. Oppenheimer's personal loyalty and devotion to this country in order to put a stop to these vicious un-American statements."[10]

Souder, of course, never got that letter. The FBI form response to any such requests was that the Bureau was strictly a fact-finding organization, took no positions, and made no judgments. Still, one imagines that the letter provided Hoover with some private amusement.

For Souder and the Bristol Township School Board, the storm clouds were just beginning to gather, a storm they would have to face without any assistance from the FBI. Opposition to the Oppenheimer naming manifested itself immediately and before long began to take on an uncomfortably organized, orchestrated quality, despite its pretensions to spontaneity.

One of the board members who had voted against the Oppenheimer name, R. Philemon Stout, offered the view that a school shouldn't be

named after someone who was still alive. "We know what a person who is dead has accomplished but a living person may do something which may embarrass the school board," he explained with impeccable logic.[11]

Some parents seemed to feel that the board had hastily named the school entirely on its own initiative, without taking into account the feelings of the school district's tax-paying residents. One PTA member thought the choice had been "railroaded" through, claiming that the board had previously promised to ask the local PTAs for suggestions before settling on a choice. "All of a sudden they decided to name the school—which I feel should not be named for a man who was cited as a security risk." Souder explained that a name for the school had to be chosen quickly so that official forms needed for approval could be filed with the state before deadline, and that the board had been discussing possible names for several months already. Where had all the folks with other suggestions been in the meantime? John Densham, the school board member who had come up with the Oppenheimer name, felt "Oppenheimer had made an outstanding contribution to the country. His name will be an inspiration to students."[12]

Not all agreed. "We can't help but feel constrained to suggest that propriety would have been better served if Robert J. Oppenheimer [sic] had been forgotten in the apparently very sudden rush to name the new $3,000,000 high school," said the editors of the *Bucks County Courier Times*. "Whatever the atomic physicist's achievements and question-able fame, the fact is he has been and remains a highly controversial figure still tagged by the United States government as a security risk." The board had "permitted an awkward and embarrassing slip to show. Good taste should dictate immediate correction of the record."[13]

Souder was finally compelled to respond to the uproar in a letter to the *Courier Times*. "For those people who are sincere in their question-ing, I would like to help them understand the Board's reasoning in this matter." Souder proceeded to set out briefly Oppenheimer's biography and major accomplishments, noting that he was "not only a brilliant scientist, he is also an outstanding teacher, lecturer, administrator and above all, a truly loyal American (a fact which has never been dis-puted).

"It is indeed unfortunate that a coalition of McCarthyites and Com-

munists succeeded in driving this brilliant mind out of the service of the United States Government," opined Souder. "McCarthy (and I hope McCarthyism) is dead so it is time we give some recognition to America's great contemporary scientists rather than hold them up to ridicule for being free thinkers." Oppenheimer was not only "a great American" but also the director of "America's foremost educational establishment." His contributions, Souder said, "will be referred to for a thousand years after this school has crumbled into dust."[14]

Souder's letter only fanned the flames. One response from a resident noted that Souder had failed to mention that Oppenheimer "was rated a grave security risk by our government." McCarthy, "even though a sick man, against his doctor's orders kept fighting until his death to keep the country he loved free from the communist threat; proving that he was a real American in heart and soul, not just another politician. . . . I wish to ask Mr. Souder if our next school will be named in honor of Alger Hiss?"[15]

A late-February meeting of the township's Associate School Board, an advisory group made up of local PTA members, was besieged by several citizens protesting the Oppenheimer naming, but a motion to poll the PTA members on their own opinions failed to pass. In a sort of reverse-McCarthyist tactic, Souder countered protests that Oppenheimer had associated with Communists by declaring that he had documents proving that Oppenheimer was a loyal American. Three other school board members also attended the meeting and defended their choice, one of them stating that he was delighted with the selection because Oppenheimer "is a scholar, and very few high schools are named after scholars."[16]

By this time, the inevitable accusations of conspiracy and collusion were beginning to surface. The Republican Policy Committee of Bristol Township called for an investigation of the actions of the all-Democratic school board. As other possible candidates of "scientific achievement," the committee suggested Enrico Fermi—certainly not a bad suggestion—and, bizarrely enough, AEC chairman Lewis Strauss, who not only had no "scientific achievements" to speak of, but wasn't even a scientist. If not those, the committee argued, what about other names that "evoke unquestioned admiration such as Christopher Columbus, Washington, Abraham Lincoln. . . . just why did the majority of this

board, acting with a devious swiftness, overriding the objections of pro-
testing PTA members and other residents, ram through the name of
this controversial figure, Oppenheimer? Every patriotic citizen has the
right to know, and the duty to see to it, that this questionable decision
of the school board be reversed and the future school board activities of
those responsible be carefully scrutinized."[17]

It all came to a head at the next regularly scheduled meeting of the
Bristol Township School Board in March. If the battle for Levittown's
hearts and minds had been waged in the local press for the past month,
here was the field upon which the fight would be won or lost for the
pro- and anti-Oppenheimer factions. Despite a late-winter snowstorm
that snarled the streets and roads of the car-dependent community, over
a hundred citizens braved the weather to make themselves heard.

It turned out to be a marathon event. Souder read aloud thirty-six
letters he had received concerning the school name. Only one letter was
against it. Then the meeting was opened to public comment, and the
deluge began. One citizen told the board that five hundred signatures
had been collected on petitions against the Oppenheimer name. Some
suggested that the question be settled in the voting booth. Others of-
fered long discourses, pro and con, with the inevitable quotations from
the AEC and Gray Board decisions. Accusations flew from both sides that
either the selection of Oppenheimer's name, or the opposition thereto,
was "politically inspired."

"This man has been deeply involved with Communists," declared
one speaker, to supportive applause. "Our government has found him
unworthy of access to our secrets." Other citizens pointed out Oppen-
heimer's illustrious service to the country in his leadership of the
atomic-bomb effort and emphasized that his loyalty had been upheld
even by the government.

The debate continued until well after midnight, when Martha Kush-
lan, president of the board, closed the meeting to public comment at
about 12:40 a.m. But, reported the *Levittown Times*, "the arguments
moved outside to the hallway and the school board discussed more rou-
tine affairs." Several stalwarts remained behind for a couple more hours,
some importuning the board to change its mind and others urging it to
hold fast, until Kushlan finally adjourned the meeting at 3:12 a.m.[18]

The school board had remained adamant in the face of the public

complaints. It had not changed its mind or agreed to another vote. The new Bristol Township high school was still going to be named after J. Robert Oppenheimer.

The matter was settled. Or so it seemed. Some saw it as a healthy exercise in participatory democracy. "To my way of thinking, those raising all the furor against naming the school after Dr. Oppenheimer are as dangerous to our American way of life and philosophy as the communists," wrote a Levittown housewife to the *Courier Times* as the dust was settling. "These people are declaring Dr. Oppenheimer guilty by association. . . . these same people are the ones who want to tell us how we should think, what we should read, and who we can talk to. . . . Perhaps the Bristol Township School Board used poor judgment in selecting a controversial figure after whom to name the new high school. I do believe they should have chosen someone acceptable and worthy of edification in the eyes of all. This is despite the fact that I personally see nothing wrong in the naming of Dr. Oppenheimer. However, I am glad that the controversy was raised and am thankful that here in America we can still take opposing views and air them even if there are strong pressures to curb our freedom to think and act."[19]

The pro-Oppenheimer forces were also encouraged by some indirect support of their position from an illustrious source. Speaking before Congress once again, an activity that had become almost a second career for him ever since *Sputnik,* rocket scientist Wernher von Braun mentioned Oppenheimer. "I think the British would have knighted him," von Braun told the House Education Committee, calling Oppenheimer's treatment at the hands of his own government "an outrage." It was a telling example of the mistrust of scientists and intellectuals that had brought America to this current crisis, he said. "People must have the courage to be eggheads," von Braun declared.[20]

"I presume that the flag-wavers and the Republican politicians who would receive more 'plums' from a school board of their own faith will stage a strategic withdrawal after Dr. Von Braun's testimony," said another letter to the *Courier Times.* "Or has Dr. Von Braun become a Communist by association?"[21]

A proposal before the Levittown Civic Association to oppose the Oppenheimer naming also met swift defeat, with the president of the association noting that the supporters of the proposal were more concerned

with the way the board had selected the name than with the name it-self.[22] A few more letters to the editor in the local papers, a few more failed resolutions and protests here and there, and by the springtime, most believed that the controversy over the J. Robert Oppenheimer High School had well and truly exhausted itself.

But such optimistic souls failed to reckon with the unique staying power of an Oppenheimer-based controversy. The war was just getting started.

* * *

Naturally, not all of the forty witnesses called during the hearing supported Op-penheimer. William Borden, whose letter to Hoover had been the match that fired the kindling Strauss had so carefully laid, was allowed to read his letter of charges into the record, though both Robb and Garrison declined to question him further. At this point, Borden's specific charges were largely irrelevant.

Military figures and security agents testified to their own disagreements with and doubts about Oppenheimer. But perhaps the most notable negative witness was physicist Edward Teller, the man with whom Oppenheimer had repeatedly clashed over the H-bomb.

Teller had always been obsessed by the prospect of the hydrogen bomb, even during his Manhattan Project stint at Los Alamos, when he had insisted on working on the then-hypothetical thermonuclear question instead of contributing to the immediate A-bomb effort. Always rabidly anti-Soviet in outlook, Teller had spent the postwar years urging the development of the H-bomb even before the Russians shattered America's nuclear monopoly in 1949. Once he finally got his wish, he found his task complicated by fellow scientists who seemed to share Oppenheimer's qualms about the weapon, and was continually irritated and offended by what he saw as Oppenheimer's lack of enthusiasm.

Long before the hearing, Teller had repeatedly been interviewed by the FBI and the AEC regarding Oppenheimer, and had not hesitated to express his an-tipathies. Shortly before his appearance before the Gray Board, Teller had been briefed by Robb, who showed him some of the secret evidence against Oppen-heimer and allowed him to read testimony of anti-Oppie witnesses from the hearing. Such helpful "coaching" thus ensured that Teller's animosity and dis-trust of Oppenheimer were at their keenest edge by the time Teller walked into the hearing room.

Although Teller "assumed" that Oppenheimer was loyal to the United States, his testimony cited occasions in which Oppenheimer had acted in ways that he found "exceedingly hard to understand." Therefore, he said, "I would like to see the vital interests of this country in hands which I understand better, and therefore trust more. . . . I would feel personally more secure if public matters would rest in other hands." Asked by Gray if he felt that clearing Oppenheimer would "endanger the common defense and security," Teller responded that while he believed Oppenheimer would not knowingly endanger the country, "if it is a question of wisdom and judgment, as demonstrated by actions since 1945, then I would say one would be wiser not to grant clearance."[23]

DIRECTOR, FBI (100-18564) 6/17/59

SAC, SAN FRANCISCO (1-439)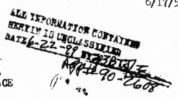

HAAKON MAURICE CHEVALIER, aka.
INTERNAL SECURITY - R AND FRANCE

At 12:45 P.M., 6/3/59, **Dr. RIDGWAYH BROTHERS**, M. D.,
603 **Mac Donald Avenue**, Richmond, California, telephone Beacon 4-
8248, called at the San Francisco Office to report the following:

On the evening of 5/26/59, there was a staff meeting at
the Richmond Hospital, and the staff group was having dinner in
connection with the staff meeting. One of the members, Dr. HERBERT
LAWRENCE, Dermatoligist, with offices at 450 Sutter Street, and also
an office in Richmond, California, mentioned that he had just
returned from Europe and had been away for four months. He continued
that while he was in France he met an individual named CHEVALIER,
and stated that this individual was going to or had written a
book exposing one OPPENHEIMER. He indicated according to Dr.
BROTHERS, that they were going to "sort of pull the rug out
from under him." CHEVALIER told Dr. LAWRENCE that he had the book
all ready for publication, but that the French publisher would
not publish it because he described it as being too libelous.

Dr. **BROTHERS** described Dr. LAWRENCE as living in Marin
County, and also owning an office building in Richmond. Dr.
LAWRENCE graduated from Stanford University Medical School in 1939.
Dr. **BROTHERS** stated that he had heard, but could not recall where,
that LAWRENCE changed his name and that it was originally SHAPIRO.
He could furnish no additional information.

The above is for the information of the Bureau. An
extra copy of this letter is being included in case the Bureau may
wish to furnish a copy to the Paris Legat (100-310).

3 - Bureau (REG.)
1 - San Francisco
DCS/lmg
(4)

150-17828

10

The Otherness of People

f, as Louis Souder had hoped, McCarthyism had been dying, *Sputnik* and the resulting panic stirred up by the beeping satellites had given it new life. In the fear and frantic self-examination gripping America as it struggled with its new sense of vulnerability and inferiority, it was all too easy to fall back on old suspicions and the comfort of familiar paranoia. And it was equally important for anyone who considered himself a "true" patriot and a "real" American to loudly and repeatedly proclaim such to all and sundry—and to attack and criticize anyone upon whom the slightest doubts had ever been cast. Oppenheimer was an easy and obvious target, always handy as an anti-American symbol.

The idea of naming a school, a sanctuary for America's precious children, after such a questionable character was more than anathema to some—it was nothing less than national sacrilege. For the American Legion, therefore, it was too tempting a cause to ignore. And the Levittown post was not about to sit back idly and allow such an outrage in its own backyard to go unanswered. It glommed on to the issue wholeheartedly and transformed it from a local squabble into a national political debate split along partisan lines.

Levittown's Post 960 labeled the Oppenheimer school naming "a flagrant abuse of public trust," declaring that the school board "has pitted neighbor against neighbor and friend against friend." The school

naming was "of such controversial nature that it should be withdrawn in the interest of community harmony." The post protested that the board's decision in the March meeting to name two other new schools after Washington and Lincoln "after paying homage to a man who is forbidden access to classified data is a slight of the greatest magnitude against two of the greatest Americans."[1]

Another Legion commander complained, "How in heaven's name can any one retain any respect for a system that glorifies this scientist? This loss of respect could have one end result; an eventual collapse of law and order through failure of moral support to constituted authority."[2] The J. Robert Oppenheimer High School, then, wasn't simply an outrage and an affront to patriotic Americans; it was a literal threat to the very fabric of American society.

The protests of the Legion surprised nobody, since in its national magazine the organization had already recently condemned the moves to reinstate Oppenheimer. Given the Legion's influence, it was only a matter of time before the issue burst beyond the local community into national prominence. Edmond J. Wilkins, the Post 960 chairman of "Americanism," however, did do Oppenheimer the courtesy of sending him a copy of the post's resolution "that official condemnation and protest be directed against the . . . Bristol Township School Board" because of the Oppenheimer naming.

Away in Europe at the time, Oppenheimer didn't respond. Stopping briefly back in the States before proceeding to the new family getaway on the island of St. John, he undoubtedly saw the letter, but there was little point in answering. He had been aware of the roiling controversy across the Delaware River in Bucks County but, as usual, kept his distance.

Later in the summer, Wilkins sent another, more personal letter, hoping to use the potential for national controversy as a blunt instrument to bludgeon Oppenheimer into submission. "Frankly, Dr. Oppenheimer, while many of our people respect your achievements in the field of science, the people of the Township are overwhelmingly against the use of your name on this school," Wilkins claimed. "The American Legion has protested the name up to the State level and will protest it on the National level in Chicago, September 1–4, at the National Convention." Wilkins told Oppenheimer that the local PTAs and other civic groups

had also been protesting, "each time stirring up the same old stories of your experiences with the 'Gray Committee.'" Worst of all, "now we have the problem of the students themselves asking what's going on."

So all the difficulty was obviously Oppenheimer's fault, not that of the Legion and the various other stalwart patriots who had been noisily complaining. And it would only get worse, because the national Legion convention "will attract National attention and no doubt, the same effect will result as in 1954 when the nations [*sic*] press had a 'field day' over your testimony at the hearings. We think we are going to have a problem explaining to the students why your name was chosen for this high school."

Given all this, Wilkins continued, "Why should you be made to suffer the indignity of having these same old stories brought up all over again?," playing the part of an innocent, concerned observer rather than one of the key parties engaged in dredging up those "old stories" again and again. But it was okay, because Wilkins had a solution: "May we suggest and urge you to notify the Bristol Township School Board that you wish to decline this honor at this time so that we can stop the protest before it goes to Chicago and attracts this National attention."[3]

Wilkins seemed to be completely unaware of, or to have ignored, the fact that since those "same old stories" had been endlessly dragged through the press by various anti-Oppenheimer factions for the past four years, surfacing almost every time Oppenheimer made any sort of public appearance, the silken threat that they might again be brought into the national spotlight was hardly going to upset Oppenheimer. By this time, he was all too used to it.

The American Legion's efforts did manage to enlist others into the crusade, however, and by the end of the summer the Levittown Civic Association and the Bucks County Republican Organization, among others, had publicly backed the Legion position, "if for no other reason than community harmony, since this has become a most debatable item and has resulted in dissension among our residents," as the LCA helpfully pointed out.[4]

Former first lady Eleanor Roosevelt begged to differ, writing to the school board that it was "a wonderful thing that you are naming your

new high school in honor of Dr. J. Robert Oppenheimer, whom I consider a most distinguished citizen of our country and worthy of the tribute you are paying him."[5]

As promised, at its Labor Day convention in Chicago, the American Legion officially issued a resolution condemning the Bristol Township School Board for naming its high school after "an individual of questionable honor and patriotism to the United States." Other resolutions warned against cutbacks in military spending, called for an investigation of the American Civil Liberties Union because of its supposed "help and assistance" to Communist and subversive organizations, and praised the late Joseph McCarthy as "a real American whose vindication is brought about by the events of our own era."[6]

Back in Levittown, matters were becoming even sillier as Republican politicians charged the beleaguered Bristol Township School Board with spending over $1,000 in taxpayer money on a twenty-page booklet about Oppenheimer and defending the board's choice of high school name. "It contains a professional propaganda story on Dr. Oppenheimer," complained one candidate. Meanwhile Wilkins and the local Legion kept up the pressure through repeated letters to newspapers and editorials. Despite Wilkins's assertion that the populace was "overwhelmingly" against Oppenheimer, most of the locals either had no opinion or simply wanted the continual bickering to end.

And many openly opposed the Legion tactics. "This Legion protest is one of the best symptoms that our present age is mentally sick," stated one letter to *The Trenton Times,* pointing to Oppenheimer's recent European tour as evidence that Oppenheimer "is welcomed anywhere in the world as the great thinker and theoretical physicist he is. Anywhere, that is, except the United States."[7]

Throughout the fall and into the winter, the pressure on the Bristol Township School Board continued. The pro-Oppenheimer members, led by secretary Souder, were beginning to show signs of wearing down. They had fought the good fight for a principle, but they were under political siege, and the reasons for continuing the struggle seemed to grow less and less compelling while the temptation to cave in and thus deflate and end the controversy once and for all became overwhelming.

Finally, just before its regularly scheduled March meeting in 1959—over a year since the entire ordeal began—the first crack in the

wall appeared. The board announced that it was planning to reconsider the Oppenheimer decision, pointedly offering no explanation.[8]

The big issue at the meeting on the evening of March 12 at Benjamin Franklin Junior High School wasn't the Oppenheimer question, but a controversy about whether or not to drop kindergarten programs in the following school year. Over 350 residents turned out to argue heatedly for most of the meeting over the issue before the board voted to drop kindergarten.

Most of the crowd went home, the major issue of the evening settled as far as they were concerned. Then, as the hour approached midnight, board president Benjamin F. Stockett Jr. moved that the Oppenheimer High School be renamed the Woodrow Wilson School. He asked for a vote from the other five board members present. Stockett "offered no reason for his action," reported the *Levittown Times*. Neither did board member Calvin Morrison, who seconded Stockett's motion. The vote proceeded and the motion passed, 4 to 2.

Bristol Township's spanking new high school, set to open the following September, would bear President Woodrow Wilson's name, not Robert Oppenheimer's.

The opposing votes had come from John Densham, the man who had started all the trouble by originally suggesting Oppenheimer's name over a year ago, and Neils Haugaard, who declared, "I felt proud last year when we named the school. We name schools for politicians. Why not name one for a scientist? I feel ashamed of the board's action tonight." Another nay vote would have come from the board's seventh member, secretary Louis Souder, but he was home sick in bed.

Stockett and Morrison, who had been among those originally favoring the Oppenheimer name, later remarked that they had given in to the pressure because of the ill effects the controversy was having on the community and the school system. "It affects the students, their parents and other factors in the schools," said Stockett. The other two votes in favor of the change came from the board members who had opposed the Oppenheimer name from the beginning.[9]

Predictably, Oppenheimer had "no comment at all" when called by reporters. He was, perhaps, disappointed, but hardly surprised. A few other people did have something to say about the matter, however. "I read of the Bristol Township Board decision to rename their new high

school after originally planning its dedication to you . . . and I was furious!" a Michigan woman wrote to Oppenheimer. "Then and there I decided to write to you and explain that there must be many other people throughout the United States who feel as I do, that the denial of your security clearance was one of the grave injustices of these times. . . . whereas Dr. Teller may have the scientific mind required of these times, he was born without the compassion and reverence for life that truly great men must have. . . . I felt that even a man of your stature might welcome a sign of confidence from an ordinary individual."[10]

A Bristol Township resident told Oppie, "I would like to offer you a feeble apology for the recent actions of my neighbors. . . . I shall never be able to understand just how a man of your great mental depth can give so freely of his time and energy in the cause of mankind when you know full well the type of rabble among us who will benefit from your work."[11]

Whatever Oppenheimer's feelings about the entire sorry episode, he remained inscrutable in public as always. By this time, he knew that anything he might say in response to such incidents would be pointless. And he was also still flush with the acceptance and warmth of his European stay, and a string of other recent engagements.

It would have been nice to know that somewhere a Robert Oppenheimer School existed. But in its own rather ironic way, the fact that it had almost happened, then been irrevocably derailed by the "same old stories" that still haunted Oppenheimer and clung to his name years after the hearing, was in itself a sort of validation, both of his martyrdom and his influence. Few other public figures would have inspired such a robust and long-lasting battle as Oppenheimer. If it proved nothing else, the Bristol Township saga provided incontrovertible evidence that, shunned by his government or not, considered a traitor by many of his own countrymen or not, Robert Oppenheimer *mattered.*

Another factor affecting Oppenheimer's outlook on the hue and cry periodically inspired by his name was that it had all become so boringly repetitive and predictable. Always there would be the inaccurate statements about his "loyalty being questioned by his government," the "lies told to security officers," the "Communist friends/wife/girlfriend/

students," the out-of-context quotations from the Gray Board report or the final AEC decision. To Oppenheimer, at least occasionally, it must have been darkly amusing.

The script was repeated several times in 1958, with the Bristol school board episode being only the most unusual and extended variation. When Oppenheimer was invited to speak at Vassar College in November, there were the usual letters of protest to the college administration and the local press, although nothing on the scale of the previous year's Harvard episode.

Although talk of revisiting the security case had died down considerably since the initial post-*Sputnik* frenzy, it continued to percolate steadily at a low but detectable level. Appearing on *Meet the Press* in April, Senator Clinton Anderson again went on the record as supporting the idea. Asked "Do you think his services should be used in any way or not?" Anderson responded, "Yes, I have said that I think he should be given an opportunity to serve. I don't think that you can conceal from Dr. Oppenheimer some of the things that he himself developed. I think that his work was exemplary when he was at Los Alamos in connection with the bomb. I think he was foolish after he got away from there, but I wouldn't be at all concerned when he was put in a position of responsibility."

But did that mean that Anderson thought that Oppenheimer's security clearance should be restored? "I would like to have him put on a program like thermonuclear research in the development of power, where we are not going to have any great amount of secrecy anyhow, and where his remarkable brain could be used for the benefit of this country. It would not bother me in the slightest."

And Oppenheimer received a vote of confidence from another, considerably more exotic and unexpected, source. No less than the legendary actress Marlene Dietrich proclaimed herself an Oppenheimer fan. "I think when it comes to people in general, Robert Oppenheimer is one of the most outstanding," she told a reporter who asked her what public figures she admired. "Not only for his scientific achievement but as a human being. He has character and modesty and the willingness to take what comes along without being dragged down into the mud."[12]

While no one would ever venture to call him lighthearted or care-free, close friends and colleagues were noticing a distinct change in the man now that some years had passed since his public crucifixion. And for the most part, the change was for the better. His next-door neighbor in Princeton, David Lilienthal, dropped in for beer and a sandwich one day. Oppenheimer "seems much mellowed from the time I first met him (in January, 1946, I think it was) when we were getting started on the Board of Consultants on International Control of Atomic Energy," Lilienthal commented in his journal. "Then he was so care-worn, and pacing, pacing."

Oppenheimer, Lilienthal noticed, wasn't without some outward signs of his recent trials. "His forward stoop is much pronounced, almost like an old man—which he is not." But now, perhaps because he no longer bore the weight of grave matters of state and atomic policy on his frail shoulders, and despite the circumstances that removed him from that role, "He looks much better; the lines of care have given away to a kind of 'success' calm." The "survivor" had triumphed, at least in some way, just as he had told the *St. Louis Post-Dispatch* reporter the year before in response to the question "Can a security risk survive?" As Lilienthal noted, "He has weathered one of the most violent, bitter storms that any human being ever went through."

Lilienthal noted another indication of the change in Oppenheimer. "For the first time I can remember he made a warm and extravagant comment directly to me. He doesn't go for that ordinarily, though I know he respects me, and is fond of me. But it isn't his way to pay compliments in private, face-to-face conversation." Their lunchtime conversation had turned to their former work on the board of atomic energy consultants after the war, and Oppenheimer told Lilienthal, in fond remembrance of the experience, "It is part of your genius that you can turn individuals into a group."

Lilienthal was right: although Oppenheimer would never begrudge anyone the appropriate credit or praise in a professional or formal setting, such a personal compliment coming from him was indeed a rare thing. For most of his career, Oppenheimer had been well known for his capacity for a sort of haughty arrogance. He didn't suffer fools gladly, and he let them know it, even in his prewar years as a young

professor. Many were the young graduate students devastated by a single cutting Oppenheimer remark in a seminar. And it wasn't only students who felt the sting of Oppenheimer's derision; at times he would unleash it against his own peers at physics conferences or meetings. Oppenheimer got away with it because, more often than not, he was right, and because his remarks, however acerbic, had a knack for penetrating through the fog that surrounded a tricky question and getting right to the point in a way that everyone could instantly comprehend.

But as Oppenheimer began to move and work in political circles after the war, his sharp tongue and studied superiority began to earn him more than a few enemies. Chief among them was Lewis Strauss, whose initial dislike of Oppenheimer blossomed into active hatred around the time that Oppenheimer smoothly and devastatingly mocked Strauss's testimony before Congress regarding the export of radioactive isotopes. For Strauss, a sensitive man who already tended to take opposing views personally, the incident sparked an animosity that soon evolved into suspicion and then an active obsession to drive Oppenheimer out of government, leading to the security hearing and the suspension of Oppenheimer's clearance.

Lilienthal was quite aware of this aspect of Oppenheimer's nature, and thus the mellowing of his friend's personality was all the more evident. The physical changes were striking too. "Remarkable-appearing man. His hair is now as silver as mine. The youthfulness that his slight figure and brilliant eyes gave him thirteen years ago, when we first met, has been accented rather than diminished by his years."

And again, Oppenheimer was surprising him. "Oppenheimer startled me with a sentence that I wish I had put down verbatim, but this is the best I can do (he does phrase things so strikingly at times): Men must have pity on myths. Life wouldn't be bearable if everything had to be based on provable propositions, on propositions that could be established as one does in physics."[13]

It was beginning to seem as though the "devastation" and pain caused him by the security hearing and his exile from government service that so many saw in Oppenheimer immediately after the fact had now given way to a sort of monastic acceptance, a stoic inner reconciliation to his new life. The McCarthyites and misguided patriots who

continued to yap at his heels in the public realm were becoming easier to ignore, if not totally dismiss. And many of the more powerful among them were starting to lose influence and power, or otherwise drop from the public scene. McCarthy himself had died the previous year, censured by the Senate and disgraced, and without the motivating force he provided, many of the worst excesses of anti-Communist fervor had diminished. The Republican administration was still reeling from the shock of *Sputnik*, not to mention a faltering economy, and many citizens were beginning to come around to the belief that it had gone too far in some of its actions—kicking distinguished scientists out of government service, for example.

For Oppenheimer personally, the most significant shift in the Washington power structure came with the retirement of Lewis Strauss as chairman of the Atomic Energy Commission. Strauss wasn't leaving government completely; he was soon tapped by Eisenhower to take over as acting secretary of commerce. But his departure from the AEC signaled to some that the prospects for Oppenheimer's reinstatement were better than ever. Without Strauss at the helm to obstruct a new hearing or demand "new evidence," and with the professed support of congressmen such as Clinton Anderson and the others who had called for a review of the case after *Sputnik*, the time for Oppenheimer's vindication seemed near.

Almost as soon as Strauss's successor, John McCone, was named AEC chairman in June 1958, Anderson asked him to reevaluate the Oppenheimer case. McCone assigned Loren K. Olson, AEC general counsel, to scrutinize all the records of the charges, the hearing, and all the other voluminous AEC files on Oppenheimer, and analyze the entire saga in exhaustive detail.

What Olson found surprised him. He discovered that the Oppenheimer case was "a messy record from a legal standpoint, that the charges kept shifting at each level of the proceedings, that the evidence was stale and consisted of information that was 12 years old and was known when a security clearance was granted during World War II." In short, the proceedings against Oppenheimer had been nothing less than "a punitive, personal abuse of the judicial system."[14]

So all of the criticisms advanced by Oppenheimer's supporters ever

since the AEC verdict had first been announced and the hearing transcript released were true. There was one problem: the AEC couldn't act on its own initiative to clear Oppenheimer, particularly in the current political climate. If anything concrete were to happen, Oppenheimer would still have to be the one to kick off the effort, by requesting a new hearing from the AEC, a congressional review, or one of the other avenues that had been suggested to him by enthusiastic supporters.

And Oppenheimer, having expended so much of himself and suffered so severely coming through the fire, was showing no great eagerness to submit himself to that wringer once again. It was all very easy for caring friends and colleagues to urge him to try again. But they hadn't been forced to sit in a hearing room for three solid weeks while every detail of their lives was scrutinized, criticized, and found wanting.

He had come through the process and survived, and against all expectations was now thriving, at least reasonably so. He had carved out a new life for himself at the Institute and a new role as America's philosopher-poet of science. Was it worth losing all that, risking everything he had managed to salvage of his wrecked life and career in the past several years, merely to regain an AEC "Q" security clearance? What if he subjected himself willingly to that ordeal once more—and was again denied, rightly or wrongly? What then?

No. Not yet. A presidential election was on the horizon, and with it a change in administration, bringing perhaps an administration that would be more sympathetic and receptive. For now, it was still too soon, and not worth the risk of failure. Oppenheimer had not only himself but also his family to consider, and if he needed any evidence of the damage the security episode had already wreaked in that department, he had only to consider his own wife's alcoholism and other health problems, and the resultant pressures on his children.

Even if Strauss was out of the AEC, he was still in government, still powerful, and still had the ear of the president. That, however, was about to change. Strauss had been collecting his own dedicated corps of enemies and inspiring his own smoldering resentments during his past years in Washington. And in a manner eerily reminiscent of the downfall he had engineered for Robert Oppenheimer, he was about to face a very public and very humiliating reckoning.

* * *

At long last, on May 6, the hearing quietly closed and the Gray Board adjourned to consider its judgment. By the end of the month, the board issued a split decision: Gordon Gray and Thomas Morgan voted against clearing Oppenheimer, while Ward Evans voted in favor.

The board's report was a marvel of contradictions. All three members agreed unequivocally that Oppenheimer was completely loyal, and displayed "a high degree of discretion, reflecting an unusual ability to keep to himself vital secrets." Yet Gray and Morgan found that "Dr. Oppenheimer's continuing conduct and associations have reflected a serious disregard for the requirements of the security system" and "regretfully concluded" that he had been "less than candid" during his testimony to the board.

Regarding the H-bomb question, Gray and Morgan agreed that Oppenheimer "did not oppose the project in a positive or open manner, nor did he decline to cooperate." But because his opposition to the H-bomb had become widely known, "his attitudes undoubtedly had an adverse effect on recruitment of scientists. . . . if Dr. Oppenheimer had enthusiastically supported the thermonuclear program . . . {it} would have been pursued with considerably more vigor." In other words, the problem was not that Oppenheimer had actively tried to stop the H-bomb; it was that he had simply not been enthusiastic enough about it.

Ward Evans's minority report was concise and sharply worded. He criticized the AEC for investigating Oppenheimer for charges on which he had previously been cleared in 1947. Oppenheimer "did not hinder the development of the H-bomb, and there is absolutely nothing in the testimony to show that he did." Evans acknowledged that Oppenheimer had left-wing and even Communist friends, but "the evidence indicates that he has fewer of them than in 1947, when he was last cleared." Moreover, "he is not as naive as he was then. He has more judgment. . . . it is better now than it was in 1947, and to damn him now and ruin his career and his service, I cannot do it." He concluded that failure to clear Oppenheimer would be "a black mark on the escutcheon of our country."[15]

Evans was crying out into the wilderness, and he knew it. His words would make no difference. The case wasn't technically over yet, but Strauss and his AEC allies were delighted with the Gray Board decision. Harold P. Green, the former AEC counsel who had actually drafted the letter of charges but soon af-

terward removed himself from any involvement in the case as he realized first-hand the underhanded tactics being used by Strauss, noted that "the AEC prosecutors and FBI aides {who had assisted Robb during the hearing by spying on Oppenheimer and his lawyers} joined in a victory dinner at the Chevy Chase Country Club when the Gray Board announced its decision."[16]

STANDARD FORM NO. 64

Office Memorandum • UNITED STATES GOVERNMENT

TO : **Mr. A. H. Belmont**

DATE: **August 11, 1959**

FROM : **Mr. F. A. Frohbose**

SUBJECT: **REQUEST FROM SENATOR CLINTON P. ANDERSON, JOINT COMMITTEE ON ATOMIC ENERGY, FOR INFORMATION CONCERNING DR. J. ROBERT OPPENHEIMER**

Tolson _____
Belmont _____
DeLoach _____
McGuire _____
Mohr _____
Parsons _____
Rosen _____
Tamm _____
Trotter _____
W.C. Sullivan _____
Tele. Room _____
Holloman _____
Gandy _____

By letter dated August 8, 1959, Senator Clinton P. Anderson, chairman, Joint Committee on Atomic Energy, requested the Bureau to furnish him with a list of all reports, memoranda, and summaries of information concerning Dr. J. Robert Oppenheimer during three separate periods of time.

Pursuant to instructions, Mr. Bartlett of the Liaison Section discussed instant matter with Mr. Henry Roemer McPhee, Assistant Special Counsel to the President. Mr. McPhee said this looked like a continued attempt on the part of Senator Anderson to "get his foot in the door" in requesting information from the Executive Branch of the Government; that he does not know what Senator Anderson is up to in this particular matter, and that he would suggest very strongly that prior to complying with the Senator's request the Bureau should discuss the matter with the Attorney General and seek his advice.

ACTION:

For information.

1 - Mr. Belmont
1 - Mr. Wacks
1 - Liaison
1 - Mr. Bartlett

OHB:mtb
(5)

REC- 21

23 SEP 2 1959

11

A Good Augury

As 1959 began, Lewis Lichtenstein Strauss (rear admiral, USNR, retired) was a proud, self-made man who had it all and was about to acquire even more.* He had started out working for Herbert Hoover, made a fortune as an investment banker, achieved the rank of rear admiral in the Naval Reserve in World War II, and then moved into public service. As one of the original AEC commissioners appointed by President Truman in 1947, Strauss had been an insider in the early postwar atomic program, and became acquainted with Oppenheimer both through his AEC work and through his position as a trustee of the Institute for Advanced Study. Strauss had even recommended Oppenheimer for the directorship of the Institute in 1947.

The relationship between the two men was cordial and correct, if not warm, at the beginning. But they soon recognized that they harbored fundamental differences, not only of opinion and outlook but of personality, and began to find themselves at odds on various issues, with Oppenheimer's advice as chairman of the AEC's General Advisory Committee frequently clashing with Strauss's own views on atomic and

* Strauss insisted on pronouncing his name "Straws," supposedly because this was how it was done back in his home state of West Virginia. Others suggested it was out of some unconscious residual shame at his Jewish background.

defense-policy issues. Aside from being a sensitive man with a prodigious capacity for holding grudges, Strauss also began to view Oppenheimer's opinions and advice as motivated by something other than honest, scientifically objective considerations. The scientist was arrogant, influential, and self-important, all qualities that were irritating enough to Strauss. The fact that Oppenheimer also had a questionable leftist background, coupled with his vocal opposition to obviously necessary (to Strauss) steps such as building the H-bomb as soon as possible, and Oppenheimer's support of measures to reduce rather than increase government secrecy, made him even more suspect in Strauss's eyes. At the very least, Oppenheimer had become Strauss's personal bête noire, the person who always seemed to be in his way, blocking his pet projects, opposing his strongly held beliefs, a constant and unrelenting political thorn in his side.

When President Dwight Eisenhower picked him to be his new AEC chairman in 1953, Strauss suddenly found himself with the power to pluck that thorn out of government. He warned Eisenhower that Oppenheimer "was not to be trusted" and, after contacting FBI director J. Edgar Hoover to obtain the Bureau's latest information on the scientist, set the investigative wheels of the government in motion to dig up more dirt on Oppenheimer, to add to the FBI's already voluminous file.

Then, on the evening of November 7, 1953, William L. Borden, former executive director of the Joint Congressional Committee on Atomic Energy, mailed a letter to Hoover that detailed his "exhaustively considered opinion, based upon years of study of the available classified evidence, that more probably than not, J. Robert Oppenheimer is an agent of the Soviet Union."[1] Although the FBI found nothing substantially new against Oppenheimer, Borden's letter provided Strauss with the magic bullet he needed.

Armed with Borden's accusations, Strauss was able to convince the president to order that a "blank wall" immediately be placed between Oppenheimer and government secrets, and Strauss suspended Oppenheimer's security clearance. Oppenheimer requested a hearing, and six months later, Strauss achieved his ambition: Oppenheimer's

influence within the United States government had effectively been destroyed.

Strauss had eliminated one enemy from his sight, but he had an uncanny knack for making more. Over the next several years after Oppenheimer's downfall, Strauss's antagonistic, holier-than-thou style managed to alienate most of his fellow AEC commissioners, most notably Thomas Murray, as well as much of Congress, particularly New Mexico senator Clinton P. Anderson of the Joint Committee on Atomic Energy. "Mr. Strauss seems to be at odds these days with just about everybody who counts in official Washington," observed *The New York Times* in mid-1958, as Strauss's term as AEC chairman approached its end. He seemed "to be attempting with new vehemence to prove that he has been right on everything from 'clean' bombs to continuation of atomic tests," said *The Times,* noting only two of the more contentious issues of Strauss's reign.[2]

As the end of Strauss's term neared on June 30, 1958, speculation brewed in Washington circles and in the press about whether Strauss would be reappointed. He was known to enjoy Eisenhower's confidence and trust, and the president had even considered appointing Strauss as AEC chairman permanently. But Strauss was sixty-two years old and had wistfully been hinting to reporters about retiring to his farm, weary of the vicious political brawling he seemed continually to inspire. And reappointment as AEC chairman would require confirmation by the Senate, a process that promised to be ugly considering the bad blood Strauss had stirred up on the Hill during his tenure. Yet, as even his wife commented, Strauss was not one to surrender power easily.

Finally Strauss suggested a solution to Eisenhower: he would leave the AEC as scheduled, but would remain in the administration as a special civilian adviser to the president on atomic energy. Eisenhower liked the idea, and Strauss left the AEC at the end of June 1958, much to the relief of many in Congress and government, including most of the AEC itself. For Strauss, it was a shrewd move that provided a means for him to stay close to the president and the power that he craved while avoiding the spotlight and political battles of his previous job.

The peaceful period didn't last long. When Eisenhower's secretary

of commerce resigned his post under a cloud of scandal in the fall of 1958, the president immediately chose Strauss to take over as acting secretary. Strauss was forced from the shadows of the administration back into the glaring light. This time, as usual, he would stir up controversies and ill will, if over different sorts of issues than when he was AEC chairman, inspiring a whole new set of resentments and enemies.

In January 1959, Eisenhower submitted Strauss's name to the Senate for confirmation as permanent secretary of commerce. It promised to be a tough fight: the Democrats had just won a convincing midterm congressional victory to maintain their dominance of the House and Senate, and Strauss's old nemeses were still there and still powerful, including Anderson, now chairman of the Joint Atomic Energy Committee. But Strauss was confident about his confirmation. He knew he had the backing of the president and the rest of his administration, and in the entire history of the United States, the Senate had rarely failed to confirm a cabinet nomination. Strauss was smart and experienced enough to realize that the hearings probably wouldn't be a cakewalk, but he had no real reason to expect defeat.

Lewis Strauss was about to reach the pinnacle of a distinguished career in public service. But first he had to submit himself to questioning by the Senate Committee on Interstate and Foreign Commerce, a process that, judging from past example, should take several weeks at most.

But Strauss had underestimated the depth and pervasiveness of the enmity he had sown during his years in government. Now he was going to place himself squarely in the sights and at the mercy of many of his most powerful political enemies. For most of his career, Strauss had believed that his close associations with the rich and powerful, not to mention his own unquestionable righteousness, would protect him from the worst. He was about to learn otherwise.

Partly because of health problems with the committee chairman and partly out of sheer political obstructionism by the Democrats, Strauss's confirmation hearings were delayed a full two months. Then, after a mere two days, the chairman recessed the hearings for another month.

The delays provided Strauss's numerous adversaries with ample time to build a case against him.

The nation's editorial pages were already marshaling the arguments against Strauss. Noting his performance as acting commerce secretary and his conflicts with the State Department, *The Louisville Courier-Journal* observed, "He is following his familiar practice of making decisions which should be guided by the over-all interests of foreign policy entirely on his own. . . . It is fatiguing to think that this contentious man is already stirring up his own brand of interdepartmental mischief." Obviously nothing good would come of Strauss's confirmation: "Our relations with the rest of the world are now so delicately balanced, so difficult for so many reasons that, although Mr. Strauss seems to be only on the periphery of foreign relations, it is appalling to think of the number of ways in which, by meddling, he can worsen them."[3]

Others in the press, including veteran Strauss foe Drew Pearson, expressed similar sentiments. By the time the hearings resumed in April, the issue of Strauss's confirmation was the biggest story and hottest cocktail-party topic in Washington.

The opening days of the hearings had been routine, but now the attack on Strauss began in earnest. Strauss biographer Richard Pfau writes: "Day after weary day for the next four weeks Strauss heard himself reviled, as his attackers combed through his career for evidence against him. Committee members, other senators, scientists, even columnists accused Strauss of misconduct. . . . As the pressure continued, it etched lines of care into his smooth face and slowed his step. Strauss was on trial for his political life. Since the age of twenty-one he had built a reputation for integrity, risen to the pinnacle of American public life, and become one of the handful of close confidential advisers to the president. Honored with a cabinet post, known widely, respected for his wisdom, and even feared for his power, Strauss enjoyed the homage he received."[4]

But now Strauss was experiencing the downside of power and influence. Now all the hostility, all the resentment, all the hatred he had created, had come together in one place and at one time to focus like a blinding hot beam of sunlight upon him.

And whether one believed that Strauss was finally getting his just deserts or was the hapless victim of political opportunism, one towering irony, one inescapable comparison, could not be ignored. "Like Oppenheimer five years earlier, Strauss faced a review of his career that could lead to his dismissal," Pfau points out.[5]

Oppenheimer wasn't called upon to testify at Strauss's hearing, nor did he make any public statement on Strauss's fitness for the job. But as he read the daily reports and summaries of the proceedings, the eerie parallels between his own ordeal five years earlier and Strauss's current roasting could hardly have escaped him. Nor did they escape Strauss's awareness. Whether he drew them consciously or not, he certainly noted the "nightmarish quality of the proceedings" in his memoirs.

Strauss remarks that the special counsel to the committee "enjoyed the reputation of being a successful prosecuting attorney"—exactly like Strauss's choice for chief AEC counsel at Oppenheimer's hearing, Roger Robb. Strauss complains about a statement read by one witness against him, "a document containing many assertions at second hand by persons who were not identified and also a number of untrue statements." Such documents were one of the chief weapons used by Robb against Oppenheimer and other witnesses at the AEC hearing. Strauss continues, "A witness testified against me at considerable length with a prepared statement containing allegations, many introduced by such expressions as 'It is believed,' 'It was reported,' 'It is generally credited,' 'The impression was' and an assortment of innuendoes." Strauss could have been describing the great majority of the FBI reports and other statements brought against Oppenheimer at his own hearing.

Strauss must also have recognized another favorite Robb tactic at his confirmation hearing. "As the hearing progressed, much was made of the fact that I was unable to recollect the details of a letter dated some three and a half years previously," he complains. At Oppenheimer's hearing, much was made of the fact that Oppenheimer couldn't remember the details of a letter from a GAC member from almost five years previously, with Robb all but implying that Oppenheimer had willfully "forgotten" it or was lying about not remembering it. "The circumstance that I could not recall all the details of such a letter . . . was characterized as 'a

shocking lack of truthfulness,'" says Strauss. Perhaps a scientist like Oppenheimer was expected to have a better memory for years-old correspondence than a mere administrator like Strauss.

Then there was the trademark Robb move of using evidence and statements from classified documents unavailable to the defendant or his attorneys, as was done throughout Oppenheimer's hearing. Strauss found himself hoisted on this particular petard when a question came up about Strauss's alleged presence at a certain AEC meeting and he was unable to answer: "as the Commission wished to preserve the precedent of keeping its minutes privileged, the transcript was not made available to me to rebut the charge that the letter had been 'discussed' in my presence.

"It was now clear," Strauss writes, "that this was to be not a hearing so much as an inquisition, with the attorney for the prosecution brought in by the chief judge."[6] Not even Oppenheimer's staunchest defenders could have come up with a more apt description of the Oppenheimer hearing. Some of those defenders couldn't help but relish Strauss's ordeal. One of them, Bernice Brode, a friend of Oppenheimer's and the wife of one of his Los Alamos colleagues, made it a point to attend the hearings and wrote to Oppie: "It's a lovely show—never thought that I'd live to see my revenge. In unchristianly spirit, enjoy every squirm and anguish of victim. Having *wonderful* time—wish you were here!" She even included a sketch of the hearing room showing Strauss's position surrounded by hostile senators.[7]

One crucial difference between the Strauss confirmation hearings and Oppenheimer's previous ordeal, and one that undoubtedly made the proceedings all the more hellish for Strauss, was that his hearings were completely open to the press and public, while the Oppenheimer proceeding had been conducted in secret (even if its existence had become public knowledge almost as soon as it began). Strauss thus had to withstand not only the questioning from senators during the day but the commentary and criticisms in the press every evening. Still, it was a double-edged sword. If Strauss's detractors were having a field day, then so were his supporters, who rushed to defend the admiral against every alleged contradiction or slip of memory.

But as the hearings progressed, it was clear that the forces aligning against Strauss were far more vocal and dominant. Many of these were from the scientific community, not only out of sympathy and support for Oppenheimer, but also because many scientists believed that Strauss had done considerable damage to the fraternity of scientists and their relationship with the government.

Dr. David R. Inglis, the new chairman of the Federation of American Scientists, told the committee that Strauss's "anti-intellectualism and overzealousness" had harmed scientific development and progress, and through "personal vindictiveness" against Oppenheimer, Strauss had dragged scientific freedom "into the dirt." Another scientist charged that "many misstatements can be found in his [Strauss's] comments on the dangers from radioactive fallout and on the degree of information released to the public." According to the scientist, David Hill, "most of the scientists in this country would prefer to see Mr. Strauss completely out of Government." In the midst of the hearings, Strauss kept a commitment to speak at a meeting of the American Physical Society, limiting his speech to the innocuous topic of the metric system. Many APS members stayed away out of protest anyway.[8]

Strauss's performance before the Senate did little to help his own cause. He fell into some flagrant inconsistencies and self-contradictions, but in fairness, few individuals could withstand such critical questioning without a few lapses here and there. But Strauss made it worse for himself by his characteristic arrogance and self-righteousness, which made him almost constitutionally unable to admit a mistake or misjudgment. "In the hearings Strauss proved himself to be vain, arrogant, and self-righteous in defense of his record. . . . Strauss's stubborn attempts to defend himself led him into twisted, legalistic positions that made him look untruthful," says Pfau.[9]

Strauss's agony was intensified by his paranoiac streak, which made him worry whether he had become the target of the same sort of surveillance he had previously demanded for others, including Oppenheimer. Were his enemies spying on him? Richard Pfau writes, "He feared that they had tapped his telephone at the Shoreham [Hotel in Washington, where Strauss was living], and one day when his

wife could hear him talking on one of their lines while she talked over the other, he called the FBI. No taps or microphones were found."[10]

Soon after the scathing testimony of Strauss archenemy Senator Clinton Anderson (a man Strauss so despised that even in his own memoirs, he cannot bring himself to use Anderson's name, referring to him invariably as "the Junior Senator from New Mexico"), the committee voted. Somehow, despite all the animosity and rancor against Strauss, the admiral squeaked through, the committee voting 9 to 8 in favor of recommending his confirmation to the full Senate.

The first weeks of June would be the decisive period. Meanwhile, the debate on Strauss continued in the public forum. Many pundits, both pro- and anti-Strauss, feared the long-term effects of the drawn-out and bitter confirmation saga. "Republican Senator Prescott Bush of Connecticut warned that the prolonged inquisition might have damaged the nation already because Strauss's ordeal would make good men reluctant to serve their country," Pfau observes in his Strauss biography.[11] The same concerns, of course, had engulfed the scientific community ever since the Oppenheimer debacle five years earlier.

In the wee hours of June 19, 1959, the final vote was taken: 46 for Strauss, 49 against. Strauss's public career was over. Somehow, it seemed appropriate that it had ended in the same sort of bitterness, ill will, and pointless partisan wrangling that Strauss had stirred up and thrived upon throughout that entire career.

Like Oppenheimer, he had been destroyed, apparently completely and utterly. Like Oppenheimer, he had in many ways brought the worst upon himself, choosing noisy confrontation over quiet retreat: Oppenheimer could have accepted the cancellation of his security clearance without fuss, but chose to fight and requested a hearing; Strauss could have remained a presidential adviser and avoided his ordeal by refusing appointment to the cabinet.

Yet Oppenheimer's downfall, especially now viewed in retrospect, had been only partial. The loss of his clearance meant the end of his government career, but he still had his second life—actually, his first

and most important life—as a respected scientist to fall back on. His status as a world-class physicist was unaffected by any taint of supposedly being a "security risk," and his position as a scientific administrator and statesman was unassailed and decisively confirmed when he was kept on at the Institute for Advanced Study. Whatever the wounds of the hearing—and they were deep and painful—there was still solace to be found in science, the one safe haven that was always there, the accepting mistress who would never reject him.

But for Strauss, the truth was altogether more bitter and final. Public service had been his entire life for over forty years, and now that the opportunity to continue had been torn from him, he had no real alternative but the quiet retirement to his farm that he had long contemplated, a deeply hurt, broken, shamed man. "In eighteen years of almost continuous responsibility for national defense, Strauss had become testy, irascible, and increasingly intolerant of opposition," Pfau observes. "He probably should have turned down the president's offer to join the cabinet. . . . instead, he exposed himself to the exhausting and demeaning inquisition that capped his distinguished career with disgrace."[12]

Unlike Oppenheimer, who was able to forge himself anew as a scientific spokesman, there would be no public renewal for Strauss's image. "Most Americans knew him as the destroyer of J. Robert Oppenheimer, opponent of TVA, and rigid cold warrior, and the long months of debate over his nomination only exacerbated those negative impressions," writes Pfau.[13]

According to *The New York Times,* Strauss was the first cabinet nominee to fail to be confirmed since 1925, a humiliating coda for any career. *The Times* speculated that the Democrats' defeat of Strauss might hurt them politically in the long run and that "the Strauss affair may become an issue in the 1960 Presidential campaign—and it may boomerang against the Democrats."[14] But by the time the 1960 campaign swung into high gear, Strauss was already a forgotten man, the partisan nature of his public defeat swept aside by more immediate and pressing issues.

Strauss's decisive and final expulsion from government served as more

encouragement for the advocates of his old nemesis, Robert Oppenheimer. Among them was Senator Clinton Anderson, the major force behind Strauss's recent defeat.

Anderson was well known as supporting the reinstatement of Oppenheimer to public service, and now that Strauss's influence and power had been decisively destroyed, many believed that the time was ripe for another go at an Oppenheimer rehearing. One motivating factor for Anderson was a series of pro-Strauss newspaper editorials in the wake of the confirmation hearings that inaccurately portrayed Strauss's role in the Oppenheimer case; in a phone call to Oppenheimer's secretary, Anderson said that the editorials "should not be allowed to go unchallenged." One way to clear up the misstatements would be a senatorial investigation.[15]

Meanwhile, Anderson had brought several other Democratic senators on board who were willing to support the reopening of the Oppenheimer case, and were assured they had the blessings of the Democratic leadership to proceed. The plan was to put Strauss on the witness stand and grill him regarding his conduct on the Oppenheimer case, hoping to expose him as a liar and master manipulator.

But Oppenheimer would also have to offer up a "simple dignified statement of regret" about his past indiscretions and possible "thoughtlessness" regarding security regulations. And if things didn't go smoothly, the Democrats would have to walk away from the entire endeavor, leaving Oppenheimer twisting alone in the wind: no one was about to toss away a political career for him.

By the time Anderson attempted to contact Oppenheimer with these somewhat dubious propositions, the scientist had already departed the country for his summer sabbatical in St. John, so Oppenheimer's secretary, the tireless Verna Hobson, referred the senator to Lloyd Garrison. Garrison told Anderson in a phone conversation that Oppenheimer would definitely "be averse to any public retrial" of his case, but that Garrison would contact his client and find out his feelings on the matter. Anderson agreed not to proceed with anything without Oppenheimer's knowledge and full approval.

Despite Anderson's enthusiasm, and even with the removal of Strauss

from power, Garrison was unimpressed. "My own feeling is that a public rehash of the case would serve no good end," he wrote to Oppenheimer in the Virgin Islands. It would "simply reopen old wounds that have been healing and readvertise chapters of the past that are being forgotten." And although Garrison believed that Anderson "is convinced that a very great injustice was done to you," his primary objectives were political: "My impression, however, is that he has not thought the matter through very far and that his dominant motivation is to show up Strauss rather than to vindicate you."[16]

Oppenheimer responded as soon as Garrison's missive wound its leisurely way to him across the Caribbean to St. John. Again, he was electing to stay above the fray. "I quite generally agree with you," he wrote. "For many clear reasons, I would welcome the restoration of security clearance. I would hope that one day this might be done on the basis of the very full record that exists, and of my conduct since the revocation of clearance, with a minimum—or no—further explanation and clarification. I am not hopeful of such action on the part of the present administration." Oppenheimer thought that any attempt to restore his clearance through some kind of formal congressional proceeding would be "if not . . . impossible," then at best "a doubtful, protracted, and perhaps needlessly embittered" affair.

Vague promises from Senator Anderson were not enough. Oppenheimer was "in some doubt as to the precise form" of just what Anderson was proposing, and some of the possible purposes of such an investigation "clearly have little to do with me." Because of this, Oppenheimer would not "either promote and encourage . . . nor . . . oppose" Anderson's efforts. If Anderson's investigation did proceed, Oppenheimer would remain "wholly uninvolved" and would do "all that I could, within the limits of duty and responsibility, to remain disengaged from the proceedings."[17]

No doubt it was exceedingly frustrating for Oppenheimer's champions to be faced with such studied reluctance and lack of support from their man. But as much as he appreciated such efforts and the goodwill and faith behind them, Oppenheimer was determined to avoid any repeat of those three grinding weeks in the spring of 1954. No matter

how sympathetic the judges might be this time, no matter how much the political winds had shifted, no matter how nearly certain a favorable outcome seemed: he wasn't going to go through all that again.

As far as he was concerned, once was enough. The facts, the testimony, the truth, everything was there in the 992 pages of the published hearing transcript, in the reams of legal argument submitted by Garrison and others, in the example of his own life before and after the hearings. That, Oppenheimer believed, should be more than enough for anyone to realize the injustice done to him and to rectify it properly.

And there was another thing to consider. Suppose he did submit himself to another hearing, and for whatever reasons, a fluke, a legal technicality, a misunderstanding—he *wasn't* cleared? What then? What future for a man condemned not once, but twice, as a security risk—and the second time in a proceeding in which, unlike the first, he had been given every chance, every advantage?

The risk wasn't worth taking, not for himself, nor for his family. And anyway, it wasn't necessary. The political climate *was* changing, had changed in the five years since the hearing, and it was possible that with the coming of a new administration, those newly in power would be more willing to reconsider and correct the wrongs of the past.

So Oppenheimer would continue to bide his time and await the future. He would not risk his present life, so laboriously built up and restored from the ashes, on the wispy promises of ambitious politicians or ailing crusaders.

And, perhaps, it might be wise to allow a little more distance to fall between himself and his past. Particularly when certain people still persisted in refusing to allow that past to die a natural death.

* * *

The Gray Board report went to AEC general manager Nichols, who reviewed it and sent it on to the AEC commissioners with a cover letter of his own, containing his own interpretations of their arguments and his recommendations. Nichols totally disregarded the accusations of stalling H-bomb development and focused

instead on Oppenheimer's "veracity" and "consistent disregard of a reasonable security system." His letter invented new accusations, groundlessly speculated on various matters and drew conclusions as if based on fact, and pointedly ignored aspects of the Gray Board findings that didn't support his positions. Garrison and Oppenheimer's other lawyers might have been able to refute Nichols's tactics, but they were never given a copy of the Nichols letter or even told that it existed.

But Oppenheimer was within his rights to appeal the Gray Board verdict, and after being denied the opportunity to make an oral argument before the AEC commissioners, Garrison filed a written brief. As the wait began for the final decision on Oppenheimer's fate, the debate in the press and on the public stage continued.

On June 29, the AEC commissioners issued their final verdict. Lewis Strauss and three other commissioners ruled against Oppenheimer, citing "fundamental defects in his character" that made him "not entitled to the continued confidence of the government." Strauss held that Oppenheimer "has consistently placed himself outside the rules which govern others" and "repeatedly exhibited a willful disregard of the normal and proper obligations of security."

Strauss's remarks about Oppenheimer's "defects of character" are most revealing, because they betray how much the charges against Oppenheimer had shifted from their original version. Strauss and the other commissioners piously insisted that their censure of Oppenheimer was of course not at all based on his professional or personal judgments about the H-bomb or anything else: "Dr. Oppenheimer was, of course, entitled to his opinion." Instead, the commissioners zeroed in on his many supposed "falsehoods, evasions, and misrepresentations."

Chief among these was the Chevalier incident. One admitted lie—the version of the incident that Oppenheimer had related to security officer Boris Pash involving three contacts, the Soviet embassy, and so on, that Oppenheimer had explained as due to his "idiocy"—had been blown up from an innocent casual conversation in a kitchen to a possible major espionage attempt involving an entire ring of imaginary Soviet agents—with Oppenheimer in the middle of it all, thanks largely to Robb's characterization of it as "a whole fabrication and tissue of lies" and his ruthless cross-examination tactics, which wrung repeated admissions of lying from Oppenheimer.

From a single white, or at most gray, lie, thoughtlessly tossed off in a foolish attempt to protect a friend, and several other incidents that were characterized as

lies or obfuscations but were simply normal human lapses of memory, Strauss and the other commissioners concluded that Oppenheimer was a habitual liar with "fundamental defects of character" that made him unworthy of the nation's trust.

Date: April 1, 1960

To: Mr. Robert L. Bell
 Director of Security
 National Aeronautics and
 Space Administration
 1512 H Street, Northwest
 Washington 25, D.C.

From: John Edgar Hoover, Director

Subject: UNKNOWN SUBJECT
 DR. J. ROBERT OPPENHEIMER
 ESPIONAGE - X

A confidential informant who has furnished reliable information in the past
has advised that on March 28, 1960, he obtained the following information from
████████████████████████ Washington, D.C.:

Oppenheimer, Director, Institute for Advanced Study, Princeton, New Jersey,
advised Abe Spanel, President, International Latex Corporation, New York
City, that the individual in charge of the Atlas missile project, a personal
friend of Oppenheimer's, had related that in the development of missiles the
United States is not far behind the U.S.S.R.; that in the short-range missile
field the United States is ahead of the U.S.S.R.; and that the United States
is not more than six months behind the U.S.S.R. in its long-range missile
endeavors. Oppenheimer also told Spanel that once the United States starts
producing the Atlas, Polaris, and Titan missiles, the United States will have
more missiles than the Soviets will ever have. Spanel cautioned ████████
not to use Oppenheimer's name with regard to this information since
Oppenheimer was a "crucified man."

Oppenheimer is the scientist who in 1954 was denied clearance for access to
classified atomic energy data by a majority vote of the Atomic Energy
Commission commissioners because of information indicating character defects
and imprudent association with communists on the part of Oppenheimer.

 1 - Assistant Chief of Staff for Intelligence
 Department of the Army
 Attention: Chief, Security Division

 1 - Director of Naval Intelligence

 1 - Office of Special Investigations
 Air Force
 Attention: Chief, Counter Intelligence Division

NOTE: The above information has also been furnished to the Vice President by
letter 4-1-60. State was furnished this information via liaison on 3-30-60
and authorized further dissemination by Bureau. It is noted ████████ was
instituted at request of State. Classified Confidential since the source is
████████████ which is most delicate.

- 2 -

CONFIDENTIAL

12

A Kind of Humanity

Although Oppenheimer took no satisfaction—at least publicly—in the fact, his worst enemy had been stripped of power and position, and many of Strauss's allies were facing a similar waning of their power and influence. With each passing year, the McCarthy era faded in its power to evoke the old animosities and suspicions. Already the Red-baiters were beginning to sound quaint and archaic, almost laughable in their jeremiads. Charges of disloyalty and subversion were now met more often with demands for evidence and proof rather than with knee-jerk agreement. Who cared about someone's naïve dalliances with Communist front organizations twenty years ago when America faced a clear and present danger from a revitalized, militarily strong and technologically advanced Soviet Union, and needed all the expert help it could get?

As the 1950s drew to a close, Oppenheimer's critics, the ones to whom his every word and action were suspect, the ones who never failed to recite the litany of the many "defects of character" the AEC had pointed out or to remind the American public that the scientist was a "security risk," were sounding more and more hollow. They still had their true believers, and on occasion those believers rose up in force and made their feelings felt, as in Bristol Township, Pennsylvania, but most average citizens no longer seemed to care one way or the other. To most people, Oppenheimer was a famous scientist who'd had a few problems

a few years ago, and that was about it. They didn't care about long-ago indiscretions, arguments about the hydrogen bomb, or the "Chevalier incident." There were more immediate concerns to worry about, the flagging economy and the missile gap among them.

But Oppenheimer had made a new enemy, one who cared very much about Oppenheimer's past, because he had been intimately involved in it. He was Haakon Chevalier, the center and instigator of the "incident," and he believed that Oppenheimer's handling of that brief moment in both their lives had irrevocably changed them both. Once he had considered Oppenheimer a dear friend, as close as a brother; now he felt himself utterly betrayed, his life literally destroyed by him. He had tried to seek some sort of explanation or reparation from Oppenheimer personally, but to no avail; the friendship had been destroyed.

But while Oppenheimer moved on, though with regret and sorrow, Chevalier nursed a festering sense of rage and hurt, his feelings of betrayal blooming into a hatred as intense as that of a spurned lover, to the point where, in his eyes, the entire remaining course of his life had been determined and doomed by Oppenheimer's actions.

In the fall of 1959, Chevalier made his personal betrayal public. The former French literature professor and noted translator of Malraux published a novel with the revealing title *The Man Who Would Be God*. The title character, Sebastian Bloch, is an arrogant, charismatic atomic scientist working on America's World War II weapons program. Bloch also harbors Communist sympathies and works secretly in Communist front organizations. A young FBI agent infiltrates Bloch's university to get close to him and ends up becoming intellectually "seduced" by Bloch, striking up a genuine friendship with the scientist that causes the agent personal conflicts, and later costs him his career and livelihood when Bloch eventually betrays him for selfish political and personal gain.

Although Chevalier claimed in the book's foreword that "any resemblance to actual persons or events is unintentional and fortuitous" and denied that the book was intended as a roman à clef, he wasn't fooling anybody who had the slightest familiarity with the Oppenheimer case and Chevalier's role in it. Oppenheimer was clearly Bloch, and Chevalier the idealistic young security agent ultimately betrayed by him. "So

striking and precise are the allegedly 'unintentional and fortuitous' re-
semblances to the actual case history of Oppenheimer and Chevalier
that it is almost impossible for a reader to think in other terms or for a
critic to comment on the book as a novel rather than as a polemic,"
wrote one critic.

If Chevalier had hoped that *The Man Who Would Be God* would win
him sympathy and understanding, recognition as an innocent and in-
jured party, or even decent book sales, he soon found himself sorely
disappointed. The parallels between real life and Chevalier's portrayal
were so obvious, so lacking in subtlety, that the novel was almost uni-
versally panned. In fact, Chevalier had faced considerable difficulty
finding a publisher for the original European edition, since some of the
editors he approached feared a libel suit from Oppenheimer.

Instead of coming across as an incisive analysis or literary portrait of
a compelling character based on a real-life figure, Chevalier's book was
perceived as little more than a fumbling attempt at scoring some sort of
personal revenge, almost childish in its naïveté and lack of tact. "It is as
if Judas were to write a 450-page novel telling how badly betrayed he
had been by the Crucifixion," said the *Chicago Sun-Times*. "And a clum-
sily written novel at that." The book might indeed be, "as its publisher
predicts, one of the most widely discussed novels of 1959. It is unques-
tionably one of the shoddiest." The *New York Herald Tribune* called it "A
Bitter 'J'Accuse' Written as a Novel."[1]

Oppenheimer's opinion of *The Man Who Would Be God* is not re-
corded, nor is it known whether he ever read it. The friendship had
ended bitterly some months after his security hearing in 1954, after
Chevalier found himself "shattered" by the revelations of the published
hearing transcript and the facts that subsequently emerged in the press.
That was when Chevalier finally learned the source of the shadowy ac-
cusations and suspicions that had dogged him throughout his postwar
career, leading to FBI interrogations, mysteriously withdrawn job of-
fers, and other unexplained misfortunes: it had been Oppenheimer
implicating him in an alleged espionage conspiracy. The fact that Op-
penheimer had done so inadvertently, and that he had complicated his
own situation by refusing to name Chevalier and trying to protect him
for as long as possible, was lost on the aggrieved Chevalier. The two
men had not communicated since late 1954, when Chevalier had begun

working on the novel and even mentioned it to Oppenheimer in their final correspondence.

So for Oppenheimer, dedicated as he was to leaving behind the mistakes of the past and moving on with his new life, Chevalier's book must have seemed fairly pointless, a futile expression of hurt feelings, a needless dredging up of old injuries about which nothing further could be done. If Chevalier had intended his book as a means of direct or indirect revenge against his perceived betrayal by Oppenheimer, the public and critical response showed that his intentions had backfired spectacularly. If anything, Chevalier had only enhanced the sheen of noble martyrdom that by now was an integral part of Oppenheimer's image.

J. Robert Oppenheimer was not only striving to move forward, he was simply *moving,* almost constantly. The speeches and addresses to distinguished gatherings and conferences continued unabated throughout 1959 and into 1960. He had become a dedicated globe-trotter, something for which he had enjoyed little time or opportunity during his years in government service.

Oppenheimer returned to Paris in September 1959 to help his colleagues there get the French Institute for Advanced Study up and running. He also took a week out to devote to a group with which he had become increasingly active, the Congress for Cultural Freedom.

Formed in Berlin in 1950, the CCF was a group of distinguished, politically liberal intellectuals dedicated to promoting ties between the European and American intellectual communities and battling the spread of Communist influence in world culture. Among its members were former ambassador to Russia and now IAS faculty member George Kennan, historian Arthur M. Schlesinger Jr., and an impressive crowd of European writers, historians, and thinkers.

For Oppenheimer, the CCF provided a group of like-minded allies on his own intellectual level who shared both his deeply philosophical and his practical concerns for the state of the world. "Oppenheimer deeply empathized with the Congress' liberal anticommunist message," write Kai Bird and Martin Sherwin. "Oppenheimer was now in the company of intellectuals dedicated to dispelling the illusions of 'frivolous fellow-travelers.' "[2]

At the CCF conference on the banks of the Rhine near Basel, Switzer-

land, Oppenheimer spoke on nuclear power and nuclear weapons. Perhaps feeling unusually comfortable and welcomed in this cosmopolitan environment, far from the clouds that followed him in the United States, Oppenheimer allowed himself to express some quite dark and direct ruminations, pronouncing himself to be "profoundly in anguish" that the dangers of nuclear weapons weren't being discussed in anything other than very abstract, "prudential and game-theoretic" terms. "What are we to think of such a civilization?" he asked. Of course, he admitted in a rueful nod to his removal from government, he was "not now very deep in these things."

But as stimulating as it may have been for Oppenheimer and the other participants, very few practical solutions or proposals ultimately came out of the CCF conferences and the similar high-level get-togethers in which Oppenheimer frequently participated. To many observers, such ivory-tower idylls seemed little more than an opportunity for high-powered intellectual types, far removed from the down and dirty cares and concerns of the real, everyday world, to indulge themselves in guilt-ridden hand-wringing over abstractions and lofty theories and thus help themselves feel noble. As historian Charles Thorpe caustically notes, "Oppenheimer offered to weep for the world but not to help change it."[3]

Perhaps as an acknowledgment of his new man-of-the-world status, Oppenheimer was picked to represent the International Atomic Energy Agency at 1960's Tenth Annual High Energy Physics Conference in Rochester, New York. Oppenheimer had been attending the annual conference for years already, but now he would be doing so as an official representative of a United Nations organization. Since the IAEA concerned itself with peaceful atomic energy applications, it was not an appointment that required any sort of security clearance, but it was something of an honor and indication of a new official cachet that Oppenheimer had been chosen for the position.

One minor distraction from the whirlwind of intellectual touring that Oppenheimer's life had become was a small fire at his Princeton home, Olden Manor. It started one April morning in a second-floor dressing room and, aside from some damage to a rug, some furniture, and some books, caused no major problem. But it was indicative of Oppenheimer's undiminished ability to make the newspapers that *The New York Times* carried a brief story on the incident the next day.[4]

Although it was the only such incident that made the pages of *The New York Times*, it was far from the first such "accident" at Olden Manor. Kitty (and, on occasion, Robert) had a bad habit of smoking in bed, often after having had too much to drink. The *Times* report mentions no cause for the fire, but chances are good that Kitty's habit caused the April 1960 incident. "Almost every night she fell asleep in bed smoking," Bird and Sherwin observe in *American Prometheus*. "Her bedding was full of cigarette holes."[5] Her alcoholism, a proneness to accidents, and Oppenheimer's unwillingness (or inability) to do much to rein in his volatile wife made the Oppenheimer home a frequent victim of minor domestic mishaps—not to mention a focus of sometimes amused, sometimes nasty gossip in the circles of Institute faculty and Princetonian society.

For those who knew the Oppenheimer family, Kitty was as polarizing a figure as Oppenheimer himself. She was either loved or hated; there seemed to be no middle ground. She was alternately described as "overbearing," "conniving," "manipulative," "a gossip," even "evil" by some, and "strong," "courageous," "intense," and "fun-loving" by others.

IAS professor Freeman Dyson thought she was "great," and that she "certainly kept Oppenheimer going. She was a much stronger character than he was." Dyson agrees that Kitty had a drinking problem but says that "it wasn't visible in much of her life."[6] Yet, another Institute member, Abraham Pais, states plainly that Kitty was not only an alcoholic, but "the most despicable female I have ever known." But he acknowledges that she was fiercely loyal to and supportive of her husband, who seemed to tolerate and excuse Kitty's sometimes erratic behavior. "Today, we would call them co-dependents," Pais observes.[7] The dichotomy in Kitty's relationships with others extended to her own children: while she and daughter Toni enjoyed a close bond, she was constantly in conflict with Peter, and the rift between mother and son later drove Peter to leave home as a teenager.

Nineteen sixty would be a notable Oppenheimer year for other, more salutary reasons. Aside from his high profile both internationally and nationally, and the fact that his appearances finally seemed less dogged by controversy and contention, there was the impending presidential election and the changes it would bring. No one, least of all Oppenheimer, was saying it out loud yet, but if the new president turned out

to be the young Senator Kennedy from Massachusetts, Oppenheimer's stock might go up considerably. After eight years of a Republican administration, Oppenheimer's allies looked forward eagerly to the prospect of a new, more liberal Democratic government that would sweep away the last vestiges of McCarthyism, including Oppenheimer's exile from government. But of course, it was also quite possible that Vice President Nixon would be taking the reins come January, and if that happened, the prospects for vindication would be much less rosy.

But there would be plenty of time later to worry about such matters. Almost coincidentally, Oppenheimer found himself marking the end of another sort of era and the beginning of a new one when, in the fall of 1960, he traveled to perhaps his most unlikely destination of all: Japan. Even more unlikely, he did so not over the objections of the only people in the world to be subjected to Oppenheimer's bomb, but with their direct and enthusiastic invitation.

The visit had been in the works at least informally for some time. A year earlier, Oppenheimer's friend Harold Taylor, president of Sarah Lawrence College, returned from an extended trip to Japan and wrote Oppenheimer: "I discovered that a considerable body of intellectuals is very much interested in having you come over to Japan for three months, the three prime people being Matsumoto, Takagi and Yukawa, with the physicists and natural scientists particularly anxious and the university community in general all hopeful that you might be persuaded." In case Oppenheimer had any reservations about lingering resentments on the part of the Japanese, Taylor assured him, "You will find a very warm welcome, and a deep hunger for serious communication of ideas between the American community and the Japanese."[8]

The idea intrigued Oppenheimer, not only because of sheer curiosity, but also for professional reasons. A small but vibrant scientific community had sprung up in Japan since the war, and Japanese physicists were making exciting contributions. It was high time for someone to begin reaching out and strengthening the ties of friendship and collaboration between Japanese scientists and those in the United States and Europe. Who better than America's first envoy of science?

Not everyone thought it was such a charming idea. After all, only fifteen years earlier, the collective fruit of Oppenheimer's leadership, the supreme achievement of his life, had wiped out thousands of Japanese

lives and caused the ultimate defeat of the empire. Hiroshima and Na-
gasaki had been rebuilt, yes, fences had been mended and old animosi-
ties healed, yes, and Japan was now a staunch ally and friend of the
United States. But no people had ever before been subjected to such a
"rain of ruin," as Truman had called it, such a literally unprecedented,
unimaginable horror from a clear blue sky, as had the citizens of Hiro-
shima and Nagasaki. Fifteen years was hardly any time at all. How
would the Japanese people receive the man who had created the terrible
weapon that had defeated them?

The prospect of Oppenheimer touring Japan was made even more
dodgy by recent anti-American protests that had taken place in the
country because of an impending security treaty with the United States.
A planned visit by President Eisenhower had to be canceled when angry
demonstrators threatened an advance party, including Eisenhower's
press secretary. Matters calmed down somewhat after the treaty was
ratified, but American-Japanese tensions continued to simmer at an
uncomfortably high level. On top of all this, as Charles Thorpe points
out, "Oppenheimer's visit was potentially a direct and painful reminder
both of wartime defeat and of postwar subordination to the United
States."[9]

No, some told Oppenheimer. The invitation was a nice gesture, ad-
mirable and generous in spirit, but no one could predict what might
actually happen if Oppenheimer went there. All the contempt and de-
rision and vitriol hurled at him over the past years from the McCarthy-
ites might pale in comparison: rather than just rhetorical threats, in
Japan there was the possibility of literal physical danger. Better to re-
spectfully decline the invitation and stay home.

Oppenheimer disagreed. He would be going to Japan not as a repre-
sentative of the American government or military, but as a scientist, a
member of a profession that knew no bounds of parochial nationalism.
Those who had invited him were friends and colleagues, and he had
already hosted many Japanese scientists at the Institute. What had hap-
pened in wartime was over. To forgo such an invitation would be a be-
trayal of his own ideals and philosophies. Besides, he had never been to
Japan, and would probably never again have a better opportunity.

So on September 5, 1960, at the invitation of the Japan Committee
for Intellectual Interchange, Oppenheimer arrived in Tokyo for a

three-week lecture tour. Despite the colossal irony—or some might say, impropriety or arrogance—of the putative father of the atomic bomb paying a visit to the land that had been the bomb's first victim, Oppenheimer was met not with protests but with warmth and enthusiasm.

Oppenheimer didn't see his visit as a pilgrimage or act of contrition, but merely as a logical extension of his continuing efforts to bridge the gap between science and culture and to facilitate communication, the same concerns he had been addressing at least since his Reith BBC lectures in 1953 and his Columbia University address in 1954. "Because of the complexity of science, it has some contributions to make to the unity of man," he told reporters after his arrival.

But some questions just had to be asked. At a brief and, according to one newspaper, "terribly ill-planned" press conference in the crowded, overheated International House in Tokyo, Oppenheimer faced them gamely. No, coming to Japan didn't cause him any greater regret over his role in the creation of the atomic bomb. It hadn't changed his "sense of anguish" about the bomb. Still, "it isn't that I don't feel bad; it is that I don't feel worse tonight than last night."

What about Hiroshima? Would Oppenheimer visit that ill-fated city? He would like to, he explained, but it wasn't on his official itinerary, and "it is not clear that it will be practical." But he would be visiting Kyoto, Osaka, and some other cities, giving lectures to specialized audiences of scientists and to the general public.

The Japanese newspapers noted that some of Oppenheimer's appearances were attended by individuals who, "by the faintly starry-eyed look in their eyes were thought to be members of 'peace' and 'anti-bomb' organizations."[10] If so, he certainly said much in his more general lectures to warm their hearts and chill their bones. Noting that one of his talks had been given the title "The Future of Civilization in the Scientific Age," Oppenheimer remarked, "I do not use this phrase easily for I am one of those who share with my many colleagues at home and here in Japan profound doubts of the very existence of a future."

He observed that "[m]any of us talk about ridding the world of atomic weapons. I sympathize with this aim; but we cannot by such action or by any action recreate the world of 20 years ago. Men know how to make such weapons. This knowledge cannot be driven away. It

cannot be buried away. It is here, and whatever arrangements we make for saving ourselves from the bombs we must make in light of the fact that this is always imminent, virtually present in the world of men from now on."

All of his less technical talks in Japan followed much the same theme; in fact, they were variations of the same basic lecture. "In asking how we may try to bring effective improvement to our lives it is natural for me to think of what the loose group whom you and I represent, called intellectuals, can do, what our duty is, we who are teachers, artists, statesmen, scientists," he pointed out, stating what had become one of his primary obsessions in his new life. "It is our duty not least to help create a world in which despair and cynicism are complemented and partly replaced, not by optimism, but by a courage and by hope."[11]

All his lectures were met with the packed houses that had become standard by now for an Oppenheimer talk, with extensive press coverage and copious quotations of the "savant"'s words. Oppenheimer's more scientific talks met with an equally rapturous and respectful response. "As the slender and somewhat aristocratic scholar elaborated his suggestive and up-to-date—even to physics experts themselves—theory to intent Japanese students of physics whose academic position is highly appreciated in the world, he talked as if he were at his institute in his country," marveled the *Mainichi Daily News.*[12]

One of the definite highlights for Oppenheimer occurred late in the trip, on the day of his public lecture in Osaka, when he had the opportunity to meet the parents of a former student. Shuichi Kusaka was a young physicist who had attended Vancouver University and then done graduate work with Oppenheimer at Berkeley before World War II, and Oppenheimer had helped Kusaka with his work visa arrangements. After Pearl Harbor, Kusaka had been caught up in the internment program of Japanese living in the United States, but Oppenheimer managed to wangle his release from internment camp by arranging for him to study at Princeton University. Kusaka went on to become an associate professor at Princeton, but tragically died in a swimming accident at the New Jersey shore in 1947. Oppenheimer later helped to establish a scholarship fund in Kusaka's name.

Kusaka's parents were elderly and unable to travel, so Oppenheimer's visit to Japan provided them with the perfect chance to finally meet

and thank this man who had done so much for their son. "Dr. Oppenheimer told the aged couple their son was a distinguished scientist and a good man," reported the *Asahi Evening News*.[13]

Oppenheimer had another notable encounter during his Japan excursion, this one with an expatriate American. By 1960, the issue of atomic testing and widespread fallout had aroused worldwide outcry, and passionate protests were routinely in the news. One of the more dedicated acts of protest came from the Reynolds family, who purposely piloted their yacht *Phoenix* into the test zone during a series of atomic tests in the Pacific at Eniwetok atoll in 1958. The Reynoldses were now living in Hiroshima, and the head of the family and *Phoenix*'s skipper, Earle Reynolds, sent his son, Ted (who had also navigated the yacht during the 1958 protest voyage) to carry a letter to Oppenheimer. The letter was an invitation to Hiroshima.

"We have followed closely through the press your activities here in Japan, and note with regret that you do not plan to visit Hiroshima," wrote Reynolds. "We can understand the delicacy of the situation, but I do hope your decision was not dictated by any feeling that you might meet with personal unfriendliness." Reynolds assured Oppenheimer that the people of Hiroshima "bear no animosity toward any individual for the tragedy which overtook them. . . . their only hope is that there will never be another Hiroshima."[14]

The twenty-one-year-old Ted Reynolds journeyed to Osaka to intercept Oppenheimer, who accepted the letter from him. Oppenheimer admitted to Ted that while he would have wished "to have quietly visited the city," the Japan Committee for Intellectual Interchange, sponsoring his trip, had indeed feared negative reaction and publicity, so Hiroshima wasn't going to be on the itinerary.[15] Oppenheimer would never set foot within either of the cities, Hiroshima and Nagasaki, whose destruction marked the culmination of his Manhattan Project leadership.

Aside from the lecturing and scientific schmoozing, the tea parties and receptions held in their honor, Oppenheimer and wife Kitty found time to play tourist, visiting palaces and gardens, and catching the sights. Most of the sightseeing was terribly formal and always escorted. But Oppenheimer made the most of it, perhaps feeling that this would be his only visit to the island nation. "We have a double duty," he said

in one of his last lectures in Japan. "One is to do our work, to retain our skill, to be as good as is given us at our specialty. This is where we live as craftsmen and as man, and this is our anchor in history. We also need a great openness and friendliness to things with which we are not intimate, to listen to a friend or a stranger, with all the strength that we can bring to it. This is hard."

He continued, "If it is possible at all, it is because of things that we are not purely intellectual, because friendship and love soften the hardness of our isolation."[16] Perhaps these words, as much as any, explain why he willingly agreed to go to Japan, and what he hoped to accomplish, both personally and in the larger sense, by going there.

After a brief stopover in Hong Kong, Oppenheimer and Kitty returned to the United States at the end of September. Shortly over a month later, America would elect a new president. Some saw it as a herald of a new and more humane era, one that might bring vindication to Robert Oppenheimer. Others, including Oppenheimer himself, weren't so sure.

There would be changes, yes. But whether they would be enough to erase the mistakes and misjudgments of the previous decade remained to be seen.

* * *

Strauss and the majority also made much of Oppenheimer's questionable "associations," particularly his continued friendship with Chevalier, including a visit with him in Paris as recently as the previous December. It didn't matter that, as far as Oppenheimer knew and had testified, Chevalier had abandoned all of his Communistic ideas and associations years before, or that, in fact, their December meeting had been set up by their mutual friend, the ardent anti-Communist writer and de Gaulle adviser, André Malraux. There were also brief, passing encounters in the postwar years with other former leftist friends, in such innocent circumstances as a chance meeting on a Princeton street. No matter: these were enough to prove that Oppenheimer had continued a pattern of suspicious associations with unsavory characters up to the present day, obviously yet another "fundamental defect" in his character.

Unlike the Gray Board decision, which is almost regretful and respectful in tone, the AEC majority decision is merciless, almost gleefully savage. "It would

be difficult to find a sorrier example of an ungenerous judgment," says John Mason Brown. "The decision may seem to show moderation in granting Oppenheimer the right to his opinion on the H-bomb. Yet the opinion it states of Oppenheimer's defects in character is devoid of tolerance. So brutal is it as a condemnation that it sounds like outrage turned into cruelty."[17]

Only one commissioner, Henry DeWolf Smyth, dissented from the majority findings against Oppenheimer. He argued that the only question before the AEC was whether Oppenheimer would intentionally or unintentionally reveal secrets, and "there is no indication in the entire record that Dr. Oppenheimer has ever divulged any secret information," even though Oppenheimer had been "investigated, reinvestigated and under actual surveillance" for years. Smyth held that the security system "is nothing to worship. . . . if a man protects the secrets he has in his hands and his head, he has shown essential regard for the security system."[18]

But the decision had been made. J. Robert Oppenheimer would never again serve the United States in any official capacity. His enemies had set out to destroy his influence and remove him from the corridors of power, and they had won. Perhaps there is no more telling indicator of the times, and the damage that McCarthyism had wrought, than what was reported in the New York Daily Mirror *the day after the AEC verdict was made: "When the commission's decision was announced to the House late this afternoon by Chairman W. Sterling Cole (R-NY) of the Senate-House Atomic Energy Commission, there was considerable applause."[19]*

COURAGE AND HOPE

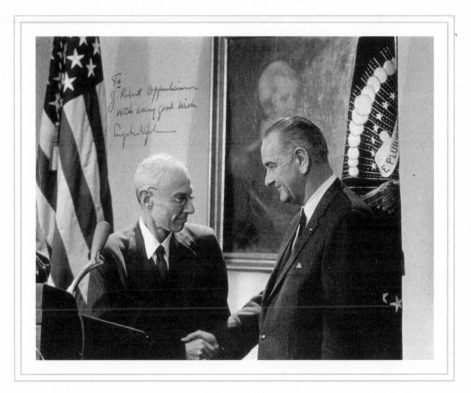

Vindication or consolation prize? Oppenheimer accepts the Enrico
Fermi Award from President Lyndon B. Johnson, December 1963.

We should try to look toward our future without flinching,
without lying, and without despair.

—J. ROBERT OPPENHEIMER
TO NICOLAS NABOKOV, 1961

LEWIS L. STRAUSS

Mercury Building
1925 K Street, N.W.
Washington 6, D.C.

2 February 1961

Mr. Tolson
Mr. Mohr
Mr. Parsons
Mr. Belmont
Mr. Callahan
Mr. Conrad
Mr. DeLoach
Mr. Malone
Mr. McGuire
Mr. Rosen
Mr. Trotter
Mr. Evans
Mr. W.C.Sullivan
Tele. Room
Mr. Ingram
Miss Gandy

Dear Edgar:

In the book that I am writing
I am engaged on a chapter dealing with
the Oppenheimer case. I would like to
illustrate it with a facsimile of the
letter which William L. Borden addressed
to you and which started the case. The
letter is in the public domain as it was
introduced as evidence in the hearings
which were published by the Government
Printing Office, and it has appeared
in print a number of times but not in
facsimile. Could your office send me a
photostat of it? I would be grateful.

Faithfully yours,

Lewis

Lewis (Strauss)

Honorable J. Edgar Hoover
Director
Federal Bureau of Investigation
Washington 25, D.C.

EX 101

REC- 4

100-17828-2360

5 FEB 14 1961

CRIME RESEARCH

13

Honor and Respect

On January 20, 1961, John Fitzgerald Kennedy became the thirty-fifth president of the United States. In his inaugural address, he urged his fellow citizens, "Let us begin anew," and challenged them to "ask not what your country can do for you, ask what you can do for your country."

In the case of Robert Oppenheimer, a man who had already done considerably more for his country than most citizens could ever aspire to, one could forgive him if he had wondered fleetingly about what his country might do for him now, after almost seven years of official exile. Certainly his friends and allies allowed themselves to ask that question as the new administration settled in, populated by many blatantly pro-Oppie individuals in high places such as McGeorge Bundy, Arthur M. Schlesinger Jr., and even the new secretary of state, Dean Rusk. As Kennedy had proclaimed, the torch had been passed to a new generation, one with a fresh outlook and daring ideas. It was a new decade, a New Frontier, and thus, it seemed, time to ask: what would be done now to correct the old wrongs done to Oppenheimer?

At first, at least officially, the answer appeared to be very little. After all, as some pointed out, Kennedy and his New Frontiersmen hadn't exactly been awarded a ringing mandate from the American people: JFK had won in the closest election in American history, a victory that

many (including JFK's opponent, Richard Nixon) suspected was not completely legitimate. Such a narrow triumph didn't encourage any overtly daring or controversial moves on the part of the incoming administration. And JFK already had a full plate: Cuba, an increasingly belligerent and restless Soviet Union, segregation conflicts in American cities. Finding time to review the years-old security case of one beleaguered atomic scientist, even someone as prominent as J. Robert Oppenheimer, had to rank fairly low on the agenda. Perhaps, as some quietly advised, it would be best to avoid stirring up such long-slumbering but volatile controversies, at least until after the midterm elections in 1962.

Oppenheimer could afford to bide his time, and in any event, he was already busy enough. He was involved in a new round of speaking engagements, which now seemed to take up just as much of his time as his governmental advisory work had done a decade earlier. He spoke at a tribute dinner for the late Henry Stimson, under whose guidance as secretary of war during World War II Oppenheimer had worked on the Manhattan Project and who had consulted Oppenheimer on the use of the bomb.

But if Oppenheimer was too busy giving erudite speeches to worry about regaining his security clearance, the champions of his cause were anxious to pick up his banner for him. Kennedy had barely settled into the Oval Office before the Americans for Democratic Action declared that the president should order a review of the Oppenheimer case, not to mention various other questionable personnel security cases of the past administration, and set up a special task force for the purpose. This, said Joseph L. Raub, ADA vice chairman for civil rights, would help America recover from "a bad hangover of McCarthyism."[1]

The retired Lewis Strauss, busily working on his memoirs but still keeping a watchful eye on matters Oppenheimer, noted the tiny article about the ADA action in *The New York Times* and, just to make sure that his good friend J. Edgar Hoover hadn't missed it, clipped it and sent it along to Hoover's office. "To be sure that it did not miss your eye," Strauss wrote helpfully. While incidentally noting that Raub had for many years been "most articulate in his criticism of the Government's loyalty procedures and has attacked the Bureau on a number of

occasions for participation therein," the FBI filed the *Times* clipping away in Oppenheimer's still-closed file, but in case the ADA decided to press the issue with Kennedy, and "since there may be additional publicity in this regard," the Bureau decided that "it appears advisable to point out to the Attorney General pertinent data concerning Oppenheimer, including a capsule summary of just what our investigations of the subject disclosed."

The Bureau proceeded to send a précis of the Oppenheimer file along to the new attorney general, Robert Kennedy. It contained the usual litany of charges and accusations quoted by everyone from congressmen to columnists to Lewis Strauss himself: "The Atomic Energy Commission Personnel Security Board hearing . . . recommended clearance for access to Restricted Data be denied. . . . Oppenheimer's continuing conduct and associates reflected a serious disregard for the requirements of a security system . . . susceptibility to influence which could have serious implications . . . conduct in the hydrogen bomb project sufficiently disconcerting . . . doubt as to whether his future participation would be clearly consistent with the chief interests of security . . . less than candid in several instances in his testimony . . ."

Then there were the earlier wartime investigations, which showed that "Oppenheimer contributed large sums of money to Communist Party officials. . . . associated with many prominent Communist Party officials . . . his relatives were Communist Party members. . . . he was affiliated with and contributed money to various Communist Party front groups. . . . described himself as a 'fellow-traveler' . . ." There was the requisite description of the Chevalier incident, capped with the information that "Oppenheimer opposed the development of the hydrogen bomb by the United States and he refused to support the Department of the Air Force long-range detection program for determining atomic explosions in the Soviet Union," the two charges that had caused the majority of the United States military-industrial complex to align against him.[2] All old news, and no doubt already quite familiar to Bobby Kennedy, who didn't bother to do anything further with the information, undoubtedly already quite busy planning the invasion of Cuba with his brother.

In mid-1961, Oppenheimer added more stamps to his passport when the Organization of American States invited him to tour Latin America under a visiting-professor program, lecturing in Mexico, Brazil, Uruguay, Argentina, and Chile. Although the OAS was a Latin American body, it was partially funded by the United States, and predictably the diminishing contingent of McCarthyite holdouts complained about the "disgraced Oppenheimer" getting a grand tour of Latin America at taxpayer expense, as if Oppenheimer were going on vacation rather than serving as an official representative.

But America's taxpayers could take heart in the fact that Oppenheimer's Latin American excursion was a resounding success. Wherever he went, *"el padre de la bomba atómica"* was met with great enthusiasm, rapt crowds, and various honors. Aside from brief past visits to Brazil and Puerto Rico, it was Oppenheimer's first time in Latin America, and accompanied by a translator, he embarked on his usual whirlwind of scientific and public speeches, met with students and professors, and as in Japan, did a little sightseeing when time permitted.

Meanwhile, Oppenheimer's angels were busily at work behind the scenes in the new administration, and the FBI's informers were keeping the Bureau apprised of new developments. One of them, with an apparent connection to the White House and code-named 67D, informed a Bureau liaison officer in October that "pressure" was being brought to bear in order to secure White House clearance for Oppenheimer. According to 67D, "a move has now begun by certain members of the scientific community, who urge the White House to use Oppenheimer's talents in connection with a study that the White House will soon begin."

The study in question was a survey of United States higher education, a topic that by its very nature would be unclassified, so that Oppenheimer's lack of clearance would not be an issue. The informant pledged to "do everything in his power to keep Oppenheimer away from any White House connection."

"This appears to be a move on the part of a group of scientists to give Oppenheimer White House recognition, particularly by the use of the 'foot in the door' tactics of suggesting that he be used on an unclassified project," noted the FBI's report. Once again, the FBI decided to let the attorney general know what was going on, although the Bureau admit-

ted that "[i]t is not known who is responsible for this latest effort to have Oppenheimer once again assist the United States Government." A letter was also dispatched to Kenneth O'Donnell, special assistant to the president, setting out the basic facts re Oppenheimer, just in case he happened not to know.[3]

Oppenheimer had no inkling of the intrigue or the efforts proceeding in his name. And yet, he found himself hosting occasional visits from perfectly respectable and friendly FBI agents at the Institute for Advanced Study, despite the fact that he was no longer under official, purposeful surveillance.

The visits were routine and uneventful, generally concerning information on foreign nationals who might be visiting the Institute or other foreign contacts or activities with which Oppenheimer was involved as Institute director. Given Oppenheimer's history as a favorite target of the Bureau's attentions over the years, it's difficult to interpret these periodic FBI visits scattered throughout his appointment books as completely benign. Biographer Martin Sherwin speculates that these casual drop-ins by FBI agents at Princeton were Hoover's way of attempting to keep Oppenheimer in line, of reminding him that even if he was no longer under constant scrutiny, he had not been forgotten by his erstwhile friends at the Bureau. Unofficially, at least, they were still keeping an eye on him.

Still, Oppenheimer struggled to keep his own eyes above it all, on the lofty, rarefied ideals of community, peace, and scientific progress he continued to espouse in his speeches and writings. "For myself, there are at least two things that I should look for: an image of a world that responds to the changing needs and hopes of men without resort to the institution of war, indeed without its possibility; and a world in which, despite the vastness, the complexity, the rapid change in the circumstances of our life, and the knowledge which underlies it, the scope and depth of human responsibility and human nobility grow instead of shrinking," he wrote to his friend, CCF leader Nicolas Nabokov, as 1961 ended. "We should try to look toward our future without flinching, without lying, and without despair."[4]

Despair and the possibility of war, however, were much on the minds of both the Kennedy administration and the American people in early

1962. Kennedy's summit meeting with Khrushchev the previous summer had been a disaster, with the Soviet leader belligerently rejecting Kennedy's attempts at negotiation and resorting to his trademark posturings. The hot summer became considerably frostier shortly afterward as the crisis over Berlin intensified and the infamous wall was erected, dividing the city.

As Oppenheimer traveled to Canada to deliver the Whidden Lectures at McMaster University in Ontario, Americans were debating the pros and cons of a national civil defense program, fallout shelters were being identified and stocked in public buildings, and many citizens considered building their own backyard shelters. Even while privately acknowledging that it was pointless, administration officials publicly and enthusiastically pushed the civil defense evangel. After all, it *might* actually save a few lives, and at least it was doing *something* to help alleviate the apocalyptic fears gripping the American psyche.

Asked by the Canadian press for his thoughts on civil defense, Oppenheimer said, "I am passionately opposed to the thought of nuclear war for which an effective defense is difficult, if not impossible. The assertion that nuclear war will not be so bad, if believed, will distort our beliefs and behavior. . . . it is when civil defense is married to something like the Berlin crisis that it becomes a piece of idiocy."

Still, civil defense had its place. "I do not think that anyone believes that nuclear war can be made good clean fun. As long as people hold a realistic view of the degree of protection they can obtain, the fallout shelter campaign cannot be said to increase the danger of nuclear war."[5]

Oppenheimer's casual attitude toward the notion of fallout shelters wasn't simply a matter of public pronouncement; he practiced it in private as well. In the midst of America's shelter hysteria, an Ohio man wrote rather whimsically to Oppenheimer: "I have been arguing with my neighbor about bomb shelters. He is building one in the basement— I say it is useless. Anyway, I told him that if you had a bomb shelter and believed in them, then I would give up and build one myself." Oppenheimer's response no doubt saved his correspondent considerable work and expense. "We do not have a bomb shelter, and have no plans for one," he said.[6]

Certainly there were few people who realized more clearly than Op-

penheimer that the main benefits of civil defense and bomb shelters were psychological rather than practical. He wasn't going to go against the administration line too strongly, but neither would he prevaricate to an honest citizen asking him a direct question on the issue.

By that spring the Kennedy administration was beginning to feel comfortable enough to make what many interpreted as the first substantial overtures to right the wrongs of the McCarthy era. As Arthur Schlesinger writes in his history of the Kennedy presidency, *A Thousand Days,* JFK had quietly, gingerly, been making behind-the-scenes moves to repair the damage done to several individuals whose careers and livelihoods had been ruined by false accusations of subversion or disloyalty. "[Kennedy] was vigilant in his opposition to any revival of McCarthyism," says Schlesinger. "He took particular pleasure in the rehabilitation of government servants who had been punished for independence of thought in the past."[7]

Without much publicity or fanfare, cases had been reviewed, and unjust, ill-supported decisions had been reversed. Now, urged some in the administration, might be the time for more public steps involving more prominent persons. A perfect opportunity would be a gala state dinner and reception at the White House for American Nobel Prize winners. Aside from the honorees, other distinguished guests would be invited. Why not, asked McGeorge Bundy, include J. Robert Oppenheimer among them?

Kennedy agreed, and on Sunday, April 29, 1962, forty-nine Nobel Prize laureates and a small group of additional guests—including Oppenheimer—attended a formal White House reception and dinner. One of the honorees, scientist Linus Pauling, actually made it to the festivities a little late: as a dedicated leader of the international effort for a comprehensive nuclear test ban, he had been busy picketing with other protesters outside the White House just before the dinner.

Resplendent in formal garb, Oppenheimer mingled with luminaries such as astronaut John Glenn (fresh from his historic orbital spaceflight), novelist Pearl Buck, poet Robert Frost, and the widows of Ernest Hemingway and General George C. Marshall, among many others, in what JFK wryly referred to as "the most extraordinary collection of talent, of human knowledge, that has ever been gathered together at

the White House, with the possible exception of when Thomas Jefferson dined alone."

It was a milestone for Oppenheimer for several reasons. For his public image, it provided a clear and unmistakable signal that in Washington, he was no longer persona non grata. It was an unofficial, informal acknowledgment from the powers that be that Robert Oppenheimer might be okay after all. After almost a decade of exile from the halls of power, the White House dinner served as a sort of coming-out party for Oppenheimer, at least insofar as the government's formal recognition of his existence and preeminence in his field.

It was also a sure sign that there were new people and new ideas in town. "Nothing could better signalize the difference in intellectual climate between the two Administrations than the presence of the man who would have been counted the Prince of Darkness in the earlier one, having been dismissed as a security risk in 1954, and who is today brought out of his isolation as a distinguished mind," wrote Max Lerner in the *New York Post*.[8]

Aside from being a message to the public and to Washington insiders that Oppenheimer was no longer considered officially untouchable, the dinner invitation was intended as a message to Oppenheimer himself that the Kennedy administration was more liberal, more forgiving, more tolerant, than the previous one—and, quite possibly, more receptive to the idea of clearing his name.

Yet practical political realities still made it difficult for the administration to act unilaterally. Any presidential proclamation clearing Oppenheimer, any congressional hearings such as those previously championed by Clinton Anderson, would be unlikely, especially with critical midterm elections on the horizon. Which meant that if redemption was to be had, Oppenheimer would have to initiate the process himself.

That was made clear at the dinner by Oppie's friend Glenn Seaborg. A former colleague from Berkeley, the Manhattan Project, and the General Advisory Committee, Seaborg was now serving as AEC chairman. Kennedy's appointment of a distinguished (and Nobel Prize–winning) scientist to that position, rather than an administrator and politician such as Lewis Strauss, had been yet another indica-

tion of the new president's affinity for intellectuals, science, and liberal thinking.

At one point during the after-dinner festivities, Seaborg took Oppenheimer aside for a quiet word. Obviously things were a lot better now than ten years ago, the political climate had changed, Oppenheimer once more had friends in high places, said Seaborg. The chances for reinstatement of Oppenheimer's security clearance and his return to government service were probably better now than they had ever been before. But the formal, legally prescribed procedures still had to be followed, which meant that if Oppenheimer wanted to regain his clearance, he would have to submit once more to a Personnel Security Board hearing. Would you be willing to do that? asked Seaborg.

Oppenheimer didn't have to think twice about his answer. "Not on your life."

Seaborg didn't push the issue. He knew as well as any of Oppie's friends how the 1954 hearing had scarred the man. No one had the right to ask a friend to subject himself to that once more. In the end, there were no guarantees, and if the new board somehow ruled against Oppenheimer again, even on a whim or technicality, then Oppenheimer would have endured it all again for nothing.

But whether the White House had invited Oppenheimer to the dinner hoping to encourage him to make the attempt to regain his clearance, or as a trial balloon to test the reaction to a possible administration action on his behalf, many saw his mere presence as a portent of imminent rehabilitation. "His invitation to the White House dinner was viewed by some as a possibility that this Administration might seek to restore his security clearance," said *The New York Times.*[9]

Many thought it long overdue. "Wherever—in heaven or elsewhere—balances are kept of life's injustices and redresses, it would make sense to tip the balance back by restoring to Oppenheimer his security clearance," wrote Lerner.[10] Others were more circumspect, such as the *New York Herald Tribune:* "There was speculation, but nothing that could be deemed official comment, on the significance of Dr. J. Robert Oppenheimer's presence as a guest—eight years after the atomic physicist's dismissal from government as a security risk."[11]

The journal *Science* noted in an editorial that shortly after JFK took

office, he had asked a "high official" whether anything was being done about the Oppenheimer case. "The answer was that it was difficult to see exactly what could be done that would be in Oppenheimer's best interest. The view, perhaps a sound one, was that any overt action would do as much harm as good to Oppenheimer by opening the door to a public raking-over of all the old charges. . . . Oppenheimer's invitation to dinner at the White House presumably was intended as a modest compromise between the political and personal problems inherent in a formal reinstatement and the needs of conscience."

Ironically, some of the policies and ideas for which Oppenheimer had been condemned by his enemies had been subsequently proven right. "On several . . . issues, such as the need for continental air defense, tactical nuclear weapons, and conventional non-nuclear forces, Oppenheimer's position has since become accepted national policy."[12] This fact was not lost on many in the new administration, which was another factor contributing to the idea of finding some way to make amends to Oppenheimer.

Whether Oppenheimer was to be officially "forgiven" or not, his presence at the dinner was a harbinger of great changes. A *New York Post* editorial entitled "Eggheads at the White House" mused: "A White House dinner for Nobel Prize winners is in itself a novel event, indicating how far we have moved from the period when to be an egghead was to be automatically suspect. . . . The invitation to Robert Oppenheimer represents an even more dramatic contrast with the years dominated by the know-nothings."[13]

As might be expected, not all thought that Oppenheimer rubbing shoulders at the White House was something to be celebrated. Senator Karl E. Mundt of South Dakota called it "unfortunate but not surprising" and sneered to the press: "I hope, but not confidently, that Alger Hiss won't be the next one invited."[14] The *National Review* couldn't resist weighing in with predictable sarcasm: "J. Robert Oppenheimer, too, was in the attendant court, the man whose soul has roamed the cosmos in discontent, ever since the pygmies told him that fire was not for him alone to play with. . . . While Edward Teller, whose vision and arduous work gave us a song without which Lorenzo would by now have lost his palace and all his earthly goods, was not

there. He had not been asked. But who are we to question the wisdom of the Court?"[15]

Edward Teller may not have been invited to the White House dinner, and many of his own allies were now out of power temporarily, but he had quietly been building a new circle of friends and supporters. He had achieved his own brand of prominence not only as the ostensible "father of the H-bomb," but in the popular lore as Robert Oppenheimer's personal archenemy (at least now that Lewis Strauss had been put out to pasture). Neither Oppenheimer nor Teller did much to encourage or promote such a perception—although Teller was decidedly more sensitive to any perceived or overt references to Oppenheimer or his supposed opposition to Teller's pet ideas and projects.

In a spring 1962 television interview on New York's *Open Mind* show on WNBC, host Eric Goldman, a history professor from Princeton University, asked Teller point-blank for his opinion on the possibility of Oppenheimer's reinstatement. The topic had come up in the natural course of the interview, and Goldman decided to press his luck. "I'd like to ask you this," he said to Teller. "In view of the high respect in which Dr. Oppenheimer is held in many American scientific circles today, and his very high reputation in a number of circles abroad, both as a scientist and as a humanist, are you still opposed to granting him clearance and letting him serve the Government of the United States?"

Teller had obviously not been expecting such a hard fastball question. He said nothing. He simply sat in silence for an uncomfortable period (thirteen seconds, by Goldman's watch), struggling for an answer that wouldn't come.

"I take it you do not want to discuss this matter?" Goldman finally prompted.

Apparently Teller did not, still declining to answer. Goldman let him off the hook and continued with the interview, changing the subject. Teller later asked Goldman to cut the question and his nonanswer from the taped interview before it was broadcast.

Goldman obliged, but somehow news of the incident got out anyway, making the national papers. For Teller, who had suffered the rejec-

tion and contempt of many of his colleagues ever since his testimony at Oppenheimer's hearing, it was another painful and embarrassing interlude.[16]

Teller seemed to recover from his speechlessness fairly quickly, however. Some months later, Edward R. Murrow producer Fred Friendly sent a curious note to Oppenheimer: "In the strangest of all possible conversations, Ed Teller told us he would be willing to have a television conversation with, of all people, the same man with whom Ed Murrow had his historic conversation." Friendly playfully gave Oppenheimer a multiple-choice form at the bottom of the note, asking him to check off his response. "Please check: (a) No. (b) Let's talk about it. (c) Well, I'll be damned!" Oppenheimer checked (a) and (b), crossing off "about it." There would be no television encounter between Oppenheimer and Teller, that year or any year afterward.[17]

But the two men would shortly be tied together again, although this time under much happier circumstances—at least for Oppenheimer.

* * *

The general feeling, at least initially, was that Oppenheimer had received what he deserved, even if many of the editorial writers who said so weren't quite as gleeful in their expression as the applauding congressmen. After all, Oppenheimer hadn't had to fight; he could simply have resigned quietly instead of exposing himself to the trauma of a security hearing. Even Einstein had said that Oppenheimer should have told Strauss and the AEC that they were fools and gone home, refusing to participate in such a farce.

Perhaps so. By 1954, Oppenheimer was doing very little consulting work for the AEC or anyone else in government anyway; even the AEC commissioners noted that for the past several years, ever since he left the GAC in 1952, he spent only a few days in active government service. For Oppenheimer the man, such speculations were purely academic. It was true that many other innocent people had lost their jobs and livelihoods after being accused of disloyalty or being "security risks." But Oppenheimer lost something deeper and more profound. He had been publicly humbled, removed from public service, knocked off his lofty oracular perch, the clouds of suspicion and mistrust that had always followed him now given the official imprimatur of his own government. He

had survived what historian John Mason Brown vividly described as a "dry crucifixion."[18] *The immediate and most pressing question that he faced, and that his colleagues and friends, the press, and the interested public were asking, was, what next for Robert Oppenheimer?*

Mrs. R. Victoria Ubil

April 7 - 1963

Mr. J. Edgar Hoover,

Dear Mr. Hoover,

 As a very concerned citizen, I am writing to you, first to thank you for the wonderful and loyal work you have done for our country. Second to ask you if there is anything private citizens can do to stem the flood of Communism?

"They" say Mr. Robert Oppenheimer was a Security risk in the last war. Doesnt he bear watching?

 All Best Wishes to you,

 Sincerely,

 /s/ Mrs. R. Victoria Ubil

14

Charity and Courage

T welve days before the Italian-born Nobel Prize–winning physicist Enrico Fermi died of cancer in 1954, the Atomic Energy Commission and President Eisenhower bestowed upon him a special presidential award for his lifetime achievement in physics, including the first controlled nuclear chain reaction. Two years later, the award was made permanent, to honor Fermi's memory, intended for individuals who made noteworthy contributions to nuclear physics or otherwise benefited humankind through the development and promotion of atomic science and technology.

It was an enormously prestigious honor given for a lifetime of achievement by the president of the United States, consisting of a citation, a gold medal with Fermi's likeness, and, not incidentally, $50,000 tax free from the U.S. Treasury.

Even a mere six years after it was instituted, the list of Fermi Award laureates was a literal who's who of the most eminent scientists in physics: John von Neumann, Ernest O. Lawrence, Hans Bethe. In 1962, Edward Teller was selected to receive the award for his hydrogen-bomb work.

No one begrudged Teller the award. Whether one supported or detested the volatile Hungarian—like Oppenheimer, he was a man who inspired faithful followers as well as bitter opponents—Teller's contributions to physics and the development of the hydrogen-bomb program

couldn't be denied. But such recognition for Teller, particularly coming from a president and an administration known to be not especially enamored of his political attitudes, raised an intriguing possibility.

Oppenheimer had unequivocally rejected the notion of going through the usual formal AEC channels to regain his security clearance, and no one could blame him. That reluctance severely limited the options of those looking to find some way to redress the tawdry history of the Gray Board hearing. The Nobelist dinner invitation had done some good, but in the view of most, not enough. Highly placed Oppenheimer advocates McGeorge Bundy and Arthur Schlesinger knew that direct action by the White House would be too politically risky. But what about something else—something considerably more substantial and prestigious than a mere invitation to a fancy dinner? What if Oppenheimer got the Fermi Award?

"We thought of the Fermi Award as a good opening," said an unnamed White House official in a *Life* magazine article about Teller and Oppenheimer. The fact that Teller had received the award in 1962 made giving it to Oppenheimer "a real possibility." At first the AEC informally considered giving a joint award to Oppenheimer and Teller in 1962, but that idea was quickly shot down. But, said the official, "The two names go together; they're so closely associated, you can't think of one without the other. . . . So there was a sort of conditioned reflex when Teller got the award in '62 and the word began to float around, 'Why not balance the ticket in '63?' The possibility was brought up with President Kennedy."[1]

Fermi Award recipients had to be formally nominated by the General Advisory Committee of the Atomic Energy Commission (which Oppenheimer had once chaired), and then the final selection was made by the president. The White House quietly made it known to the GAC that Oppenheimer's nomination would be met with no resistance.

Recommendations for the award were gathered from scientists, policymakers, and officials—among them, a vote for Oppenheimer from Teller himself, who saw it perhaps as a way to atone for some of the ill feelings he had caused over the years—and the GAC unanimously nominated Oppenheimer. The nomination was duly submitted and approved, and on April 5, 1963, it was officially announced: that year's Fermi Award would go to Dr. J. Robert Oppenheimer. If the tradition

of the previous years was followed, the presentation would be made on December 2, the date when Enrico Fermi first achieved his historic controlled chain reaction under the squash courts of the University of Chicago in 1942.

Oppenheimer was enormously pleased. "Most of us look to the good opinion of our colleagues, and to the goodwill and the confidence of our Government. I am no exception," he said in an official statement. He became a bit less formal when reporters tried to wangle a more personal comment from him: "Look, this isn't a day for me to go shooting my mouth off. I don't want to hurt the guys who worked on this." He may not actively have supported the efforts of those who had been working behind the scenes for so long to win him some kind of vindication, but he had always appreciated their attempts, and he wasn't about to say anything to cause them personal or political strife.

Suddenly, Oppenheimer was all over the news again, and more prominently and persistently than at any time since 1954. But with a difference: this time both the coverage and the reason for it were overwhelmingly positive. Headlines across the country declared that Oppenheimer was being "redeemed," "rehabilitated," "vindicated." *The Boston Globe* compared Oppenheimer to the victims of Stalin's purges who had been recently "rehabilitated" by Khrushchev, calling him an "American Phoenix" whom the AEC, through the award, was helping to "rise . . . from the ashes to which it had consigned him in 1954."[2] For *The New York Times,* the award was "a generous if belated acknowledgement of Dr. Oppenheimer's enormous contribution to this country and to science. It is also an indirect effort by the AEC to restore Dr. Oppenheimer's good name."[3]

Surprisingly, there was little initial reaction from Washington insiders or Congress, save for longtime Oppie booster Clinton Anderson. "This is a wonderful recognition, long overdue," Anderson gushed. "I am pleased that the awards committee was broad-minded enough to forget unpleasant incidents of the past and recognize his work for what it was worth to the nation." A few prominent Republicans were reported to be "greatly disturbed," but no shrill outcry of protest was heard. Part of the reason for the silence was no doubt the fact that Congress happened to be out of session and many senators and congressmen weren't in town to register their pleasure or outrage publicly.[4]

Oppenheimer steadfastly turned down an onslaught of interview requests, believing that his prepared statement was enough. But that didn't allay comment and a fair amount of good old Monday-morning quarterbacking regarding the implications of the award. "Selection of the controversial scientist . . . immediately opened two avenues of speculation," declared an Associated Press report. Those speculations were "that the government may ask him [Oppenheimer] to do secret work and that the administration wishes to see dispelled the cloud that enveloped Oppenheimer in the 1954 security case."[5]

The Washington Post thought that "the America which honors Robert Oppenheimer seems a great deal healthier than the America which dishonored him a decade ago."[6] The *Boston Herald* believed that "nothing could be more appropriate." Even though the Fermi Award "doesn't restore Dr. Oppenheimer's security clearance or prove that those who removed it nine years ago were wrong," it did indicate "a maturer attitude on the part both of the AEC and the public. It is belated recognition that a great man may break the rules and still be honorable and worthy of respect."[7]

"For almost a decade the case of Dr. J. Robert Oppenheimer has roiled the consciences of many Americans," noted *Newsweek*. "Some of them, wise neither in politics nor science, simply wondered how the man who was trusted to develop the atomic bomb could suddenly be unworthy to know the country's nuclear secrets. His friends among scientists couldn't bring themselves to believe that shy and bookish 'Oppie,' the theoretical physicist, was a Communist tool. Politicians, too, began to doubt the methods and conclusions of security investigators. All of these, working stubbornly to clear Oppenheimer's name, clutched a symbol of victory last week." According to *Newsweek,* one staffer at the Institute for Advanced Study "burst into tears" of joy upon hearing the news.[8]

"Time has a way of making things possible that, earlier, seemed impossible," observed the *Oakridger* of Oak Ridge, Tennessee, a town that, as one of the wartime centers of the Manhattan Project, had perhaps a more personalized interest in Oppenheimer. "Thus, it has been deemed possible now to, finally, do honor where formerly dishonor was done." The editors pointed out one aspect of the affair that had perhaps been overlooked. "During the eight years since the AEC decision, we are

not aware of one word of bitterness or resentment being uttered by Oppenheimer himself. Indeed, there has been bitterness and resentment expressed by others, as there has been ugly jubilation on the part of some on the other extreme of the controversy. Through it all, however, Oppenheimer himself has remained a giant of composure and, quite possibly, compassion and understanding for those who voted against him. And there, really, seems to be the human measure of the man whose essential greatness within the nuclear field was never really questioned. . . . now, however, we can read between the lines of the Fermi Award's qualifications and find not only nuclear but human greatness as well."[9]

Then there was the mail. While Oppenheimer, like any prominent national figure, had always received a lot of mail—a fair amount from the crackpot contingent, of course, but also a good deal from average thoughtful citizens with questions, comments, or good wishes—the bags of letters that arrived in Princeton after the Fermi Award announcement were surpassed in bulk, number, and weight only by those that had come on the heels of the security hearing.

First were the congratulations of friends and colleagues, who saw in the award announcement varying degrees of vindication and righteousness. Fellow physicist and gadfly Leo Szilard kept his well wishes short and simple: "Congratulations! There is a limit to everything, even ingratitude, which is just as well."[10] John Lansdale, the former Manhattan Project security chief who had testified on Oppie's behalf at the hearing, wrote: "I noted with a great deal of interest and pleasure your designation to receive the Atomic Energy Commission's Enrico Fermi Award for 1963. You must have derived more than usual satisfaction from this designation. I have read in full the Commission's elaborate release on this matter and note no reference at all to what must have been the most unpleasant episode of your career."[11] Physicist I. I. Rabi, who had always been one of Oppenheimer's most faithful supporters, was especially pleased: "You must feel like a voyager on a ship when after a long year the sailor on the crow's nest cries, land, land! I wish the reaction to the award could have been a simple Congratulations but there is too much history for simple rejoicing. The dismal years when injustice, paranoia and hypocrisy seemed to prevail remain all too vivid in the memory. Now in addition to our gratification perhaps we can

hope for better things to come."[12] Even the New York Mineralogical Club, to which a precocious twelve-year-old Oppie had once delivered his first scientific lecture about his rock-collecting hobby, sent its best wishes.

Greetings also came from some less expected quarters. Edward Teller dropped Oppenheimer a hasty note scribbled on an Eastern Airlines flight: "I just heard on the radio that you are getting the Fermi Award of 1963. . . . I had often been tempted to say something to you. This is the one time I can do so with full conviction and knowing that I am doing the right thing. . . . With sincere wishes for good luck—which we all need."[13]

Whatever ill feelings might yet have existed between the two men, it was only proper for Teller to acknowledge the award both as a previous recipient and as one who had recommended Oppenheimer for it. But Oppenheimer must have been truly startled to receive a laudatory telegram from none other than Lewis Strauss, even if the admiral was still on the Institute board of directors. "While you will no doubt be hearing individually from the members of the board, I would like to extend on behalf of the board of the Institute and personally congratulations on the great honor just announced by the president in recognition of your intellectual attainments and your outstanding contributions to the scientific achievements at the Los Alamos laboratory under you as director during World War Two."[14] Although the Fermi Award was being given for more than Oppenheimer's Los Alamos tenure, it's notable that Strauss confined his recognition solely to Oppenheimer's wartime achievements, ignoring those that came afterward during his years of conflict with Oppenheimer.

Commentators of a right-wing and conservative bent reacted as might be expected. "The government isn't giving the Fermi prize and $50 thou to Oppenheimer as a gesture of retroactive gratitude for his great work. . . . it is giving it to him as a step in the program to reintegrate him into the Establishment, and to undermine a security program which the Establishment had bitterly and consistently opposed," William F. Buckley wrote in his *National Review,* after the usual dismal recitation of Oppenheimer's "Communist past."[15] Stanton Evans, in another *Review* piece, made the tiresome comparisons with Alger Hiss and noted that Oppenheimer, who "has presumably been meditating in

injured quietude at the Institute for Advanced Study" since his security hearing, had been the object of "strenuous agitation designed to prove Oppenheimer an American Dreyfus persecuted by willful men in Washington." Again, the quotations from the Gray Board decision followed, with the conclusion: "That's the man who, thanks to the Kennedy Administration, will soon pocket $50,000 of the taxpayers' money."[16]

But as many pointed out, the award, however appropriate and welcome, didn't completely heal the scars of the past. "Complete exoneration of Dr. Oppenheimer, a slim soft-spoken man, would require another hearing to determine if his security clearance should be restored," noted the *National Observer*.[17] "For complete 'rehabilitation,' Dr. Oppenheimer's full clearance would be of far more value than the monetary and honorary award," said *The Boston Globe*.[18] *The Christian Science Monitor* was optimistic about "the arrival of the American people at a new high level of political maturity." Supposedly, a "new balance" had been established "between defending the independent world against the spread of the Communist power system on the one hand, and defending the values of American democracy on the other. A new maturity has been developed. . . . When a man cannot redeem himself and prove his redemption, and is pursued with vengeance for the past, something vital has gone out of American civilization. It now stands happily restored by the Fermi Award and there is every reason to hope and anticipate that a distinguished thinker will once again be given security clearance for a role in American policy planning."[19]

But this "redemption" of Oppenheimer, whether real or not, wasn't necessarily a cure-all for the excesses of the past decade. "If it marks, symbolically, the end of the virulent phase of McCarthyism, the question that remains is whether the consequences of that era of fear, suspicion and hatred are not still evident—in excessive and even spreading secrecy, in conformity and timidity," observed Marquis Childs in *The Washington Post*. "Oppenheimer believes that the attention on him as symbol is irrelevant to his own continuing concern over secrecy and its cramping effect on science and the intellectual life of the Nation."[20]

Any confirmation that Oppenheimer was about to be officially welcomed back into the fold with a formal restoration of clearance remained elusive, and Oppenheimer's more dedicated supporters soon

began to demand more than the symbol of the Fermi Award. "Mc-Carthy is dead, but his ghost still walks," declared *The Nation*. Noting that the Federation of American Scientists had been pushing for official review of the Oppenheimer case since at least October 1961, but that the AEC had yet to respond, the magazine concluded that the timing of the award to Oppenheimer was nothing more than an empty gesture. First came the Nobel Prize dinner invitation to test the waters, and then, with the midterm elections safely over, "it was decided to give the Fermi award to the 'security risk,' in the hope that this compromise might let sleeping dogs lie. . . . a shabby thing was done and it cannot be corrected in this sleazy and roundabout way." In fact, since Oppenheimer "needs no reward for his part in developing the atomic bomb . . . nor does he particularly need to have the record corrected and the entire proceeding [the security hearing] acknowledged to be what it was—an unconscionable abuse of governmental power," perhaps he should have declined the award completely.[21]

The Federation of American Scientists had indeed petitioned the AEC as far back as October 1961 for a review of Oppenheimer's case, and although the commissioners now under their new chairman, Glenn Seaborg, were receptive, the proposal had become embroiled in political discussion and argument about how best to address it, not to mention delays and procrastination because of the midterm elections. Seaborg's offer of a new hearing to Oppenheimer at the Nobel Prize dinner was one attempt by the AEC to resolve the issue, but Oppenheimer's refusal ensured that it remained a political hot potato for the Kennedy administration.

"The Seaborg question and the Oppenheimer response pointed up the basic problem confronting Administration officials—that of finding a way to 'clear' Dr. Oppenheimer without reopening the hearings and subjecting him to another round of interrogation," explained a *New York Times* analysis. After Oppenheimer refused a new hearing, some officials "believed it would be unwise to take any action that might make the Oppenheimer case an issue in the upcoming Congressional election." That effectively precluded any congressional hearings. "After the election, there was renewed activity within the commission and the office of Dr. Jerome B. Wiesner, the President's science adviser. In recent weeks officials have been indicating privately that action could be expected shortly."[22]

Now the FAS was pressing for something concrete, hoping that the Fermi Award wasn't all they could expect. A memo sent to FAS council members shortly after the award announcement urged, "If you think the Government should take the next step and restore Oppenheimer's clearance, please write to the President and to AEC Chairman Seaborg expressing your congratulations for their action on the Fermi Award *and* urging them to act to upset the 1954 decision revoking clearance."[23] According to *The Washington Post,* FAS representatives had discussed the matter with Attorney General Robert Kennedy and "found him agreeable to their objective."[24]

The prospects were still far from certain, but they were looking good, better than at any other time in the past ten years. Some believed that there were options beyond running Oppenheimer through another hearing. Loren Olson, the former AEC general counsel who had reviewed the case upon Seaborg's appointment as chairman, was now himself an AEC commissioner and advanced an idea that he had first suggested back in 1960: the AEC could simply hire Oppenheimer all over again. That way, he would undergo the same routine clearance procedures as any other new hire, with no hearing or other such indignities. Assuming no fresh detrimental information was uncovered, the AEC could simply choose to disregard all the old information about Oppenheimer that had led to the original hearing (and for which he had already been cleared anyway) and welcome him back into the AEC fold.

But political repercussions, criticism, and second-guessing would be unavoidable, and it was unclear how bad it might be. No matter how friendly the administration and the new AEC leadership, there would be consequences, both for those who championed Oppenheimer and for the man himself. Would they be worth it?

Oppenheimer had spent the past decade creating a new life for himself, one that allowed him not only to make valuable contributions to science and to learning, but to travel the globe as a lecturer and scholar, to dedicate himself to thinking, teaching, and trying to change the world through intellectual and cultural avenues. Did he really want to toss himself—and his family—back into the relentless, unmerciful turmoil of public life? Did he really want to sit again on countless committees and advisory boards, giving advice and rendering technical and

policy judgments that might just as well be ignored for political convenience? Might he not be able to do more good now as a private citizen who was free to speak his mind rather than as a governmental employee bound by political concerns and security regulations? What, in the end, was more important to Oppenheimer: the symbolic redemption provided by the Fermi Award, or a complete eradication of past injustices through a full reversal of the AEC decision?

As Oppenheimer and his allies pondered such questions, other, less friendly types were doing the same. One of them, Republican representative Craig Hosmer of California, worried publicly whether the Fermi Award indeed meant that Oppenheimer was about to reenter government service, and declared to his congressional colleagues that "it may readily be seen that it could be a matter of some embarrassment to the President of the United States personally to confer an award carrying this prestige and importance to a man who is not the beneficiary of a security clearance." Hosmer observed that "President Kennedy has an obligation to bear whatever personal embarrassment may be occasioned when the award is presented," but helpfully suggested that Kennedy "make certain matters very clear and definite" at the award presentation, including that "the award does not condone the recipient's actions which lost him his security clearance" and that, even with the award, "Dr. Oppenheimer shall not be considered eligible for government employment of any kind."[25]

One assumes that Hosmer meant any form of government employment that required a security clearance, and would not have objected to Oppenheimer taking a job as a mailman. Hosmer also claimed that it would be "a most grievous miscalculation" to believe that bringing Oppenheimer back into government service "would be tolerated by even a small minority of the American people."[26] He failed to explain how he was so certain of the wishes of more than a "small minority" of Americans.

Hosmer was assuming that Kennedy would present the Fermi Award personally, since that had been the tradition followed in the previous years; JFK had handed the award in person to Hans Bethe in 1961 and to Edward Teller in 1962. But even that was subject to question in Oppenheimer's case. Some within the administration felt that giving Oppenheimer the award was enough. No need to risk the president's

image any further by having him present it to the controversial scientist. It could just as well be done by the vice president, perhaps, or by AEC chairman Seaborg. As the initial excitement over the award announcement subsided and the press and Oppenheimer moved on to other things in anticipation of the actual ceremony, the question of JFK's participation in that ceremony remained enigmatically unclear.

But the ceremony was still in the future, and there were myriad other matters to keep Oppenheimer occupied. Among them was another brief trip to Europe, during which, on one quiet Sunday in Paris, Oppenheimer met with his "fan," actress Marlene Dietrich. Dietrich had sent her good wishes upon the news of the Fermi Award: "Your photograph is in the Paris papers today and I thought this was a good day to tell you that I still feel what I said long ago . . . not only still but more and more. I wish you well." Before their meeting, she sent him a note to make arrangements, confessing that "I am writing to you because I would probably be tongue-tied on the phone." That the legendary screen goddess could be so flummoxed by the Oppenheimer charisma is a resounding testament to its power.[27]

Continuing his role as intellectual ambassador, in late spring Oppenheimer helped organize and participated in yet another learned conference, sponsored in part by the Congress for Cultural Freedom at the estate of Mrs. Agnes Meyer, the widow of former *Washington Post* publisher Eugene Meyer, in Mount Kisco, New York. Like the CCF confabs and other conferences in which Oppenheimer participated in Europe and elsewhere, it was a distinguished international gathering of high-powered intellectuals dedicated to discussion and learned analysis of the problems of war, peace, and poverty. Although it proved a stimulating experience for the participants, so much so that the "Seven Springs farm conference," as it would become known, named after the Meyer estate, was held repeatedly in later years, it produced nothing concrete, nothing serious that could actually be implemented or considered by the self-serving, realpolitik-thinking governments of the world.

But Oppenheimer could always be counted on for quotable statements about big issues. In an examination entitled "Morality USA," the editors of *Look* quoted Oppie on the ethics of nuclear war. "The notion that we could have a great war and not use the stuff is even more

dangerous. Virtuous nations are not virtuous when at war, although this is still a view held by some—despite Hiroshima." And just in case anyone misunderstood, he noted the irony of the nuclear age: " 'Thou shalt not kill'—but a general says we can kill 400 million human beings."[28]

Back home in the tranquillity of Princeton, Oppie's former AEC colleague and friend David Lilienthal found him as enigmatic and sometimes confounding a personality as always. Both men were important and insanely busy, and they didn't see each other nearly as often as might be expected for two next-door neighbors, which usually inspired Lilienthal to make special note of their encounters in his journal.

One day, walking the Institute grounds, he noted a "familiar shabby convertible" coming up the hill, and instantly recognizing the driver because of his "flat porkpie hat that *is* Robert Oppenheimer." Beside Oppenheimer, as usual, was wife Kitty. They stopped to trade a few words of friendly conversation with Lilienthal. "A tragic pair," Lilienthal mused that night in his diary. "The trail from Los Alamos, and Alamogordo is a long and terrible one, a Golgotha indeed." Lilienthal wondered what the world would be like if Oppenheimer had failed at Los Alamos: "Suppose some of his calculations had been wrong. Suppose the Alamogordo test had been a dud." How different would the world be, for Oppenheimer, for everyone? "There would be nightmares, but not nuclear ones."

Not that such idle thoughts mattered, as Lilienthal was perfectly aware. He, as well as Oppenheimer, knew that the genie was inescapably out of the bottle, as one popular metaphor had it. And, Lilienthal observed, despite everything, Oppenheimer was a different man than he had been at Los Alamos or in the immediate postwar struggle for control of atomic weapons and policy. He describes a leisurely visit with Oppenheimer in late fall, an hour of conversation that was "not only pleasant but relaxed," with Oppenheimer "looking much, much better physically than I have seen him in a long time." A man who had always held Oppenheimer in near reverence, Lilienthal now found himself less intimidated by the man than ever before. "I can see that the awe of him I once felt, that made relations with him those of a high school sophomore talking with a college professor, no longer prevents me from being natural, or being able to differ, or offer a variant viewpoint."[29]

Lilienthal wasn't the only one to make such observations; other old friends had noted a different Oppie, a sort of mellowing, a new maturity, a composure that some described as almost monklike, or with similar religious and spiritual imagery. Perhaps it was the validation of the impending Fermi Award, coupled with the new respect and dignity he had found for himself in his new public role. Perhaps it had something to do with his family, a better condition of the illness-plagued Kitty, a stronger relationship with his children. Perhaps it was the fact that he was about to turn sixty years old in several months.

Whatever the reasons, most thought it a welcome change. Some still saw the stigmata of tragedy in his lined, thin face, frail frame, and gray hair, a whisper of anguish that never quite went away. Yet even they had to admit that somehow, Oppenheimer had found in himself some way to accommodate the suffering. There was a certain peace, a sense of calm, in him that wasn't there before. He could still be just as cutting and ruthless in criticizing a wayward scientific argument in an Institute seminar, but somehow the arrogance, the faint edge of cruelty that had once terrorized the graduate students of Berkeley and Caltech, were now gone. Injustice or not, some ventured the opinion that in the long view, his security ordeal was the best thing that ever happened to him.

The world had indeed changed massively in the twenty years since Oppenheimer had been swept up into the Manhattan Project. Much of that change, of course, was directly due to his work and that of the people he had led. But even with all the terrible dangers, hope remained, not only for Robert Oppenheimer personally but for the world. Not all was darkness. Sometimes, a shaft of light still glittered in the void.

One such ray of light was the announcement that, after much speculation and second-guessing, President John F. Kennedy would indeed present the Fermi Award personally to Dr. J. Robert Oppenheimer on what had become the traditional date, December 2, the anniversary of Fermi's triumph in Chicago. Kennedy had disregarded the advice of some of his more circumspect advisers regarding the possible political implications and decided that he was not about to give in to the paranoia of the past or the timidity of the present. Almost ten years before, another president had decreed that Oppenheimer was not to be trusted.

Now another president was risking his own political standing to honor that same man.

It was another indication of how much the world had changed, and happily, in this case, for the better.

The announcement from the White House came on November 21, 1963. It appeared on the front page of *The New York Times* and America's other newspapers on the morning of November 22, as President Kennedy arrived in Dallas, Texas.

Only a few hours later, everything would change again.

<p style="text-align:center">*　*　*</p>

What would Oppenheimer do now? It seemed to be the question of the hour in the summer of 1954, now that the larger issue of Oppenheimer's security status had finally been settled. For some, the answer seemed obvious, even before the AEC had laid down the ultimate word. "Dr. J. Robert Oppenheimer is reliably reported to be planning to accept an offer to teach at Cambridge University in England," reported The Christian Science Monitor *of June 19, 1954.[30] In England, Henry Hynd of the Labour Party insisted to Parliament that Britain should invite Oppenheimer, "whose services as an atomic scientist are not required by the United States Government, to put his knowledge at the disposal of this country."[31]*

For a man who had been so humiliated by his own government despite its official belief in his "loyalty," such a move didn't seem wholly unreasonable. Perhaps Oppenheimer could find peace and a measure of renewed dignity as a prominent expatriate, a continual reminder to the United States of its own folly in driving him away.

Oppenheimer, however, would have none of it. On July 3, an Associated Press reporter visited him in Fuld Hall for the first full interview after the AEC decision, and asked about the rumors of Oppenheimer leaving the country for good. "It is not true that I have ever thought of leaving this country, nor can I imagine circumstances under which I would," he said firmly.[32]

His deep feelings on the question were more profoundly and less formally expressed to his good friend and Institute colleague George Kennan, who recalled in his memoirs: "He was at home, I pointed out, in other parts of the world. . . . he had many friends in the European academic world; there was not a university anywhere across the globe that would not welcome him with open arms.

"He stood there a moment, tears streaming down his face. Then he stammered, with a corniness of which he was as well aware as I was but the very helplessness of which increased the forces of the statement: 'Dammit, I happen to love this country.'"[33]

BOARD OF EDUCATION • THE METHODIST CHURCH

EDITORIAL DIVISION

201 Eighth Avenue, South

TELEPHONE CHapel 2-1621

Nashville 3, Tennessee

Henry M. Bullock
Editor, Church School Publications
General Secretary, Editorial Division

Horace R. Weaver
Editor of Adult Publications

Harold L. Fair
Associate Editor
Daisy L. Dozier
Harold D. Minor
Freddie H. Schisler
Maxine C. Stout
Editors

August 27, 1963

Mr. J. Edgar Hoover
Director of the F.B.I.
Washington, D. C.

Dear Mr. Hoover:

 I am in need of information about the final attitude of the F.B.I. toward Dr. Robert Oppenheimer. Could you please tell me if he is still considered a security risk?

 Any information you can provide will be helpful.

Cordially yours,

Harold D. Minor

Harold D. Minor
Editor, <u>Adult</u> <u>Teacher</u>

REC- 66 100-17828-2372

SEP 9 1963

CORRESPONDENCE

ex to Minor 9-9-63
DTP: bal/mek

15

Darkness and Light

"How utterly horrible, how evil.

"President Kennedy dead, murdered.

"The TV voice is still booming away. But why listen to anything more. Irrevocable. God forgive the hatred in men's hearts that produces such cowardly barbarism. . . .

"What a grievous blow to us all. . . .

"This day ends in anguish."[1]

So David Lilienthal recorded in his journal the tragic events of November 22, 1963. For his neighbor and friend J. Robert Oppenheimer, the shock and sorrow were no less profound.

The news came to Oppenheimer while he was alone in his office at the Institute, working on his acceptance speech for the Fermi Award. His distraught son, Peter, knocked on the door and came inside to tell his father that Kennedy had been shot. A moment later, Oppenheimer's secretary, Verna Hobson, dashed in with the news that the president was dead.

As a stricken Oppenheimer ordered the Institute to be closed down for the day and prepared to go home with his son, he predicted, "Now things are going to come apart very fast."

For Robert Oppenheimer, it seemed, there could be no vindication without qualification, no triumph without tragedy, no happiness without pain. He admitted that JFK's violent and sudden death shocked

and saddened him like nothing since the death of Franklin D. Roosevelt in 1945, just as the Manhattan Project was approaching its culmination, the man who had initiated it not surviving to witness its war-ending triumph. Kennedy's willingness, indeed his true enthusiasm, to personally present the Fermi Award to Oppenheimer in the disapproving face of the McCarthyite holdouts in Congress and the press was to be the icing on the cake, the sweetener, the extra gloss on and the final confirmation of the prestige and honor represented by the award.

Now an assassin's bullet had stolen that away. The irony was highlighted by a congratulatory letter written by Justice Felix Frankfurter that morning of the twenty-second and obviously already mailed before the events of that afternoon: "I am gladdened by the Fermi Award to you and its presentation by the President of the United States in person will of course underscore its significance. . . ."[2]

But, perhaps, in appearance only. Lyndon Johnson abruptly ended idle speculation and well-meaning advice as to whether he would still, now as president, honor Oppenheimer. In no uncertain terms, in his best inimitable LBJ style, he told reporters that yes, he would be giving Oppenheimer his award at the White House on December 2, just as planned. Deciding to do so had been one of JFK's last official acts as president, LBJ explained, and it had meant a lot to Kennedy personally. The pundits and critics be damned: Johnson was going to fulfill the murdered president's wishes.

Yet, despite citizens mourning their president, despite the general mood of uncertainty and fear for the future that pervaded the country in those weeks immediately following the JFK assassination and leading up to the December 2 Fermi Award ceremony, there remained those who insisted on using the occasion for political posturing and to remind anyone who might have forgotten that the ghost of McCarthy was still slinking about in the corridors of power.

Iowa Republican Bourke Hickenlooper, as a member of the Joint Committee on Atomic Energy, had been invited to the Fermi Award ceremony as a matter of course. Instead, Hickenlooper made a great show of indignation by turning down the invitation, saying that he could not "in good conscience" attend, because it was "unthinkable" to him that the award should go to Oppenheimer. In a letter to the AEC

secretary that was later made public, supposedly against Hickenlooper's wishes, the senator explained, "I fail to see how anyone who has any respect for the security system of the United States could support this award."

Fair enough, but Hickenlooper added, "I don't know of any specific accomplishments he contributed to atomic energy that put him in the top flight of those who already have received the award." Incredibly, Hickenlooper said that he was "unable to find convincing evidence of any outstanding contribution to atomic science" made by Robert Oppenheimer.

Editorial commentators and letter writers helpfully pointed out Oppenheimer's many scientific accomplishments to the senator. The distinguished science writer Lincoln Barnett, after a lengthy recitation of Oppenheimer's career in *The New York Times,* concluded: "It is tragic that at a time when bitterness in the scientific community caused by Dr. Oppenheimer's mistreatment is being repaired, the ranking minority member of the Joint Committee on Atomic Energy should proclaim to his country not only his lingering bias but his lamentable ignorance of the work of this great American scientist."[3]

Hickenlooper wasn't missed at the award ceremony in any case, because almost everyone of importance in Oppenheimer's life who was still breathing was there instead. Aside from Kitty and the two children, there was AEC chairman Glenn Seaborg; former AEC commissioner Henry DeWolf Smyth, Oppenheimer's sole defender in 1954; Senator Clinton Anderson, his best friend in Congress; and even, much to the surprise of many, Edward Teller. David Lilienthal was also present "to witness the new president pouring the sacramental water of absolution on Oppie," as he put it in his diary.

Next to the tall, robust LBJ in the Cabinet Room of the White House, Oppenheimer appeared to everyone to be more frail, small, and humble than ever before. Lilienthal thought him "tragic in his intensity," compared to Kitty, who was "a study in joy."

"I know every person in the room grieves with me that the late President could not give this award as he anticipated. . . . I take great pleasure and pride that I substitute for him," said Johnson, declaring that signing the award to Oppenheimer was "one of President Kennedy's most important acts." Then, as photographers snapped pictures ("It

was almost impossible to get into the Cabinet Room" because of the gaggle of press, said Lilienthal later: "There were more men of this calling in the Cabinet Room than guests"),[4] Johnson handed Oppenheimer the citation (signed by Kennedy before his death) and gold medal, along with the $50,000 check, which Oppie quickly passed on to Kitty, behind him.

He held on to the citation and medal, however, staring at them for a moment or two, as if reassuring himself of their reality. Then he made the quiet speech he had been composing when he heard of Kennedy's death, speaking of "the brotherly spirit of science" of which Thomas Jefferson had written, admitting that "we have not . . . always given evidence of that brotherly spirit" because of the great struggles of the time, including the quest to "live without war as the great arbiter of history." Noting that "no one bears a greater responsibility" in such struggles than the president of the United States, Oppenheimer added, "I think it just possible, Mr. President, that it has taken some charity and some courage for you to make this award today. That would seem to be a good augury for all our futures."[5] Johnson thanked him, mentioning that Kitty also shared the honor with Oppenheimer and noting wryly that she "got hold of the check!"

Then, at the reception immediately after, came the tense face-to-face between Oppenheimer and Teller, the first time the two men had met in person since the hearing in 1954. According to columnist Drew Pearson, Teller jumped on the occasion as a photo opportunity. He "stood for a time at the end of the refreshment table munching hors d'oeuvres. Suddenly, seeing the news photographers unlimbering their cameras, he bolted toward Oppenheimer, elbowing his way through a crowd of well-wishers." Flashbulbs popped and Teller grabbed Oppenheimer's hand. Oppenheimer smiled and shook it "as the man who had helped drive him from Government offered his congratulations."[6]

"I enjoyed what you had to say," said Teller.

"I'm so very glad that you came," Oppenheimer replied.[7]

It was supposed to be a picture of reconciliation and forgiveness, the final happy ending to the bitter rivalry, but the photographers did their work a little too well, also capturing the icy glare on Kitty's face next to her husband. Oppenheimer might feel magnanimous, but his wife's

expression as she regarded Teller made it clear that she did not, and never would forgive.

Teller, who later wrote in his *Memoirs* that he had "hoped that government acknowledgement of Oppenheimer's great service would help to heal the schism that had developed in the scientific community" and had therefore joined in nominating Oppenheimer for the award, would soon learn otherwise. The conflicts in the scientific community that he himself had done so much to create and perpetuate, both consciously and inadvertently, would not be banished by giving Oppenheimer a Fermi Award. "Unfortunately, the schism persisted without change," Teller noted.[8]

Not that he did much to help bridge that schism. Lilienthal wrote later that day that "Teller shook my hand as if it were a poisonous reptile."[9]

During a quiet moment in the postceremony reception, White House aides quietly whisked Oppenheimer and Kitty upstairs for about half an hour. The late president's widow wanted to meet with them personally and emphasize how important it had been to her husband that the award go to Oppenheimer, and how much he had sincerely wanted to present it himself.

And yet, as Oppenheimer and his family returned to Princeton with the citation, medal, and check (which Oppenheimer remarked to a reporter was "already spent"—soon after, Kitty went to New York and treated herself to a $10,000 mink coat), a nagging sense of incompleteness, of unfinished business, remained. As Philip Stern writes, "The 'blank wall' still stood. Officially he was still deemed unworthy of being entrusted with his country's secrets."[10] However prestigious, however wonderful that he was given the award, "the prize doesn't give him back a security clearance or return him to government service," *Newsweek* pointed out.[11]

The tune had changed somewhat from the initial announcement of the award back in April. Yes, Oppenheimer had now been officially vindicated—but only "in a sense," as a Dallas newspaper remarked when Oppenheimer visited the city for a scientific meeting later in December. Oppenheimer offered a word in defense of the city whose image had been darkened by the previous month's tragedy: "The terrible events of November could have happened in any city of the country or any city of the world."[12]

Oppenheimer friend and television producer Fred Friendly dropped him a brief note after the ceremony. "I thought your mood and words in Washington on Monday were right on the mark." Friendly alluded to a new television project involving Oppenheimer, promising that it was "not dead," but that his current problems "are those of a sick wife, a sick partner [Murrow] and an assassinated President." The project never came to fruition, no doubt because of those very problems.[13]

In the end, the presentation of the Fermi Award to Oppenheimer was a quintessentially bittersweet episode, not only because, as fate would have it, it occurred under the dark cloud of John F. Kennedy's assassination and was thus forever tainted by that event, but also because it was ultimately purely a symbol—and much as they might avoid saying so, everyone knew it. Oppenheimer now had $50,000, a citation, a gold medal, and a bit of high-level goodwill. The wounds of the past had been soothed, covered over, apologized for, but not healed.

Which is not to say that Oppenheimer was not deeply grateful for all that his friends in the administration had done on his behalf. But there was also an awareness that this was probably about as far as it could reasonably go. Particularly now with JFK gone, and a new president burdened not only with the near-impossible duty of helping the country carry on but with ominous new problems, including a bitter and increasingly violent civil rights struggle and an escalating war in Southeast Asia, there was little time, energy, or courage left for anyone to push harder for Oppenheimer's sake. The people wanted to forget and move beyond the excesses of McCarthy and his anti-Communist crusades, not continue to dwell on their sad legacies. In many ways, and more so as time went on, the Fermi Award began to look like what it was: a consolation prize, a belated apology cloaked in formality, a way to bandage over an injustice without addressing its cause.

Oppenheimer's shadow clung to the Fermi Award after he received it. Lingering resentments caused Republicans on the Joint Atomic Energy Committee to charge that the Fermi Award was being "abused" and that, because the candidates were chosen by the GAC (the AEC's main scientific advisory group), "a small group of scientists were just passing the award around among themselves." Some believed that $50,000 tax free was too much money and questioned whether the con-

tributions of Oppenheimer and other recipients were actually worth that much (presumably this didn't include Edward Teller). Ironically, it was Lewis Strauss who had originally set the monetary amount. Committee members also complained that not enough consideration was being given to the contributions of engineers and later scientists.

The following year, the award amount was cut in half and the role of the GAC in the selection process was reduced. The 1964 Fermi Award went not to a scientist but to Admiral Hyman G. Rickover, the father of the nuclear submarine. Rickover was a strongly controversial figure himself with lots of enemies, but more because of his irascible and confrontational nature, not because anyone had ever cast a Communist taint upon his good name.[14]

The New York Times claimed that the Fermi Award "served to write *finis* to the controversy surrounding Dr. Oppenheimer."[15] But if so, it was only superficially, only in a practical, functional, tying-up-inconvenient-loose-ends sense. It gave license for everyone to breathe a sigh of relief and say, Thank God that whole nasty Oppenheimer thing is finally over and done with. It can stay back in the fifties where it belongs, back with Ike and McCarthy, instead of staining the promise of the New Frontier. Oppenheimer got his medal and his money and went back to Princeton. Time to move on.

As Oppenheimer celebrated his sixtieth birthday in 1964, it truly did seem that there would be nothing more, and that the symbolic redemption of the Fermi Award was the best that he was going to get or could expect. It remained to be seen whether the scars of 1954 would ever finally fade, either on their own or by some as-yet-unknown outside intervention.

As the nation attempted to recover from the shock of the assassination and carry on into an uncertain future, Oppenheimer seemed to spend much of 1964 revisiting the past in one form or another, even after the Fermi Award had supposedly allowed him to lay to rest an unfortunate piece of it. He enjoyed two important homecomings in 1964. The first was to the University of California in Berkeley, where Oppenheimer had been invited to deliver a series of lectures on the late physicist Niels Bohr. Although he had been back to Berkeley at various times since leaving to join the Manhattan Project over twenty years previously, this

was his first full-fledged official and public visit since 1949, and as such was played up heavily in the local media.

Oppenheimer had learned a few things about the world since his early times in Berkeley, and he made them clear in a letter to the school before his arrival: "I would prefer to have no dealings with the press. I have nothing very newsworthy, and believe that I should devote my time in Berkeley to my lectures, and to renewing and extending my relations with my many colleagues and associates." Regarding the local TV stations that wanted him for interviews, Oppenheimer declared, "I have an arrangement with CBS which forecloses my appearing on television." It's unclear whether this refers to his long-standing friendship with Friendly and Murrow at that network, whether he had any sort of formal agreement with them not to appear elsewhere, or whether he was merely being politely evasive.[16]

By all accounts, Oppenheimer's formal return to Berkeley was a touching experience. "A shy philosopher came home to Berkeley last night, after 15 years crowded with a painful desecration of his name that would have beaten an ordinary mortal," said the *San Francisco Examiner*. The "strangely hypnotic physicist" spoke to an audience of 12,500: "I am very pleased to be back home. I lived here a long time and to those of you to whom a choice is offered, don't go away."[17]

Oppenheimer spoke eloquently and passionately about the life and work of Bohr, both his scientific contributions and his work for a peaceful world. If Bohr's vision of an "open world" had been followed, said Oppenheimer, "we might perhaps have become free of our rather sleazy ideas of omnipotence, and have turned our vision to the development of a society with a future worth living for."[18] The standing ovation and applause for Oppenheimer after his speech were so sustained that Oppenheimer had to return to the podium and urge the reluctant audience to go home.

Oppenheimer moved on to southern California and visits to his other former academic homes at Caltech and UCLA, and then, on May 18, to another homecoming that was, perhaps, the most emotionally complex of them all: Los Alamos. Again speaking in tribute to Bohr, he was moved almost to tears by the standing ovations given by the audience of scientists and Los Alamos staffers.

It was not the first time he had been back since the war, but it was

his first official public appearance there since turning over the reins of leadership to his successor, Dr. Norris Bradbury. Oppenheimer toured the laboratory facilities, took in the exhibits at the museum, and again sat in his old chair, noting that it was "still very hard." He pointed out that the chair in the museum exhibit was actually from his former Santa Fe office, and that the one he had used at Los Alamos was "a good deal more comfortable, and it still is. It is now in my study at Princeton."[19]

Perhaps exhausted from the homecomings, his advancing age, and his relentless schedule, Oppenheimer was beginning to more frequently turn down requests for appearances, lectures, interviews, and the like. He had always received many more such requests than anyone could possibly accommodate, many of them trivial or obviously impractical, but now he found himself forced to turn away many that in the past he might have seriously considered.

He remained an obligatory phone call for reporters when any new development arose in the world of atomic weapons, energy, or warfare, such as when Communist China joined the nuclear club by exploding its first atomic bomb in October 1964. As had become his custom, his statement to the reporters who pressed him after the initial sketchy reports of the Chinese success was a masterpiece of tactful caution: "I think that it might be well to wait until the experts in our Government who are charged with studying things like this are able to assess just what has happened."[20]

CBS producer Friendly tapped Oppenheimer to participate in a television special commemorating the one-year anniversary of JFK's death, with the theme of "man's quest for peace in the atomic age" and Kennedy's specific contributions to that quest. So, on an August afternoon at the Institute, Oppenheimer sat down once more with a CBS camera crew, this time to be interviewed by Friendly associate Arthur Barron. Oppenheimer discussed his thoughts at the first bomb test and the immediate attempts to control the weapon, once more invoking Niels Bohr and his efforts to create an open world free of scientific secrets.

Barron observed that "whether or not you have been actively at work in government of late, you have always been concerned with the problems that control nuclear arms and peace." What of Kennedy's efforts in

that arena? "I certainly thought about it," Oppenheimer responded, alluding with not a little irony to his previous life as an adviser: "Even when you have very little power, it's hard to lose the sense of responsibility once so deeply acquired." Kennedy was "enormously vigorous" and "very well prepared" to deal with nuclear issues, and he did so with a "disciplined, courageous and devoted concern." But except for praising Kennedy's famous "Peace" speech at American University, Oppenheimer refrained from specifics: "I have nothing fresh to say." He recalled the words he had written to speak to Kennedy at the Fermi Award ceremony, that "it has taken some humor, some charity, and some courage for you to make this award today" (which he later altered after the assassination by removing the word "humor"), and that it was those qualities he saw in Kennedy of humor, charity, and courage that "are going to have to make the new world."[21]

Nineteen sixty-four also saw the publication of a new Oppenheimer book, *The Flying Trapeze: Three Crises for Physicists,* which consisted of the three Whidden Lectures he had delivered at McMaster University in January 1962. A bit more esoteric and less accessible than his previously published lectures, the book didn't sell quite as well, although it garnered good reviews, such as from C. P. Snow, another man concerned with both science and its philosophical implications: "These lectures catch the tone of the scientific discourse of our time. . . . these essays ought to be read, or really listened to. They speak with a voice that is authentic, living and belonging to one man alone."[22]

Oppenheimer's support and promotion of Bohr as one of the tragically unsuccessful architects of what might have been a formula for world peace in the atomic age emerged again when a British historian published a book on the history of the British nuclear program. The book revealed that both Churchill and Roosevelt had been deeply suspicious of Bohr's activities and even his loyalty, suspecting him of perhaps leaking secrets to the Soviets, and had considered placing him under arrest or otherwise confining him during the war.

Oppenheimer swiftly came to Bohr's defense in an impassioned article, essentially an abridged version of the lectures he had been giving on Bohr, in *The New York Review of Books,* arguing that Bohr's intentions and actions had been sadly misunderstood. Bohr had not only foreseen the present-day arms race, said Oppenheimer, but he had tried

mightily to prevent it by advocating a policy of openness between the atomic powers. "He was clear that one could not have an effective control of atomic energy . . . without a very open world."

At no time, Oppenheimer argued, did Bohr propose sharing atomic secrets with the Russians until it was clear that they would agree to shared responsibility and authority. The depth of Oppie's feelings on the subject is made quite obvious by the fact that, even though his *Review* piece was prominently listed on the front page of the magazine, Oppenheimer complained to the editor immediately after publication, "Although you did your best to conceal the Bohr story, I did manage to read it." The editor replied respectfully that to the contrary, the *Review* considered the article very important, as evidenced by its mention and excerpting in many other newspapers.[23]

Whether or not one considered him "reformed" or "redeemed," Oppenheimer still enjoyed a distinct presence as a public figure. For the most part, it was on his own terms: he couldn't control everything that might be said about him, but he could pick and choose what interviews he would grant, where he would lecture, what publications in whose pages his writings might appear. But 1964 was also the year in which Oppenheimer was forced to confront the contradictions between his own personality and identity and what had become the larger world's image of him.

He had been carefully managing and nurturing a certain public persona to one degree or another particularly since the security hearing, and had managed to do so in a manner that allowed him to create a fulfilling new life for himself. Now he would discover how perceptions of a public figure could become distorted and misrepresented in ways that had little to do with truth or historical reality. Fittingly and also ironically, the process would begin when his already iconic stature was transformed into a dramatic character.

* * *

Another offer of sanctuary came from India, when a representative of the Indian consulate general visited Oppenheimer in Princeton with a message from Prime Minister Nehru. According to secretary Katherine Russell's record of the conversation, "The message from the Prime Minister was to invite Dr. Oppenheimer to

come to India, for a short visit, a month or two or longer, or permanently. . . .
Dr. Oppenheimer said that he was deeply moved by the Prime Minister's letter
and invitation; and that he would always have it in mind; that he did indeed
hope to visit India, but that right now he thought his place was clearly here."
The Indian diplomat assured Oppenheimer that no atomic-bomb work was tak-
ing place in India, but Oppenheimer told him that wasn't a consideration in his
decision. Instead, Oppenheimer thought that "were he to leave the United States
now, this action could be misconstrued in such a way as to be very dangerous
and indeed harmful to the good relations between the two countries."[24]

But others were not as convinced of Oppenheimer's resolve to stay in
America—or feared that he might even be forced to leave against his will. As
Martin Sherwin and Kai Bird point out, Lewis Strauss, with J. Edgar
Hoover's support, pressured the FBI to maintain its wiretaps on Oppenheimer
even after the conclusion of the case, and to keep FBI agents physically shadow-
ing him for almost twenty-four hours a day. The surveillance continued not only
at home in Princeton but when Oppenheimer traveled.

Oppenheimer knew about the FBI's eyes on him, of course. He had been living
with the yoke of security around his neck for years, since he became scientific
head of the Manhattan Project. The presence of "watchers" and armed guards
was obvious, and he was astute enough to assume even before his security hearing
that at least his official telephone conversations were monitored. Until his secu-
rity clearance had been suspended, a huge and rather obtrusive safe had been
parked in the hallway just outside his Institute office, filled with top-secret AEC
and other classified government documents, attended by at least one armed
guard around the clock.

By this time, for Oppenheimer and even his wife, such measures had become
part of their daily landscape, even a source of rueful amusement. When they
escaped for a brief weekend away from Washington during the security hearing,
a wire service reporter encountered them on the train back to Princeton. "I found
and dined with Dr. J. Robert Oppenheimer for three and a half hours last night
under the watchful eyes of two mystery men who followed his every move," wrote
INS reporter Jack Lotto. Oppenheimer and Kitty invited Lotto into their private
compartment, but as the reporter noted: "Flanking the door . . . the two 'tails'
sat. They gave me the once-over as I went inside the room." Later, one of them
also followed the three to the dining car, where, Lotto reports, he "took the seat
directly in back of mine. . . . the 'shadows' dogged the footsteps of the couple even
when they went to the rest room or into the club car to order a drink."

Oppenheimer politely fended off the reporter's questions about the ongoing security hearing, insisting he couldn't talk about it because it was secret. But he readily joked about his watchmen. "You saw what my wife ate. . . . that's not classified. We can talk about that." Lotto dutifully noted that as Oppenheimer and Kitty got off the train in Trenton at 11:08 p.m., "their two 'shadows' got off the train."[25]

UNITED STATES GOVERNMENT

Memorandum

TO : Mr. Rosen

DATE: July 9, 1964

FROM : G. H. Scatterday

1-Mr. Rosen
1-Mr. Malley
1-Mr. Peelman

SUBJECT: J. ROBERT OPPENHEIMER
NAME CHECK MATTER

Name Check Section is in receipt of a name check request from Assistant Chief of Staff for Intelligence, Department of the Army, regarding J. Robert Oppenheimer. Request is for subversive derogatory information.

Colonel W. B. Cox, ACSI, on 7-7-64, advised Liaison Agent that request concerns a contemplated invitation to Oppenheimer as a guest speaker at the United States Military Academy, West Point. Colonel Cox advised that if results of the name check produced any derogatory information regarding Oppenheimer, Oppenheimer in all probability would not be invited. On a memorandum Wannall to Sullivan, 10-21-63, the Director approved furnishing, in reply to name check request, the Office of Security, Department of State, a summary of information as revealed by our investigations of Oppenheimer. State was also referred to the printed record of a hearing by the Atomic Energy Commission, which resulted in subject's clearance being removed. The summary contained information regarding subject being contacted to furnish information to the Soviets, affiliations and associations with subversive groups and persons, including his relations.

The results of the investigations of Oppenheimer are contained in 169 reports.

ACTION: Summary of information that was approved for dissemination to State has been furnished to ACSI. ACSI will be supplied with reports upon request.

RECOMMENDATION:

For information.

JSP:bss
(4)

100-17828

a JUL 14 1964

6 JUL 24 1964

16

The Public and the Private

When German playwright Heinar Kipphardt made Oppenheimer the subject of his new play *In the Matter of J. Robert Oppenheimer* in 1964, it wasn't the first time Oppenheimer had found himself incarnated as a dramatic character. The first was in 1947, when MGM Studios released a highly dramatized and not wholly accurate docudrama about the Manhattan Project entitled *The Beginning or the End*.* Played by Hume Cronyn (complete with trademark porkpie hat), Oppenheimer is portrayed as a morally conflicted Hamlet agonizing over whether the invention of the bomb means "the beginning or the end" for mankind. The film's producers were so earnest in their intention to create An Important Film that they proclaimed that the movie had been made solely to be placed into time capsules as "a message to future generations."[1]

Although Oppenheimer was reportedly flattered by his portrayal, few of the actual participants thought the film to be an honest depiction of the history involved. A Chicago screening for scientists was rocked by laughter and jeers. Leo Szilard later summed up the reaction: "If our sin as scientists was to make and use the atomic bomb, then our punishment was to watch *The Beginning or the End*."[2]

* Not to be confused with the 1957 flick *The Beginning of the End,* in which Peter Graves battles giant radiation-mutated grasshoppers attacking Chicago.

But Oppenheimer isn't really the "star" of *The Beginning or the End,* since the main narrative of the film involves two fictional characters. In Kipphardt's play, though, he is definitely the central figure. Kipphardt distilled the entire 992-page published hearing transcript down into a full-length morality play complete with photographic and movie projections to enhance and explain various historical points. The play is essentially a re-creation of the hearing, with most of the dialogue paraphrased or taken almost verbatim from the transcript, and with other public statements of the main characters incorporated into the monologues or testimony. Yet there are some important differences, and those differences aroused Oppenheimer to outraged action.

The play was first produced on West German television in January 1964 to great acclaim, and then plans were made for full theatrical productions in Berlin and Munich, with further engagements to follow in other European cities. When he finally read the text of the play over the summer of 1964, Oppenheimer made no attempt to hide his anger. He accused Kipphardt of distorting the truth and misrepresenting his words and feelings, while Kipphardt tried to defend his play as an artistic work whose purpose was to interpret, not strictly depict, historical events.

Such a defense was lost on Oppenheimer, a man who had suffered so profoundly in part because of the misrepresentation and misinterpretation of his own personal history. "I am struck by the number of instances in which you invent things which not only did not happen, but which could not happen, and are thus in some important sense untrue," Oppenheimer wrote to Kipphardt. "My principal objection is that you make me say things which I did not and do not believe."

Oppenheimer cited two specific examples that he found most objectionable. The first was a supposed remark in Oppenheimer's testimony that Niels Bohr had opposed the work of the Manhattan Project, when the facts "show with great force that Bohr approved and admired the undertakings at Los Alamos. . . . Why do you have me lie about it?"[3]

Worst of all for Oppenheimer was the closing monologue of his counterpart in the play, a contrast between art and reality that goes to the heart of the conflict between the real Oppenheimer and Kipphardt's romanticized version. "I begin to wonder whether we were not perhaps traitors to the spirit of science when we handed over the results of our

research to the military," says Kipphardt's Oppie in his final statement to the Gray Board. "We have spent years of our lives in developing ever sweeter means of destruction* . . . and I feel it in my very bones that this was wrong. . . . I will never work on war projects again. We have been doing the work of the Devil."[4]

Nonsense, protested Oppenheimer. He never said any such things, not at the hearing or at any time since, nor did he subscribe to such views. Kipphardt was quite literally putting words in his mouth, and in so doing, making him into a figurehead, a moralistic icon, a symbol for beliefs that Oppenheimer himself didn't share. It was the popular romantic image of the "tormented" atomic scientist racked with guilt over the bomb, set squarely upon Robert Oppenheimer's thin and bony shoulders.

It was true that many people thought that guilty yoke belonged there, but Oppenheimer himself had always shunned it. To emphasize that point, he reminded Kipphardt that during the recent Congress for Cultural Freedom conference in Geneva, he had been asked directly whether, knowing what we did now, he would still participate in building the bomb. "To this I answered *yes*. When a voice in the audience angrily asked 'Even after Hiroshima?' I repeated my *yes*."

Others, like Kipphardt, might try to make him into a guilt-ridden apologist for the atomic bomb, but Oppenheimer wanted no part of it. To correct any notions Kipphardt might have had that Oppenheimer was remorseful for Hiroshima, he wrote, "You may well have forgotten Guernica, Dachau, Coventry, Belsen, Warsaw, Dresden, Tokyo. I have not. I think that if you find it necessary so to misread and misrepresent your principal character, you should perhaps write about someone else."[5]

It might have ended there, had the play flopped and folded up production. Unfortunately for Oppenheimer, the play was an immediate hit. The reviews were mixed—some critics found the work stagy and pedantic, with the static quality that plagues most plays set in a courtroom—but audiences found it compelling anyway. Whether that was because of the subject matter or the play itself was another question.

* Kipphardt here alludes to Oppenheimer's famous remark in his testimony about a "technically sweet" hydrogen-bomb design.

A correspondent for the London *Times* called the Berlin premiere "a major success."[6] Sellout crowds followed the productions in Munich and Basel, Switzerland. Then came word that productions were being planned for Paris, London, Milan, Prague, Warsaw, and Brussels. While allowing that it was "not a play to see between martinis and late dinner," *The Washington Post* called it "the talk of Europe," quoting various glowing European reviews.[7]

Kipphardt's Berlin producer, Erwin Piscator, was fresh off another controversial success, a play entitled *The Deputy* that raised the question of the pope's responsibility for (or perhaps collusion in) the Holocaust. Now the Oppenheimer play had "produced assertions of a renaissance in German drama," said *The New York Times*. "Mr. Kipphardt appears to have tried to avoid black-and-white characterization. Neither Dr. Oppenheimer nor anyone else is classified as hero or villain."[8]

An incensed Oppenheimer began looking for ways to stop the play, perhaps by a libel lawsuit. He considered seeking an injunction to halt further performances: "You should not be too confident that the situation as it stands is without adequate grounds for legal action against you and the producers of your play," Oppenheimer warned Kipphardt.[9] As a Swiss friend wrote Oppenheimer, "It does seem to me that you should do something. After all, the Pope and the Vatican were not above answering Hochhuth's version of the role of Pius XII [in Rolf Hochhuth's *The Deputy*], and the fact that even serious newspapers, like the *Neue Zürcher Zeitung,* claim that the play is an accurate rendering of the hearings is alarming."[10]

Oppenheimer sent protesting letters to the various producers with vague threats of legal action, but he stopped short of taking that drastic step. Perhaps he realized that the attempt to suppress an instance of honest artistic expression, even one that he found personally distasteful and historically disingenuous, was directly at odds with the high-minded ideals of openness and free inquiry that he had championed for his entire career.

Instead he relied on a different tactic, fighting free speech with more free speech by making certain that his objections were heard loud and clear in the press. "The whole damn thing was a farce and these people are trying to make a tragedy out of it," he complained to a reporter.[11] He knew that alterations were inevitable in creating a play based on a

transcript, but Kipphardt had gone too far. Oppenheimer noted his major objections about the "serious distortions" in a press statement. Kipphardt "makes me say that Bohr disapproved of the work at Los Alamos because it would make science subservient to the military." Oppenheimer had "never said such a thing" and Bohr "understood and welcomed what we were doing." Then there was Oppenheimer's ending soliloquy "in which I am made to say that through these hearings I have learned that it was wrong to make the bomb, and that I would never do such a thing again. This is the very opposite of what I think, nor have I ever said anything that could be so construed."[12]

Kipphardt defended his artistic choices. The security procedures and loyalty checks faced by scientists like Oppenheimer were part of the "tragic aspects that confront the nuclear scientist of today." Kipphardt held that his play didn't question the necessity of the atomic bomb itself: "The physicists were morally justified in this undertaking because it served the purpose of saving our civilization from the threatening Nazi barbarism and of ending as quickly as possible the war started by Hitler." Whether dropping the bomb twice on Japan was the right thing, however, was another issue. "I have not forgotten the terrible stations of our past. . . . Naturally it is nonsense to want to excuse Auschwitz with Hiroshima and I have never supported such criminal nonsense. But even after Auschwitz, a German author must be permitted to write about the basic issues of our time. If I cannot write about such questions in a play set in Germany, it is because, happily, there never has been a German project for an atomic bomb nor, I hope, will there ever be one."[13]

The popularity of the play, and Oppenheimer's response to it, encouraged editorialists to ponder the ramifications of the Oppenheimer case once more, now a full decade after the fact. The *Washington Star* called the Oppenheimer story "one of subtle complexities" that the play completely missed, playing it "for newsreel melodrama, with several falsifications for dramatic effect. . . . there is the strong imputation of Hitlerian guilt to other people."[14]

Newsweek found the play too black-and-white a treatment of some complex questions: "The play's sympathies are never in doubt. The heavies are the AEC counsel, the witnesses hostile to Oppenheimer. . . . the heroes are Oppenheimer, his lawyers, friends. . . . Kipphardt's play

poses the questions: does the scientist have the duty to consider the uses to which his work is put? Does his duty to humanity come before his duty to country? Kipphardt's answer, like Oppenheimer's, is a resounding yes to both questions."[15]

The Washington Post found it "inevitable" that Oppenheimer should end up as a character in a play, for he and his ordeal "epitomized the guilt, anxiety and fear which spread in this country as a result of the enormity of what was done at Hiroshima." Because he was the "most conspicuous" of the victims of anti-Communist hysteria, and because he personified America's "humane impulses, its sensibilities and misgivings respecting the development of more and more dreadful instruments of destruction," he also became "the protagonist of America's redemption," as symbolized by Kennedy's bestowal of the Fermi Award. "All of this lends itself to the theater," said the *Post,* and perhaps almost too readily "to characterizations too facile, too unshaded, too lacking in the subtleties and conflicting pressures of real life. It lends itself too easily to distortions." These oversimplifications made it "understandable" that Oppenheimer should "resent" having his life spread all across the theaters of Europe. But, despite his protests that the hearing was a "farce," the *Post* argued that it was really "a morality play," and that perhaps "the world needs to see it recreated on the stage to understand its lesson and to experience its full dramatic impact."[16]

Oppenheimer responded in a letter to the newspaper that despite the *Post*'s "wise and friendly" thoughts, he had no "natural aversion to being portrayed" but objected only to Kipphardt's "wholly fictitious" words.[17] He added that he was hoping that the upcoming Paris production would correct that problem.

He was referring to one case where his protests had struck home. After receiving a copy of Oppenheimer's angry letter to Kipphardt, the famed French director Jean Vilar stopped rehearsals of the play in Paris and reworked Kipphardt's text in an attempt to address Oppie's objections. Vilar removed the "improvisations" in Kipphardt's text that Oppenheimer found so egregious and instead created a version that consisted solely of literal excerpts of the hearing transcript, without the expansive soliloquies or projected photos and film clips of the original German production. Oppenheimer found Vilar's interpretation more palatable, but critics and audiences were not as impressed.

One of the artistic criticisms that had been leveled at Kipphardt's work was that, because of its heavy reliance on a transcript, it was more of a documentary than a play. Kipphardt resisted any such description and forbade it in any publicity for the production, but Vilar's version, retitled *The Oppenheimer File,* could hardly be described as anything else. "Everyone seems to agree that whatever it is that the dramatist [Kipphardt] found among the 3000-page record of the Washington hearings, it is not a play," wrote *The New York Times*. "Already in Germany there was little point in using the term. Now, since Dr. Oppenheimer's much-publicized letter to the author, there is even less." Vilar's production was "the nearest approach to pure documentary theater that has been seen in Paris in many years." Even the program, complete with scientific diagrams, "looks more like a textbook of popular science than the usual illustrated cast list."[18]

Said another critic, "The play itself—at least in the Vilar version—is a bit too literal, failing to give the background of the period, the hysterical fever of McCarthyism . . . the general sense of mistrust and panic that was then in the air. It is thoughtful, intelligent and apparently truthful to the letter, but theatrically it is prosaic. . . . it never takes on the view that a dramatist must lend to such a proceeding."[19] The showbiz journal *Variety* decided that "despite excellent moments, the piece generally lacks dramatic progression. Vilar has staged with care, but cannot overcome the generally pedestrian quality of the material."[20]

Kipphardt felt that Vilar's version "pulls all the teeth out of my play."[21] The playwright claimed that he had tried to show all sides of the issues, with Oppenheimer a morally ambiguous figure, while in Vilar's production Oppenheimer is unquestionably a saint being persecuted by evil men. "Just reading [Vilar's version] makes me grind my teeth," Kipphardt said. "I don't accept it. I didn't polemicize." And he had explained to Oppenheimer that "a playwright is not an historian."[22]

As with all matters Oppenheimer, the play controversy provided an opportunity for various parties to grind their particular political axes. Some seemed to find ideological undercurrents in the differences between the original Kipphardt text and the Vilar version that, they theorized, had their origins in the political and personal backgrounds of the

two artists. Vilar was known to be of a leftist bent, and consequently some critics found, in his interpretation of Kipphardt and his willingness to accommodate Oppenheimer's objections, a ready explanation of why the Vilar version seemed particularly heavy-handed and weighted too much on Oppenheimer's side.

"The leading AEC lawyer bullies Dr. Oppenheimer relentlessly in the manner of a stock stage villain. Dr. Oppenheimer himself struggles loftily against his oppressors, a noble, suffering, 'broken' man. . . . The editing of the transcript has been carried out so as to emphasize all passages unflattering to U.S. government authorities," one critic complained.[23]

Kipphardt's background, on the other hand, was far from that of a French left winger: his father had been imprisoned in Buchenwald during the Nazi years, and Kipphardt himself had been drafted into the German army and served on the Russian front. After the war and the division of Germany, he worked in theater in East Berlin until 1960, when he was accused of being "deviationist" and fled to the West to escape the attentions of the secret police. Not the profile of a man who might be expected to be an uncritical supporter of an old "security risk" and onetime "Commie sympathizer" like Robert Oppenheimer.

It was a no-win situation for all of the principals involved with the play. Nobody was going to be completely happy. Either the play distorted historical truth and the beliefs of its central character, among others, while preserving a sense of moral ambiguity, or it was so numbingly literal and one-sided that it failed as drama even as it satisfied historical truth. "Perhaps it would take not a playwright but a magician to satisfy both Oppenheimer's demands for accuracy and an audience's demands for a simpler hero-villain conflict," noted the American Association for the Advancement of Science in a newsletter.[24]

As the controversy raged, the productions rolled on. By the spring of 1965, a London staging for the Royal Shakespeare Company was in the works at the Aldwych Theater. When the London producer, John Roberts, who had bought the English-language performance rights from Kipphardt, wrote to Oppenheimer to request his assistance or at least his blessing, he found Oppie as intransigent as ever. "I have not been for this play," Oppenheimer answered. "I have not wished to have it produced in Berlin, or in Paris, or anywhere else. I would hope that it

would not be produced in England, or in this country. Since the play deals with matters of public record, I have, I know, neither the right nor the power to prevent its production; but you should be clear that I am not for it." He mentioned his position that the Kipphardt text misrepresents important facts and people, including himself, "and, since several of the improvisations seem to me, in fact, rather 'anti-American,' I have protested." Oppenheimer's description of the play as "anti-American" in the press had raised some eyebrows, coming from a figure who had once been accused of the same sin himself, and who was still considered such in some quarters.

So, Oppenheimer continued, there was obviously "no question of my collaborating with you" or offering any other help. "I did, for Jean Vilar, try to keep him from textual inaccuracies, partly because there was a problem of translation involved," but Oppenheimer hadn't decided on the passages to be included or excluded. "I thus hardly see of what use I can be to you in this enterprise, since there is no problem of translation in your case, and since I want to be very resolute in having no complicity in what you do."[25]

A couple of weeks later, Roberts received a letter from Oppenheimer's attorneys that served as formal notice that Oppenheimer did not wish the play to be produced. And despite Oppenheimer's admission that he had no right or power to force Roberts to comply, the attorneys stated that Oppenheimer had written that letter "without legal advice and in ignorance of what we have now advised him to be his right to restrain the production of the play as an unlawful invasion of privacy." Any expenses that Roberts might incur in trying to proceed with the production would be at his own risk.[26]

Roberts decided to avoid those expenses of being forced to defend himself against a possible Oppenheimer legal assault, and canceled the production. London theater audiences would not see the play that had conquered the Continent—yet.

The same tactic squelched a New York production planned by the famous producer David Merrick. Oppenheimer told his lawyers that "he could not be more delighted with the word that it will not be done in New York; and I am deeply grateful that you had the wisdom to write a letter that was neither belligerent nor ineffective. Without it I think they would have gone ahead."[27] Although he didn't know it at

the time, Oppenheimer's victories in stopping the London and New York productions would be only temporary.

Why was Oppenheimer so determined to derail and obstruct an artistic work that, seen in any light and in whatever version, and whatever inaccuracies it contained, was decidedly on his side and cast him as a hero? The reasons were much deeper and more serious than the question of "whether a living person likes to be presented on the stage," as he explained to the press: "The answer is 'No,' in my case. But that is not my business, and it is the business of other people to decide if they will put on the play." Nor was his opposition solely due to the "presentation of living persons . . . which betrays and falsifies their attitudes and characters."[28]

Such distortions undoubtedly rankled, but Oppenheimer had repeatedly addressed them and publicly corrected them. By the time that the London and New York productions would have hit the boards, few theatergoers could have failed to be aware of Oppenheimer's objections. And most, if not all, would be sophisticated enough to realize that what they were witnessing was merely a play, not a documentary, just as Kipphardt had insisted from the beginning, so historical accuracy would be a minor concern to them. They were attending the play to be entertained, not educated. And Oppenheimer himself was a cultured individual who knew about artistic license and interpretation.

The Washington Post had thought it "readily understandable that [Oppenheimer] should resist the reliving of all this agony." It was a remarkably astute observation. For ten years, whenever an opportunity had presented itself for a new hearing, Oppenheimer had adamantly refused, no matter how favorable the odds on his side. Most recently, just two years before, he had flatly turned down Glenn Seaborg's offer of a new hearing, and even in the wake of the Fermi Award, he continued to resist any such proposals. Even if an outcome in his favor was virtually guaranteed, Oppenheimer was simply not going to subject himself to that experience ever again—and if that meant that he was fated to live out the rest of his days without a government security clearance, so be it.

But now that whole agonizing ordeal, complete with the minute dissections of his psyche, was being played out nightly in theaters across Europe. Just like ten years ago, Oppenheimer's life, motivations, pas-

sions, and mistakes were being discussed and debated, but this time over posttheater dinners and cocktails by strangers who had no knowledge of the real people and issues. And worst of all, their reactions and arguments and discussions weren't based on the actual evidence—the hearing transcript—but on a highly distorted and incomplete version of it. Which meant that their conclusions and perceptions would inevitably be distorted and incomplete as well.

And in being forced to confront those issues, the arguments of Kipphardt's play, Oppenheimer was in a real sense being forced to confront the original issues, events, and tribulations of the hearing all over again. He had tried to move on and leave it all behind him, yet time and again, he found himself dragged back into the whole miserable experience. Now the questions once directed at him by security officers and hostile AEC lawyers were being pondered by theatergoers out for an evening's entertainment: Why had he lied about Chevalier? Why did he spend a night with his Communist mistress? Had he slowed down the H-bomb project? Worse, the questions had now *become* part of an evening's entertainment.

All this considered, it becomes clear that Oppenheimer's strong reaction to the Kipphardt play was based on much more than a dislike of being made into a fictional character or a few historical errors of fact. The play reincarnated and perpetuated the most painful episode of his life, and reinforced it to the world at large as his defining moment. The past he had struggled to leave behind and to bury with the legacy of McCarthyism had been unceremoniously dug up and brought back to life like a Frankensteinian monster.

But just as Oppenheimer had eventually come to terms with the actual hearing and its impact upon him, so he managed to do the same with its dramatic representation. Although the Kipphardt play would remain a source of annoyance to him for the rest of his life, he finally came to accept the fact that it wasn't going to go away.

Over a year after the play first hit the stages of Europe, Oppenheimer wrote to Kipphardt: "With the passage of time, and after some discussion with friends who have become experts on the various versions of the 'Case,' I have come to feel that I was unduly harsh and unkind in what I wrote you more than a year ago." While he felt that his criticisms of the project "still seem rather sound to me," Oppenheimer was

now "quite clear that in these and other matters you meant me no harm. . . . I wish that I had written with greater restraint and kindness."[29]

One reason that Oppenheimer was able finally to find some goodwill in his heart for Kipphardt was that someone else had taken it upon himself to yet again dredge up a piece of Oppenheimer's past and subject it to public scrutiny, and this time without the softening patina of fiction.

Another figure from Oppie's past had resurfaced, and his feelings toward Robert Oppenheimer had far from mellowed.

* * *

Later that summer of 1954, just before Oppenheimer and Kitty departed for a long-overdue vacation, he dispatched a polite note to J. Edgar Hoover. "Though I do not know whether at this time you have an interest in my whereabouts, I think I should report my plans to you," he wrote. "I am planning to leave on Monday evening with my family for St. Croix in the U.S. Virgin Islands for a three or four week period of rest and sailing. Yours sincerely, JRO."[30] Whether Oppenheimer was merely trying to be truly helpful or tweaking Hoover's nose with subtle sarcasm is unknown. Perhaps it was a little of both. (The vacation seemed to do Oppenheimer some good: during his stay, he sent a wry note to his secretaries back home in Princeton: "I am beginning to have nightmares about the 'Oppenheimer Case.' They are more macabre than the public one; but they are much funnier.")[31]

In any case, when he and Kitty returned to New York, Oppie was immediately taken aside by FBI agents, who wanted to know whether Russian agents had tried to approach him while he was outside the country. Oppenheimer assured them that the KGB had left him unmolested during his vacation, but that he would certainly let the FBI know if Soviet agents ever tried to recruit him.

The incident was duly reported in the press. Among other papers, the New York Post *noted, "For 20 minutes he was questioned by three men reported to be FBI agents. Then Oppenheimer and his family drove quietly away in a private car."[32]*

However Oppenheimer may have tried to laugh off such annoyances, he probably never realized just how extensive and intrusive the surveillance was at its height, when even his confidential and supposedly privileged consultations with

his lawyers were bugged and transcribed—nor how long he continued to be watched and followed even after he was supposedly once more a private citizen rather than a trustee of government secrets.

Almost a year later, Oppie's friend David Lilienthal was on vacation at Trunk Bay in the Virgin Islands, a favored Oppenheimer getaway spot. As Lilienthal was paying his bill and he and his wife prepared to leave, the proprietor of the hotel took him aside: "Maybe I'm out of line in saying this, but I can't help it. There were some FBI fellows here last week. . . . they asked me about Oppenheimer. . . . they asked me: 'We just thought we would check up, who did he talk with, who did he see?' and so on. Well, frankly, I thought it was a hell of a thing." A shocked Lilienthal agreed, writing in his diary: "They will hound that fellow {Oppenheimer} as long as they can."[33]

Richmond, California

October 14, 1964

J. Edgar Hoover, Director
Federal Bureau of Investigation
U. S. Department of Justice
9th & Pennsylvania Avenue North West
Washington, D. C.

Dear Mr. Hoover:

Sometime ago a former F.B.I. agent (I can't recall his name right now)
spoke at our church. During his talk he told us about a case he worked
on - the case of Dr. J. Robert Oppenheimer.

He told us that they (the F.B.I.) caught Dr. Oppenheimer passing our
atomic bomb secret information to the Russians. He went on to tell us
that the present Democratic Administration had recently presented
Dr. Oppenheimer $50,000 in tax free money (The Enrico Fermi Award) as
a token of America's appreciation for his service.

Since that time I have read the same account of the Dr. Oppenheimer case
in two books ("None Dare Call It Treason", and "A Choice, Not An Echo").
Still I have talked to many "liberal" friends that say it is all lies.
One such friend told me to write to you, Mr. Hoover, and you would tell
the truth about this man and this case.

I am very interested in knowing the truth about Dr. Oppenheimer. According
to your files, is he or is he not a communist or a pro-communist?

As the Communism issue is the vital issue in this election year, I would
very much appreciate a reply before November 3.

Thank you.

100 - 17828 - 2380

Yours very truly, OCT 22 1964

Donald C. Hobbs

Donald C. Hobbs

APR 10-21-64
WAM/dlh

17

Responsibility and Guilt

I n the summer of 1964, Oppenheimer heard from probably the last person he expected to write to him. Even his correspondent admitted to a degree of incredulity at his own chutzpah.

"I had not thought ever to write you again," said Haakon Chevalier. "Our ways have parted so utterly. But a matter of some moment has arisen, which requires that I consult you."

Chevalier went on to explain that "it had been urged upon" him that he had a duty to publish "the true story of my involvement with you." Supposedly, even Oppie hero Niels Bohr had expressed such a thought to Chevalier. Although Chevalier "tried to tell the essential story in my novel [*The Man Who Would Be God*], he realized that many were disturbed by the fictional approach, so he was now writing a nonfiction account of his friendship with Oppenheimer, part of which was already in the hands of a publisher.

Then he got to the point. He planned to discuss "your and my membership in the same unit of the CP [Communist Party] from 1938 to 1942." Since, in Chevalier's opinion, this was nothing for Oppenheimer to "be ashamed of," he considered it "a grave omission not to give it its due prominence." But he considered it "only fair" to find out whether Oppenheimer had any objections first.[1]

Chevalier's letter was essentially a subtle attempt at blackmail. He was certainly quite aware that Oppenheimer had never officially joined

the CP, despite the suspicions and accusations that had dogged the scientist for the past two decades, and also had no illusions about the damage that such a contention could cause Oppenheimer if published, whether he might be "ashamed" of it or not.

Oppenheimer responded coldly and decisively. "Your letter asks whether I would have any objections. Indeed I do. . . . I have never been a member of the Communist Party, and thus have never been a member of a Communist Party unit. I, of course, have always known this. I thought you did too. I have said so officially time and time again."[2]

Oppenheimer had his lawyers (who were, what with the play and now the new Chevalier book, probably the busiest they had been on Oppie's behalf since 1954) look into the matter. They managed to get copies of prepublication galleys, discovering that Chevalier had included letters between himself and Oppenheimer, which the attorneys believed might be a way to stop the book: as Garrison told Oppenheimer in a phone conference, the "law seems to be settled that the writer of a letter . . . has common law copyright and can enjoin publication." He thought that Chevalier had written the book more "out of vindictiveness rather than vindication." Like a spurned lover who couldn't let go, Chevalier was desperately trying to find a way to punish Oppenheimer for his supposed betrayal.

The pesky dilemma was that any serious attempt to block the book's publication by an injunction or lawsuit would only give it more exposure and publicity—and as a result, there would be that dredging up of the past that Oppenheimer always tried to avoid. As he told Garrison, "Getting into this is really preparing for another hearing."

"Which you would rather not?" Garrison asked.

"Indeed not," Oppenheimer replied. "Once was enough." He also feared that becoming embroiled in legal proceedings with Chevalier "might provoke another official enquiry which I do not have the right to refuse."[3]

Oppenheimer and Garrison finally decided that the best strategy was to let Chevalier publish and be damned, and *Oppenheimer: The Story of a Friendship* appeared in the summer of 1965. The book is an odd combination of personal memoir, Oppenheimer biography, and attempted psychoanalysis of its titular figure. As such, it's a flawed but fascinating work.

Chevalier recounts meeting Oppenheimer and the development of their friendship in the leftist circles of 1930s Berkeley, the famed Oppenheimer charisma and its effects on himself and others, and, of course, the infamous "Chevalier incident." Chevalier also discusses the security hearing and its aftermath, including its effects on both men and their relationship. The overall effect of the book is that of an enormously self-indulgent exercise in self-justification.

Much of Chevalier's personal politics are on display in the book, and in more than just the recounting of his own background. For Chevalier, "the dropping of the atom bombs on Hiroshima and Nagasaki was a tragic error. . . . good men were committed to doing the wrong thing for a right reason." Oppenheimer, of course, believed no such thing, as he repeatedly emphasized, most recently to Kipphardt. Such a gulf between the essential beliefs of both men makes it clear that, Chevalier incident or not, and whatever their past relationship, they had both grown far apart anyway, so much so that the friendship Chevalier describes would probably have withered away in any case. And it demonstrates that the almost mystical connection that Chevalier seems to believe existed between himself and Oppenheimer was mostly or entirely on his part—and largely illusory.

Chevalier says that this "tragic error" was the message he intended to convey in his previous novel, but he realized that, at least in America, no one got it: "Had the true impact of the story been grasped in America, I should perhaps not have had to write the present story." And so, telling the "truth" about Oppenheimer was now his "public duty." That truth, as he saw it, was that Oppenheimer was a "Faust of the twentieth century" who "had sold his soul to the atomic bomb."

Chevalier's version of the "incident" that bears his name places him in an almost completely passive role, the better to highlight his later victimization by Oppenheimer's "betrayal." Fellow leftist and friend George Eltenton, a chemical engineer for the Shell Company, proposed to Chevalier that there should be some kind of exchange of technical information between the United States and the Soviet Union, a scientific collaboration for mutual benefit. Eltenton knew that Chevalier was friends with Oppenheimer, and in a "roundabout" way finally got to the point: would Chevalier "sound out" Oppenheimer about the possibilities?

"I told Eltenton something to the effect that whoever had thought this up had got his signals mixed . . . and that I was sure that Oppenheimer would be horrified at any suggestion of this kind." He thought that Eltenton was probably "a little naïve" to advance such an idea and seemed to be relieved to unburden himself by telling Chevalier about it.

As Chevalier admits, the next question was whether or not to tell Oppenheimer. He was sure that Eltenton wasn't a spy or involved in a conspiracy, but what about his colleagues? What if they tried approaching someone else? Shouldn't Oppie be warned? While Chevalier hesitated to get Eltenton involved by mentioning his name, he knew that wouldn't be very helpful. He discussed the matter with his wife, and they agreed that Oppenheimer should be told about Eltenton. Here his worshipful attitude toward Oppenheimer took hold: surely Oppie, if anyone, would know what to do. And Chevalier would let Oppenheimer know that in his opinion, Eltenton was probably perfectly innocent.

Not long after this came the fabled "Chevalier incident," the infamous evening at the Oppenheimers' and the brief conversation in the kitchen in which Chevalier, by his account, was only casually trying to let Oppenheimer in on something that Chevalier thought he should know about. Both men agreed that Eltenton's proposal was completely outrageous and out of the question, and "I dismissed the whole thing from my mind," as Chevalier writes. Later, of course, Oppenheimer would delay reporting the information to security officials, and then inexplicably complicate the story in a misguided attempt to shield Chevalier from involvement.

What seems to escape Chevalier completely is the striking parallel between his own actions and Oppenheimer's in the entire affair. Eltenton tells Chevalier of a suspicious proposal involving Oppenheimer; Chevalier ponders whether or not to tell Oppenheimer, but hesitates briefly because he doesn't want to get his friend Eltenton into trouble; but then he tells Oppenheimer, thus passing responsibility for the entire matter on to him. Oppenheimer sits on the information, sure it's nothing and not wanting to involve a friend he's sure is innocent (Chevalier), but finally decides it's his duty to report it to the proper authorities—which he does, while declining to name Chevalier, think-

ing to protect his friend when, of course, his delay merely increases the security men's interest in him, leading to much greater trouble for all concerned.

But if Oppenheimer "betrayed" a friend by first concocting an elaborate fiction to prevent having to give Chevalier's name to the security men, and then later finally named him to General Groves under orders, then didn't Chevalier equally "betray" his friend Eltenton by naming him to Oppenheimer? In fact, wasn't Chevalier's betrayal of Eltenton more immediate than that by Oppenheimer, who at least hemmed and hawed and delayed as long as possible before being forced—under orders—to name Chevalier? Didn't Chevalier simply "pass the buck" to Oppenheimer by telling him about Eltenton's proposal, because Oppie would "know how to handle it"? Didn't Chevalier, therefore, put his great friend Oppenheimer into an impossible position? Did he think that Oppenheimer wouldn't eventually be forced to report the matter and, in so doing, give his name?

In short—and without excusing Oppenheimer's own inexplicable behavior that he later called "idiotic"—might not the entire "Chevalier incident" ultimately be not Oppenheimer's fault, but Chevalier's? If, as was the case, Oppenheimer was forced to choose between friendship and his duty and loyalty to his country, wasn't it Chevalier who had placed him in that dilemma?

Instead, Chevalier wants to absolve himself of all responsibility for the matter and place all of it on the shoulders of Oppenheimer, who (he thinks) should have known what to do. Chevalier was only being helpful: it was solely Oppenheimer and his mishandling of the situation that led to the devastating consequences that engulfed both men. But if Chevalier had really been so certain that Eltenton was simply naïve and mixed up, and that he hadn't been suggesting a serious attempt at espionage, then why not simply keep his own mouth shut and not tell his dear friend Oppenheimer and thus put him in such a position?

Such questions are ultimately unanswerable, of course, but worth asking for the insight they can provide into such intangibles of history. We can never know the absolute truth of the Chevalier incident, because we have only the faulty human memories of the two men involved to go on (although some theorize that Kitty Oppenheimer had followed her husband and Chevalier into the kitchen and witnessed the

conversation, so that Oppenheimer's subsequent lies had always been to protect her more than Chevalier).

Chevalier's version, however, is nothing if not self-serving. As Oppenheimer colleague Jeremy Bernstein writes, "The least one can say is that this account is disingenuous. For a start, both here and throughout his book Chevalier leaves out the fact that he was a member of the Communist Party at this time. So [were] Eltenton and his wife."[4] Chevalier knew that Oppenheimer was aware of all this, and Chevalier may also have known that Eltenton was in fact a Soviet spy who had been tasked with the job of attempting to make some kind of contact with Oppenheimer. And yet Chevalier is surprised and outraged that Oppenheimer, recently named the scientific leader of a crucial war project, would report such an approach?

The reaction to *Story of a Friendship* was not what Chevalier had apparently hoped for, but no doubt heartening to Oppenheimer. *The Man Who Would Be God* had generally been panned as little more than a bad novel and clumsy *roman à clef,* but the new nonfiction book couldn't be excused as anything but a direct attempt at character assassination coming from an individual with a prodigious ability to hold a grudge.

"If at first you don't succeed in fiction, try again in non-fiction. This seems to be the formula being followed by Haakon Chevalier, the once-upon-a-time friend of J. Robert Oppenheimer," said a *Washington Post* critic. "The new book adds little to what is already on public record, save for some suppositions without factual support. It was clear during the Oppenheimer hearings that with Chevalier as a friend, Oppenheimer didn't need an enemy. This new book proves it."[5]

"For one of the victims, the 'incident' which bears his name seems a permanent obsession," observed *Newsweek*. "Like the Ancient Mariner, he seems unable to let it rest. And if his manner is self-righteous, starchily ponderous, insufferably virtuous, a trifle sanctimonious—well, that is the way men are sometimes affected by obsessions. . . . like a 'spoiled' priest turned atheist, he denounces the god-that-failed with tempestuous fury."[6]

Alistair Cooke noted that the focus of the book is chiefly the "dreadful story" of the Chevalier incident, and Chevalier says "almost nothing about the oppressive and often vindictive fashion in which the hearings were held, and invites no doubts about the bloodless rigidity of the

security system itself." Chevalier's book "treads the dangerous ground of ascribing motives, and on the crummy ground of looking for shabby motives. I, for one, would like to leave the casting of the final stone to others. Oppenheimer has had his deserts and more. And anyone who once idolized him ought, as all such pedestal builders ought, to ask himself if he doesn't now enjoy a mean satisfaction in seeing him pulled down."[7]

One of Oppenheimer's main objections to both Chevalier's book and the Kipphardt play was that both had relied heavily on Robert Jungk's account of the Manhattan Project, *Brighter Than a Thousand Suns,* which he and a number of other Los Alamos veterans had criticized as overly romanticized and historically inaccurate. Oppenheimer had even gone so far as to call it "mendacious" and to say that "it has very little relation to the truth." Jungk's book was the first account of the atomic bomb to decisively cast Oppenheimer in the role of a scientist-martyr who regretted doing "the work of the devil" (in Kipphardt's phrase) and who had, in some sense, betrayed not only himself but those around him—including, of course, Chevalier.

Books about the Manhattan Project saga that had appeared before Jungk's, notably William Laurence's *Dawn over Zero,* tended more toward traditional reportage and factual narrative. Jungk's work had aspirations far more literary and ambitious, as his subtitle, "A Personal History of the Atomic Scientists," reveals. His interest went beyond facts and figures about critical masses and slow neutrons and probed into the thoughts, feelings, and motivations of his main characters, particularly Oppenheimer.

In Jungk's depiction, Oppenheimer had found his true niche at Los Alamos because, while "his achievements might be considered exceptional in the academic world . . . in his own more critical eyes he had not done enough." Then he was suddenly placed in charge of the most important scientific enterprise in the world, chosen over Nobel Prize winners and others more scientifically accomplished. But even after succeeding beyond all expectations and producing the wonder weapon that ended the war, "Robert Oppenheimer was only a man, into whose hands a mighty, far too mighty, instrument of power had been given." When, later on, he was removed from his position of power, he became a "Dreyfus . . . that unjustly suspected French officer whose epaulets

were torn from his uniform and whose sword was broken before his eyes." He was a "conscience-stricken scientist" with "the halo of a martyr" who was "tortured by conflicting impulses," a "twentieth-century Faust" who had signed a "pact with the Devil."

As much as Oppenheimer hated such portrayals of himself and repudiated them as inaccurate, Jungk's book helped to cement them in the popular imagination, and the tormented, guilt-ridden scientist became a popular trope, with its perfect personification in J. Robert Oppenheimer. The image persisted despite the best efforts of scientists, politicians, and journalists to deny it. William Laurence, the only press eyewitness to most of the events Jungk describes, gave a scathing review of the book, calling it "an indictment rather than a history." Jungk was obviously interested "not so much in presenting an unbiased, objective record . . . but rather in summing up the case for the prosecution. . . . does Mr. Jungk mean to imply that the best interests of mankind would have been served by allowing Hitler to be the sole possessor of the atomic bomb?" Laurence points out various inaccuracies in Jungk's account, not the least of which is Jungk's picture of Oppenheimer: "Mr. Jungk presents a most unflattering portrait of Mr. Oppenheimer as an individual, which is wholly at variance with the character and qualities of this highly respected man of science. . . . in this Mr. Jungk shows not only highly biased judgment but also lamentable poor taste."[8]

Aside from Chevalier's use of Jungk's Oppenheimer-as-Faust line, the picture of Oppenheimer that Chevalier paints in *Story of a Friendship* owes a great deal to Jungk's own interpretations. Jungk had contacted Chevalier while researching *Suns,* and the two men met in Paris for a lengthy interview, as Chevalier describes in *Story of a Friendship.*

But although Chevalier credits Jungk with helping him to achieve "the final and decisive insight into Oppenheimer's character . . . the defect of character* that had caused Oppenheimer, almost overnight, to throw over all his ideals," it's clear that Chevalier influenced Jungk just as profoundly. The insight helped Chevalier in the creation of his Oppenheimer character, Sebastian Bloch, in *The Man Who Would Be God,*

* An ironic turn of phrase, whether unconsciously or purposely, from Chevalier that echoes one of the charges in the AEC's final verdict on Oppenheimer.

but the view of Oppenheimer as a figure racked with regret and guilt advanced by Jungk goes hand in hand with Chevalier's portrayal of Oppenheimer—fictional and otherwise—as a man whose hubris and intoxication with power lead him "to tell on his friends, to sacrifice his integrity." The notion of a tormented Oppenheimer led by expediency and the need for self-preservation to betray friends and confidences is a major tragic flaw of Jungk's Raskolnikovesque Oppenheimer figure.

Chevalier claims at the end of *Oppenheimer: The Story of a Friendship* that "I look back upon my friendship with Robert Oppenheimer with no regrets, and with no ill feeling." But he is speaking only of a past Oppenheimer, one whom he had known during "the time of innocence" when they "held high the banner of justice, freedom and equality, asserted the sanctity of human rights and proclaimed the cause of peace," one who was an impossibly romanticized creation of Chevalier's own heart. And to profess "no ill feeling" at the end of over two hundred pages of a studied personal attack is simply incredible.

But Chevalier was right on one count. He concludes that "future generations will have to make their own judgment" on the facts, and that his book might serve at least as a footnote to the history he and Oppenheimer had shared. Both of Chevalier's books on Oppenheimer have indeed proved little more than footnotes, their value not so much historical as psychological, as insight into the psyche of one of the many figures in Oppenheimer's life.

More than most, Oppenheimer had become a man inextricably and irrevocably bound to his past, however much he tried to escape it and move beyond it. Sometimes, as with the Kipphardt play and Chevalier book, that past besieged him in ways he might have wished to avoid.

But as he reached his later years, his past sometimes became something to embrace and to commemorate, as with two important anniversaries that would be celebrated in 1965.

* * *

If the prospect of Oppenheimer forsaking the United States was dismissed both by the man himself and most others as absurd, his continued leadership of the Institute for Advanced Study remained a more immediate and practical question. In general, the Institute didn't deal with any sort of classified information or

research; indeed, such activity would violate its near-sacred charter as an international sanctuary for open and pure intellectual inquiry. Possession of an AEC "Q" clearance or any other kind of top-secret clearance wasn't a prerequisite for the Institute directorship, so Oppenheimer's dismissal from the charmed circle should have no effect on his continued efficacy at the IAS.

But administrative technicalities and public realities could be two different things. Even before the final AEC decision was announced, speculation was rife that if the verdict went against him, as seemed increasingly likely, Oppenheimer would have no choice but to resign from the Institute, his professional credibility and standing irrevocably tarnished. Friends urged Oppie to stand his ground. Physicist Edward Condon, a man who had endured the security meat grinder himself more than once, wrote to Oppenheimer immediately after the AEC decision: "I was astonished at the suggestion . . . that it is expected that you will resign as director of the Institute for Advanced Study. Please under no circumstances allow yourself to be misled or provoked into taking any such action. Our government through the Atomic Energy Commission has made an awful mistake and in time to come that will be understood and perhaps even in some measure corrected. But because such a mistake has been made by four Washington politicians is no reason for you to give up one of the most important posts in American scholarly life for which you are ideally suited and in which you are doing such a splendid job."[9]

Oppenheimer himself seemed perfectly resolute, showing no hints privately or publicly that he was even considering leaving the Institute. As he told a reporter, "I may not be able to move freely in laboratories, but that has nothing to do with thinking freely."[10] His colleagues at the Institute had made their support known in a public statement as well.

Unfortunately, the final decision wasn't Oppenheimer's. It belonged to the Institute's board of trustees, among whom Lewis Strauss still wielded considerable clout. Strauss struggled to maintain an outward appearance of fairness regarding the Oppenheimer case, insisting that he had acted objectively and according to the facts, without any personal animosity. In a letter to Charles Lauritsen just before the final AEC decision, Strauss protested: "I, too, have been disturbed by the reports . . . that I was personally hostile to Robert Oppenheimer. Whatever the outcome of the case, I should like to have you know that this is categorically false." Strauss betrayed a hint of his characteristic paranoia as he continued: "My inquiries have led me to the conclusion that the story {of Strauss's hostility toward Oppenheimer} has been deliberately planted." He went

on to mention that "as recently as last October" he had convinced the Institute trustees to raise Oppenheimer's salary. "I think you will agree that this is hardly compatible with 'personal hostility.' "[11]

The behind-the-scenes record, however, makes it clear that Strauss was protesting too much. For some time after Oppenheimer was stripped of his clearance for good, Strauss maneuvered to have the Institute trustees fire Oppenheimer. But the united and strong support Oppenheimer enjoyed from the Institute faculty, expressed in a statement signed by all the permanent and emeritus members, was not something the trustees could ignore or deny, and Oppenheimer stayed, reelected to the directorship in October 1954 by the trustees.

THE ALL-ENCOMPASSING DARK

An aging Oppenheimer contemplates an uncertain future.

My own feelings about responsibility and guilt have always had to do with the present, and so far in this life that has been more than enough to occupy me.

—J. ROBERT OPPENHEIMER
TO DAVID BOHM, 1966

November 4, 1965.

F.B.I.
Washington, D.C.

Sirs:

I am a student at the Inter-American University here in san Juan and have to turn in a report on Dr. J.Robert Oppenheimer. I would like to know what his standing is as of now regarding him as a security risk. I know the government has partially tried to undo what happened to him in 1953, but I want to know if he is still considered any kind of risk to us, or if he is still considered a Communist by you.

I thank you for your reply, and ask you please to answer me within your earliest convenience, for I must turn the project in the 13. Thanks again.

Yours truly,

Raul A. Suarez

REC-52 100-17828-2385

NOV 10 1965

CORRESPONDENCE

1 xerox copy 11-9-65
acb 11-9-65
DTP:cns

18

The Sad Account

He had been such a towering presence throughout the twentieth century, both in science and in the general public consciousness, that it was hard to believe that Albert Einstein had already been gone for ten years. Nineteen sixty-five would be a year of remembering him and his achievements, and since Einstein had spent his entire later career in Princeton at the Institute for Advanced Study, under the leadership of J. Robert Oppenheimer since 1947, it was only natural that Oppenheimer would play a key role in the anniversary commemorations. What was not natural was that Oppenheimer's involvement would create controversy—and that instead of being instigated by the usual right-wing patriots and Commie-baiters, this time it was caused by Oppenheimer himself.

In a lecture before a UNESCO meeting in Paris, Oppenheimer tried to dispel what he called the "Einstein myth" that Einstein's work was too difficult and complex to be generally understood. But Oppenheimer perhaps went too far, saying that while much of Einstein's early work was "paralyzingly beautiful," it was also full of errors, and that the correction of those errors had delayed the publication of Einstein's collected works. Also, Einstein's personality was "wholly without sophistication and wholly without worldliness," so that in America or England he would have been thought uneducated. As Charles Thorpe explains, "Even as Oppenheimer paid his respects, it was clear that Einstein was

a discomforting figure for him. Oppenheimer could not help but come across as snobbish and condescending" when he made such remarks. Thorpe notes that while Einstein was often described as having a "child-like innocence," and that usually such remarks were complimentary, "coming from Oppenheimer, so obviously proud of his own sophistication, the observation about Einstein's lack of worldliness was far from being praise."[1]

Oppenheimer's UNESCO speech on Einstein disturbed not only many of his scientific colleagues but also Einstein's family. How dare Oppenheimer, admittedly a great scientist but hardly an Einstein, not a Nobelist, criticize the great man in such a way? The flap passed quickly, but some saw it as a sign that the old Oppenheimer arrogance was alive and well, if now cloaked behind his current facade of humbled sanctification.

The summer of 1965 brought another anniversary, this one more somber and involving Oppenheimer more directly: the twentieth anniversary of the atomic bomb, both its birth on the Jornada del Muerto in New Mexico and its first use as a weapon at Hiroshima and Nagasaki. Again, of course, Oppenheimer was the focal point for reporters and pundits looking for commentary on the first twenty years of the atomic age.

William Laurence, although now retired as science editor of *The New York Times,* still did occasional pieces for the paper, and as a journalist intimately associated with the bomb since its birth, he was obliged to acknowledge its anniversary. He contributed a piece to the *Times* Sunday magazine in which he asked a number of Manhattan Project luminaries, "Would you make the bomb again?"

The first respondent was Oppenheimer. Yes, he would make the bomb again, even after Hiroshima, he told Laurence. "From what I know today, I do not believe that we could have known with any degree of certainty that the atomic bomb was necessary to end the war," he admitted. "But that was not the view of those who had studied the situation at the time and who were thinking of an invasion of Japan." Oppenheimer says that with the peace feelers Japan had been extending late in the war, "probably a settlement could have been reached by political means. But the men who made the decision . . . were sure that the choice was either invasion or the bomb. . . . I am not sure that Japan was ready to surrender."

Oppenheimer's comments seem to sidestep neatly any personal responsibility on his part for Hiroshima or Nagasaki. But for anyone who thought that he was still suffering from pangs of guilt (Jungk, Kipphardt, and others like them aside), he added: "I never regretted, and do not regret now, having done my part of the job. . . . the existence of the bomb has reduced the chance of World War III and has given us valid hope." Perhaps it was used too quickly on Japan and without adequate warning, but "it was a damn good thing that the bomb was developed. . . . in that world, in that war, it was the only thing to do." Most of the others polled by Laurence, including Edward Teller, General Groves, and Luis Alvarez, echoed Oppenheimer's sentiments.[2]

Oppenheimer offered similarly equivocal comments to *Newsweek*. "Speaking in a hushed, cultivated voice, Oppenheimer said the bomb was developed 'two years late—it would have saved a great many lives if it had been ready sooner.'" He enjoyed working at Los Alamos: "For the first time in my life, I had only one thing to do. . . . there was uncertainty of achievement but not of duty."

Looking back, Oppenheimer was somewhat disappointed: "The twenty years since Trinity have not turned out as Oppenheimer expected," said *Newsweek*. "We all felt that this business had to stop and hope that nuclear weapons would blackmail man into peace and produce a profound cleansing of international relations," said Oppenheimer. "But we missed that bus." And yet, the bomb had created a sort of peace, he pointed out "with a great deal of knocking on wood. . . . Nobody can tell where a Vietnam will lead. This is such an unparalleled part of history that there is no basis for comparison."[3]

On the *CBS Evening News,* marking the twentieth anniversary of Hiroshima, Martin Agronsky asked Oppenheimer again whether the use of the bomb had been necessary. "This is a much traveled track, and I cannot give a categorical answer," said Oppenheimer, again detailing the point of view of the Allied leaders weighing the prospective invasion of Japan. "The ending of the war by this means, certainly cruel, was not undertaken lightly, but I am not as of today confident that a better course was then open."

Agronsky directly confronted the question of guilt and responsibility. "With all the rationalization, with all the inevitability of the decision that history demonstrates to us, you and many like you who

brought the bomb into being still seem to suffer, may I say, from the bad conscience about it. Is that true, sir?"

Oppenheimer said carefully, "Well, I don't want to speak for others because we're all different. I—I think when you play a meaningful part in bringing about the death of over 100,000 people and the injury of a comparable number, you naturally don't think of that as—with ease." Then he brought up one of his most famous, oft-quoted statements, one that had encouraged the image of him as a guilt-ridden scientific mar-tyr: his remark that "physicists had known sin." Now, perhaps, with the examples of how the misinterpretation of that statement by such as Kipphardt and Jungk had contributed to his public image, he saw an opportunity to clarify that thought.

"Long ago, I said once that in a crude sense which no vulgarity and no humor could quite erase, the physicist had known sin, and I didn't mean by that the deaths that were caused as a result of our work. I meant that we had known the sin of pride. We had turned to effect in what proved to be a majority way the course of man's history. We had the pride of thinking we knew what was good for man, and I do think it had left a mark on many of those who were responsibly engaged. This is not the natural business of a scientist."

"Dr. Oppenheimer, from all that you have said, it seems that when you contemplate the future, it is more with hope than with pessimism," said Agronsky.

"Well, I—," Oppenheimer began.

"Or is that an oversimplification?"

"I've tried to talk about the hopeful things," Oppenheimer said. "The unhopeful ones jump to everyone's mind. . . . there are a hundred reasons for seeing no hope at all. And I take it for granted that every-body can think of them without being reminded." But although it was harder to think of reasons for optimism, said Oppenheimer, "I have tried to say that however frail and however tentative, however limited, they do exist and they look to me like a bridgehead to a liveable future. But not without work."[4]

A few weeks earlier, on the anniversary of Trinity, Oppenheimer had published a brief reminiscence of the test in *The Washington Post*. He concluded, "The last two decades have been shadowed by danger, ever changing, never really receding. Looking to the future, I see again no

ground for confidence; but I do see hope. . . . it is not the mood of hope, but hope itself, that is part of our life, and thus part of our duty. We are engaged in this great enterprise of our time, testing whether men can both preserve and enlarge life, liberty and the pursuit of happiness and live without war as the great arbiter of history. This we knew early in the morning of July 16, 20 years ago."[5]

And yet, for all his proclamations that the bomb was "a damn good thing" and that he had absolutely no regrets, deep conflict haunts Oppenheimer's public statements twenty years after the bomb's birth. The conflict is present first in his persistent reluctance to comment on current issues of politics and policy because of his insistence that he was too far removed from direct knowledge of the facts. When the editorial-page editor of the *New York Herald Tribune* asked him to comment on a recent letter to the newspaper, Oppenheimer begged off: "The subject of the test ban is one on which I am profoundly ignorant and should remain silent."[6]

Asked by a television interviewer, "Could you tell us what your thoughts are about what our atomic policy should be?" Oppenheimer promptly replied, "No, I can't do that. I'm not close enough to the facts and I'm not close enough to the thoughts of those who are worrying about it."[7] He would limit any public statements to generalities, to philosophical musings, to moralistic pronouncements.

But more than his words, the conflict, the pain—and perhaps, guilt—that, despite all his denials, Oppenheimer may still have felt after two decades are most clearly evident in a remarkable interview contained in an NBC documentary entitled *The Decision to Use the Atomic Bomb* (and excerpted at the closing of filmmaker Jon Else's Oscar-nominated Oppenheimer documentary film *The Day After Trinity*). Interviewer Chet Huntley asks Oppenheimer about what he witnessed at the Trinity test on that July morning in the desert, two decades earlier.

Oppenheimer in extreme close-up, with his white hair and hollowed cheeks, appears frail, aged, like a man in his seventies instead of one who has just passed sixty. He looks not at the interviewer nor at the camera, but down and away, his eyes focused on some far distant point that only he can see. His voice is slow, halting, almost monotone:

"You knew the world would not be the same. A few people . . .

laughed. A few people cried. Most people were silent." A quick glance
to the side, chin trembling, as if he is struggling to keep his composure
for the camera; then his gaze returns to that distant point. "I remem-
bered the line from the Hindu scripture, the Bhagavad Gita. Vishnu . . .
is trying to persuade"—a bony knuckle dabs briefly at his right eye—is
he brushing away a tear?—"the prince that . . . he should do his duty,
and to impress him, takes on multiarmed form, and says, 'Now I am
become Death, the destroyer of worlds.'" He raises his head a bit, his
eyes still distant and fixed. "I suppose we all felt that, one way or an-
other."[8]

Oppenheimer had sometimes been accused of being a talented actor,
a man who could play both to the princes and to the proles, who could
be overwhelmingly charming or persuasive or indignant or whatever he
chose, whatever mood was necessary to influence whoever he felt needed
to be influenced, whether a general, a security officer, a congressional
committee, or even a president. And yet there were times when this
supposed ability failed him utterly, most notably at his security hear-
ing, when he allowed himself to be browbeaten and humiliated by
Roger Robb, much to the amazement and bewilderment of both friends
and enemies familiar with the old Oppie magic.

If, however, he was again acting in this particular television inter-
view, playing the part of tormented guilty scientist for the people at
home watching in their living rooms, trying to evoke their sympathy
and forgiveness not only for the bomb but for his supposed infelicities
and security farragoes, then it is nothing short of an Academy Award–
worthy performance. Without any exaggeration, without any hyper-
bole, it is Oppenheimer at perhaps his most vulnerable.

Far from the genial, composed, amiable Oppenheimer of the Mur-
row interview, he is a study in overwhelming emotion under steely,
stoic control. It is a stunning, moving piece of film. Watching it, it is
difficult to believe that, all his sophistries aside, the physicists' "sin" of
which he spoke had more to do with an abstraction such as "pride" than
with the inescapable awareness that he had played "a meaningful part
in bringing about the deaths of over 100,000 people."

Yet, even with such a revealing moment captured on film, Oppen-
heimer remained an enigma. He continued to speak about the bomb
saving the peace and ending World War II, while also hinting darkly

about extinction. He spoke about science to audiences as diverse as the U.S. Military Academy at West Point and the bicentennial celebration of the Smithsonian Institution, and yet, as biographers Sherwin and Bird describe, remained "oddly disconnected from the turmoil of the 1960s,"[9] an era in which a man with his moral sensitivities, charisma, and awareness could have become a leader for a new generation. While other scientists such as Hans Bethe and Leo Szilard remained deeply involved in political action, Oppenheimer shunned it.

Why? Freeman Dyson, one of Oppenheimer's first recruits to the Institute, has a simple explanation. "That wasn't his style," Dyson says. "He liked to do things from the inside. That was why he was very effective inside the government."[10] Another Institute veteran, physicist Stanley Deser, feels that "he had lost all desire to participate, if only because he knew he would never regain any decisive say in the arms story."[11]

Perhaps Oppenheimer had simply grown too weary. In the spring of 1965, he sent a note to the chairman of the board of trustees of the Institute for Advanced Study. "We have sometimes talked of the time when I would no longer be director of the Institute for Advanced Study," he wrote. "I have decided that I should retire—not from the faculty, but from the directorship—at the end of next year, the end of June 1966. I shall be talking with you of the reasons, institutional and personal, for this decision, as, next week, I shall also be talking with the Board of Trustees. To them, and very specially to you, I have been grateful for the opportunity, over the years, to preserve and enlarge this center of learning."[12]

It felt like a good time to leave. One of Oppenheimer's pet projects had just been completed: a beautiful, strikingly imagined new library for the Institute designed by Wallace Harrison, an architect and Oppenheimer friend who had not only done the UN building in New York but Oppenheimer's beach house in St. John. He would be sixty-five in several years, the age at which he would be forced to step down anyway according to the Institute bylaws.

And he was weary of the continuing conflicts with several members of the IAS faculty, particularly in the mathematics department, some of whom, such as mathematician Deane Montgomery, felt that he had allowed the Institute to drift too far from its original purposes. Oppenheimer had brought in some people, such as poet T. S. Eliot and George

Kennan, of whom the more conventional IAS types disapproved. By allowing John von Neumann to build his prototype computer at the Institute, he had violated the tradition that the Institute must remain solely a bastion of theory, not of practical experimentation. Many of the faculty members of the Institute's School of Natural Sciences, which Oppenheimer had spent his time building up, were also retiring or moving on, allowing the conflicts with other faculty members to intensify.

Another reason for stepping down was more personal: the health of his wife, Kitty, who, along with chronic pancreatic problems, had become a rather infamous alcoholic. The acrimonious Montgomery, in fact, dubbed the Oppenheimer home "Bourbon Manor"—both as a dig at Oppenheimer and his wife, and in sarcastic acknowledgment of the free-flowing liquor that always accompanied any social events there.

Oppenheimer wouldn't be quitting the Institute entirely; he would stay on as a regular faculty member, occupying the senior professor of theoretical physics post formerly held by Einstein. But the directorship chores would pass to someone else. The Institute issued a press release describing Oppenheimer's future plans: "Asked about his new role, Dr. Oppenheimer said: 'There are some things that I have wanted to do: physics of course, which is in a most dramatic and hopeful stage, and to seek an understanding, both historical and philosophical, of what the sciences have brought to human life. After 18 years as Director of the Institute, I hope to turn to these questions, unencumbered by the important problems of Institute policy and administration."[13]

It was not an entirely unexpected move. "Dr. Oppenheimer's plans to continue his studies of philosophical implications of science in modern society were not surprising to those who have followed his career," said *The New York Times*. "In fact, his concern with human equations in the atomic age has been viewed as a basis of the political attacks on him."[14]

While many were sorry at the prospect of Oppenheimer stepping down, the opinion wasn't shared by all. A 1966 article on the Institute noted, "Few . . . mourn his passing as director. 'He is a poet,' said someone who likes him, 'not a man to run things,'" an odd observation to make of the leader of Los Alamos. The article continued, "He has been criticized with some rudeness, which nearly everyone deplores, by

a few of the mathematicians and physicists, and there is a general feeling that his resignation as director is best for him and best for the Institute."[15]

Oppenheimer had reached the same conclusion. Despite his long tenure, he had found the director's job ultimately frustrating. "He had to fight for everything he wanted," recalls Freeman Dyson. "There was a perpetual war going on [with the mathematicians]. . . . Nothing he could do was right." So why had he stayed so long? Partly because of the freedom the job afforded. "It is of course a very convenient place if you want to be a public figure and have a distinguished position and don't have to spend full time doing the job," Dyson notes. "Oppenheimer could run the Institute with his left hand and do anything else he wanted to do." So Oppenheimer was free to travel and write and lecture without the burdens of a more conventional academic position. "I always took the view it really didn't matter who was director, there wasn't much to do anyway," Dyson says with a laugh.[16]

Aside from Lewis Strauss, who remained on the IAS board, and the faculty members who had clashed with Oppenheimer, some private citizens were also pleased to see him vacate the director's office. "Gentlemen," wrote one to the Institute, "I was very delighted to read on page 68 of the Sunday News that Oppenheimer has decided to quit his post. This character was denied a security clearance by the Atomic Energy Commission in 1954 and as far as I know never was fully approved by that Commission. Yet, an institution such as yours for reasons beyond my comprehension retains him in an executive capacity. Frankly, Princeton would be the last place I would send anyone for an education. I hope Oppenheimer takes up residence in some distant inaccessible part of the world."[17]

But Oppenheimer would be staying in the decidedly accessible climes of Princeton. Although he would now be obliged to leave the director's official Olden Manor residence, the board of trustees had voted to build the family a new house on the Institute campus "as a token of our affection and gratitude."[18] Apparently out of sheer vindictiveness, a quality which he seemed to possess in inexhaustible supply, Lewis Strauss maneuvered behind the scenes to scuttle this plan and almost succeeded, but ultimately the board overruled his efforts, and construction on the new Oppenheimer home began the next year.

Meanwhile, coinciding with the twentieth anniversary of Trinity, a new popular treatment of the bomb's development appeared, authored by Lansing Lamont, a Washington *Time* magazine correspondent. Entitled *Day of Trinity,* the book was an episodic account of the Trinity test, including the events immediately before and after, with background on the Manhattan Project. While Jungk's influence is notable here and there, Lamont strives for a more journalistic you-are-there feel while avoiding Jungk's moralistic impositions. *The New York Times*'s William Laurence, who never missed an opportunity to point out that He Was There at Trinity, found the book much more salutary than Jungk's, calling it "a remarkable achievement in many respects."[19] Lamont enjoyed the participation of a number of Manhattan Project veterans, including Oppenheimer, who granted him an interview in Princeton. Oppenheimer's remarks echoed much of his recent bomb-anniversary commentary, but with more of an edge.

"I have no remorse about the making of the bomb and Trinity. That was done right," Oppenheimer told Lamont. "As for how we used it, I understand why it happened and appreciate with what nobility those men with whom I'd worked made their decision. But I do not have the feeling it was done right. The ultimatum to Japan was full of pious platitudes. It wasn't a pretty world and it is always easy to enjoy another man's bad conscience. But our government should have acted with more foresight and clarity in telling the world and Japan what the bomb meant."[20]

Although engagingly written, *Day of Trinity* was also criticized by some Project veterans as sensationalistic and marred by inaccuracies. After the book's publication, Oppenheimer seemed to share that opinion. In a later letter to Los Alamos colleague Kenneth Bainbridge, he made an offhand reference to "all else that was wrong" with Lamont's book, without any specifics.[21] Maybe the main thing that was wrong was that in retrospect, Oppenheimer regretted speaking so openly to Lamont.

It might have been the thought of having such ambivalence permanently enshrined in the pages of a book, rather than in a more transitory medium such as a newspaper, that led Oppenheimer to decline participation in another major book project, one that struck even closer to the heart of things than a book on Los Alamos: an in-depth, scholarly study on Oppenheimer's security case by one Philip M. Stern, a

respected author, journalist, and fellow Harvard graduate. Stern was known to some Oppenheimer friends and colleagues, and certainly sympathetic toward Oppenheimer and deeply concerned about the issues raised by the security episode, as evidenced by his working title: *Inquisition: The Oppenheimer Case in Retrospect.*

Stern set about contacting sources and attempting to set up interviews. Writing to Jerome Wiesner, Stern described the project: "While this happens to be the history of one case involving one man, it is far more than that: it is a clinical examination of a national disease at its most virulent, a disease that found its most absurd manifestation in the case of J. Robert Oppenheimer. It is a disease from whose virus a nation never wholly rids itself, one that could return at any time—and, if history is any guide, doubtless will. Honorable men will be tempted or driven to do dishonorable things; rational men to irrational acts and decisions, just as they were at the time of the Oppenheimer case. Perhaps—not likely, but just perhaps—a vivid recollection of the case of J. Robert Oppenheimer, such as this book strives to provide, will give pause to such honorable and rational men and mitigate the onset of the national disease of fear at some future date."[22]

The idea for the book was actually suggested to Stern by Harold P. Green, the former AEC staff lawyer who had been given the onerous task of drafting the original AEC letter of charges against Oppenheimer in 1953. Green's intimacy with the case and his subsequent disillusionment with the behind-the-scenes machinations by Strauss led to his eventual resignation from the AEC. Green had always intended to write his own definitive book on the case, but bogged down by legal work and professorial duties at George Washington University, he tapped Stern in 1965 to come aboard as a coauthor. As Stern took over more and more of the work and Green's commitments continued without letup, Green turned the entire project over to Stern with his blessing, while still intending to write his own book someday.* Stern published the book under his own name "with the collaboration of Harold P. Green."

* That work, unfortunately, was never to be realized. The closest sample we have of what a Green book on the Oppenheimer case might have been is a fascinating article Green published in *The Bulletin of Atomic Scientists* in 1977.

Stern managed to win the trust and cooperation of many Oppen-
heimer friends, even including Lloyd Garrison, who contributed a lengthy
appendix detailing his work on the case. Stern recalled that "the few
who were unwilling to see me were at the extreme ends of the spectrum:
those most opposed to and those closest to Dr. Oppenheimer." But those
close to Oppenheimer who met with Stern encouraged Oppenheimer
himself to accept Stern's requests for an in-depth interview.

Oppenheimer considered it but finally declined, explaining to Stern:
"I have thought that I should not interpose my judgment as to whether
[this] will be a helpful book. Indeed I do not know. But I am clear that
the book will be better for having been written totally without my col-
laboration, suggestions, or implied approval. The subject of the book is
one on which I do not have a total sense of detachment, and on which I
have very large and central areas of ignorance. I cannot think of a more
poisonous brew."[23]

Oppenheimer interview or not, Stern would not be dissuaded from
continuing with the book, and as he proceeded with his research, he
found that his work was evolving into something unlike the several
other books that had already been published on the case, such as
Charles P. Curtis's *The Oppenheimer Case,* the Alsop brothers' *We Accuse!,*
and even Chevalier's memoir. Because of the combination of the close
perspective on the case afforded him by Green and the objective dis-
tance now possible thanks to the amount of time that had passed since
the hearing—an advantage the other works lacked, either because they
were published too soon (as with Curtis and the Alsops) or were too
personal (as with Chevalier)—his project had a scope far beyond the
immediate parameters and details of the Oppenheimer ordeal. As Stern
later remarked, "[T]he focus of my attention shifted . . . from the case
itself to the security system as a whole and its effects on the United
States."[24] This, along with the fact that Stern was working in the midst
of a period of social and political upheaval never before seen in the
United States, would give the book that ultimately resulted from his
efforts a unique resonance and importance.

The Stern project would be a faint background presence in Oppen-
heimer's life for the foreseeable future, with his tacit blessing if not his
active participation. As he wrote in a letter to David Bohm: "I have

known of Stern's enterprise for some time. I have every reason to think well of him, and of his reasons for writing this book; and he has been vouched for as a man of goodwill and good sense by many, including Wiesner and Schlesinger and Anne Wilson Marks. . . . I have told Stern I would play no part, and that I would not talk with him nor criticize nor approve what he was doing."[25]

In the foreground now for Oppenheimer were winding up his directorship work at the Institute, and the ever-ongoing speeches and travel and personal appearances, some coupled with the various anniversaries of 1965, some not. The year brought a somber end to another important part of his past and present life, namely, his friendship with journalist Edward R. Murrow, who succumbed to lung cancer in April at only fifty-seven years old.

With all Oppenheimer's difficulties and complex relationships with the press, both print and the electronic media of radio and television, Murrow had been one figure whom Oppenheimer had consistently respected, trusted, and counted as a friend, the only journalist he allowed to get close in the immediate aftermath of the security hearing, when the wounds were still raw and bleeding. And Murrow had crusaded against the same darkness of anti-Communist paranoia and persecution that had destroyed Oppenheimer's career in public service and changed his life forever.

Now he was gone, one more precious voice of reason and integrity silenced. Murrow's longtime producer and friend Fred Friendly acknowledged the special connection between Murrow and Oppenheimer with a note shortly after the broadcaster's death. "The fact that you sent me a telegram on Wednesday had special meaning. I cannot claim to be next of kin, but I do appreciate that in this moment of mutual sorrow, your thoughts included me."

Friendly added, "The truth is that no broadcast Ed Murrow ever did meant more to him than the Oppenheimer broadcast of 1955. In describing techniques here and in London he always cited this as the best interview we ever did. But, more than this, I know that he believed that this broadcast communicated an idea about a scientist and his work."[26] Excerpts from the Oppenheimer show were included in a special one-hour Murrow tribute on CBS.

Murrow, of course, had succumbed to the cigarettes that he had smoked almost continually, up to seventy a day by some accounts, and smoking was another trait that he and Oppenheimer shared. While in his later years Oppenheimer began to favor a pipe with walnut tobacco over cigarettes, his smoking continued unabated, and by the end of 1965, he had developed a noticeable smoker's cough.

The cough was not going to go away. Robert Oppenheimer's past was about to catch up with him again. This time, the confrontation would be direct—and final.

* * *

Oppenheimer tried to soldier on, resigned to the end of his tenure as a governmental adviser and authority figure. "This phase of my life is now concluded," he told a reporter with characteristic formality.[27]

Traveling to the Virgin Islands and losing himself in the academic endeavors of the Institute were conscious efforts to move on and leave the smoldering wreckage of the security debacle behind. He refused to discuss the security hearing publicly in anything more than an occasional cryptic or ironic remark to a reporter, partly out of sheer weariness and partly because he felt he simply had nothing more to say on the matter. If the Institute was an ivory tower, then he had locked himself in its deepest depths.

By the end of 1954, however, Oppenheimer was beginning to allow himself to venture out into the world again. In October, he traveled down to Philadelphia to accept the 1954 Achievement Award of the Pyramid Club, given for "unstinting devotion of his own great gifts to the end of increasing man's knowledge."[28]

More significantly, he accepted an invitation to participate in Columbia University's bicentennial celebration by giving a lecture that was broadcast nationwide on CBS Radio on the day after Christmas, 1954. This was his first public appearance since the security hearing, and whether he intended it or not, it struck a remarkably somber chord in his audience.

Innocuously entitling his talk "Prospects in the Arts and Sciences," Oppenheimer proceeded to draw a rather bleak portrait of a culture of lonely artists crying into the darkness, scientists unable to communicate the fruits of their noble work to the masses, a swiftly changing world that threatens to sweep past us in its relentless changes. Oppenheimer's usual poetic language and lofty phrasing soften the darkness of his message, but a vision of a civilization both beautiful

and threatening in its complexity and fragmentation comes through loud and clear.

"Our histories and traditions—the very means of interpreting life—are both bonds and barriers among us," he observes. "Our knowledge separates as well as it unites; our orders disintegrate as well as bind; our art brings us together and sets us apart." Comparing the arts and sciences to "villages" connected by the "superhighways" of the mass media, he says that just as the mass media are the "purveyors of art and science and culture," they are also "the means by which the true human community . . . the individual sense of beauty are being blown dry and issueless, the means by which the passivity of the disengaged spectator presents to the man of art and science the bleak face of unhumanity."

OPTIONAL FORM NO. 10
MAY 1962 EDITION
GSA GEN. REG. NO. 27

UNITED STATES GOVERNMENT

Memorandum SECRET

TO : Director, FBI (100-17828)　　　　DATE: 5-2-66

FROM : Legat, Paris (105-347) (RUC)

SUBJECT: DR. J. ROBERT OPPENHEIMER
IS - R

ALL INFORMATION CONTAINED
HEREIN IS UNCLASSIFIED
EXCEPT WHERE SHOWN
OTHERWISE

(S)

The ████████████████████████████████████ advised on 4-28-66 that they have learned that an individual named OPPENHEIMER, who is probably identical with the well-known American atomic scientist, visited Paris for several days at the end of December, 1965. During his visit he was in contact with Dr. and Mrs. PIERRE BIQUARD. Dr. BIQUARD is a French official of the World Federation of Scientific Workers.

　　　　This is furnished for the information of the Bureau.

3 - Bureau (1 - Liaison Section)
1 - Paris
NWP:HD
(4)

CLASSIFIED BY
DECLASSIFY ON: 25X

CLASSIFIED DECISIONS FINALIZED
BY DEPARTMENT REVIEW COMMITTEE (DRC)
DATE:

Classified by
Exempt from GDS, Category
Date of Declassification Indefinite

ST-101

100-17828-2389

REC-32

MAY 5 1966

55 MAY 17 1966 SECRET

19

Quartet in C-sharp Minor

R obert Oppenheimer had never been a particularly robust individual. He had been a sickly youngster, and as a young man had suffered from a mild case of tuberculosis. Under the pressures of leading the bomb effort at Los Alamos, his weight fell to 115 pounds, dangerously thin for a man just under six feet tall. Throughout his adult life he had been markedly thin, sometimes almost frail in appearance, and physical descriptions of him in the press invariably commented on it. Along with the rarefied intellectual persona he projected, the almost birdlike delicacy of his physical presence added to the Oppenheimer mystique, to the sense of his being an almost otherworldly creature. He seemed to survive mostly on tobacco and drink rather than solid food, and friends could only attribute his ability to maintain such a busy schedule to sheer nervous energy.

But now he was looking increasingly worn, tired, beaten down, much older than a man still in his early sixties. His hair had already thinned and turned gray not long after the trials of 1954, but now he also had developed a pronounced stoop and moved more slowly.

During the Oppenheimers' holiday vacation at their beach cottage on St. John in the Virgin Islands, his cough persisted, accompanied by what he described as a "terrible sore throat." By the time he returned to the United States in January 1966, neither the cough nor the sore throat

was showing signs of improvement, and it was becoming clear that Oppenheimer had more than just a bad cold.

Finally, at Kitty's urging, he went to a doctor in New York. The doctor found a small lump in Oppenheimer's throat, which was promptly biopsied.

Oppenheimer had cancer.

Soon after, he underwent surgery and then began cobalt radiation treatments during a three-week stay at Sloan-Kettering Institute in New York. The radiation treatments continued after his discharge, with Oppenheimer commuting back and forth between Princeton and New York. The radiation drained and weakened him physically, and led to a terribly dry, irritated throat, which Oppenheimer attempted to soothe with throat lozenges—but the sugary lozenges exacerbated his already-bad dental problems, forcing him to submit to painful dental work on top of the debilitating radiation treatments.

By late spring, though, things seemed to be looking up. Oppenheimer was back at work at the Institute, although on a lighter schedule, and seemed optimistic about his chances. "His voice was stronger than usual, for he has always had a disappearing voice—and he seemed vigorous and almost gay," wrote David Lilienthal in his diary.

But such times were only moments, fleeting and elusive. A little over a month later, after visiting Oppenheimer, Lilienthal noted, "Robert wasting away. A terrible thing to see. . . . For the first time Robert himself is 'uncertain about the future,' as he says, so white and—scared."

Lilienthal also witnessed at close hand the effects of Oppenheimer's decline on those closest to him, particularly Kitty. "I asked her how Robert was getting along, and she bit her lip, her frail little body stiffened, a picture of a fighting woman. I leaned over and kissed her cheek." Kitty began to cry, then caught herself and regained control. She "shook it off, looked at me with that little-girl look and asked me if she looked all right now, could we go back and join the others? I have never admired the strength of a woman more."

But Lilienthal and others who knew and worked with Oppenheimer were noticing more than simply what Lilienthal called "this picture of deterioration."[1] To Freeman Dyson, one of Oppenheimer's first and most successful recruits at the Institute, it seemed that Oppenheimer's

"spirit grew stronger as his bodily powers declined. . . . He was simple, straightforward, and indomitably courageous." Although Dyson had not worked at Los Alamos and had not met Oppenheimer until well after the war, he now saw in Oppenheimer the qualities that had made him such a successful leader of that monumental effort: "a man carrying a crushing burden and still doing his job with such style and good humor that all of us around him felt uplifted by his example."[2]

In April 1966, a *New York Times* exposé of CIA covert operations revealed that the Congress for Cultural Freedom, the intellectual organization in which Oppenheimer had participated and supported for many years, was essentially a CIA front. The intelligence agency had set up the CCF in 1950 and financially supported it behind the scenes in order to promote the spread of prodemocracy, anti-Communist ideas.

"The purpose of this new organization was to bring together non-Communist leftist intellectuals in Europe to promote democracy, to undermine Communist influence, and to defeat the neutralist tendencies of many left-of-center European intellectuals," explains former CIA officer James M. Olson. The CIA also launched and supported the CCF journal *Encounter,* and through several agents on the editorial staff, gently guided the journal away from criticizing U.S. policy, although "in general the publication had editorial freedom," says Olson. Over the years, *Encounter* had published the words of distinguished thinkers including philosopher and mathematician Bertrand Russell, novelist Vladimir Nabokov, poet W. H. Auden, and novelist Jorge Luis Borges— not to mention J. Robert Oppenheimer. Most of them, however, had no inkling of the CCF's connection with the CIA. "The participants were not aware of CIA sponsorship," Olson writes.[3]

At least, not most of them. But Oppenheimer, as a leading member of the CCF, definitely knew of the CIA connection. He felt it justified because neither he nor any of his CCF colleagues had ever encountered any untoward influence from the CIA upon their activities with the organization. If an organization whose aims he passionately shared happened to benefit from under-the-table CIA support, and as long as the CIA never attempted to seriously subvert those views or the organization's objectives, then what was the harm, Oppenheimer apparently reasoned.

Joined by fellow CCF mavens George Kennan, Arthur Schlesinger,

and John Kenneth Galbraith, Oppenheimer wrote a letter to *The New York Times* in defense of the CCF. "We have no question regarding the independence of [the CCF's] policy, the integrity of its officials, or the value of its contribution," they said, emphasizing that the CCF "has been an entirely free body."[4] Oppenheimer and his colleagues supported the independence and integrity of the CCF without specifically denying its CIA backing. For them, their own motivations, intentions, and actions were clean; if the CIA chose to support them financially because its own aims happened to coincide with those of the CCF, so much the better. Still, the revelations and subsequent outcry eventually forced the CIA to sever its connections with the CCF by 1970.

By the summer, Oppenheimer was on a liquid diet because of the ravaged condition of his throat, but the cancer seemed to be under control. He managed to make it to that year's Seven Springs conference in New York State, and more important, to daughter Toni's graduation from Oberlin College. Though hobbled by a leg brace and walking with a cane due to a pinched nerve, he also accepted an honorary degree from Princeton University in June.

Oppenheimer's life had not been completely engulfed by his illness, and he had remained engaged in the wider world beyond his health, his family, and the Institute. His successor as Institute director, economist Dr. Carl Kaysen, had been named, and Oppenheimer (who declared himself "delighted" with the choice) was busy preparing for the change in administration. At the end of the month, his term as Institute director formally expired, and he became just another member of the faculty, a welcome relief from the stresses of the top job. Although obviously weakened and drained, he seemed to be free of the cancer, so he and Kitty departed for their usual summer vacation in St. John.

Back home, the doctors were guardedly optimistic. There was still no sign of recurrence, although Oppenheimer still complained of pain, which the doctors attributed to the aftereffects of the radiation treatments. Oppenheimer took off for Berkeley and the annual meeting of the American Physical Society, where he enjoyed visiting with many of his former students.

Meanwhile, as Philip Stern continued researching and working on his Oppenheimer book, the pesky matter of the Kipphardt play popped up again later in the year. Oppenheimer and his lawyers had so far

managed to dissuade eager producers from mounting an American production, and thought they had stopped a London premiere the previous year.

The lord chamberlain, whose responsibilities included theatrical censorship, had refused a license to the Royal Shakespeare Company to produce the play, because of an official restriction against portraying living people on the stage. But John Roberts, holder of the play's British rights, found a loophole: that restriction applied only to public theaters. So he arranged a production at the Little Hampstead Theatre Club, technically a private venue not subject to the authority of the lord chamberlain.

The critics were receptive but not overwhelmed, repeating many of the remarks that had greeted the previous productions: it was too documentary in approach, "not *theatre* in any artistic sense of the word"; "a sober courtroom piece"; but still "a night to make you thoughtful." Audience response was enthusiastic enough to inspire Roberts to reapply for permission to stage a public production.[5]

For Oppenheimer, it was a continuing annoyance, but by this point he lacked the energy or outrage to do anything substantial to stop the productions. "The miserable play, in one form or another, had hundreds of productions in Europe; so it goes," he wrote to a correspondent with resignation.[6]

More important concerns were now pressing upon him. With the Institute's new director assuming his duties and moving into the official residence at Olden Manor, Oppenheimer and his family finally moved into a smaller house near the Institute campus, while construction continued on the house promised them by the trustees. Bad enough to leave what had been a beloved home for almost twenty years, but worse, Oppenheimer's cancer had returned with a vengeance, now spreading into his tongue, palate, and left Eustachian tube. It was too widespread now for surgery to be practical, but doctors still held out some hope for a new round of radiation treatments. His dental problems and already raw throat only made the further radiation more debilitating.

But somehow, Oppenheimer managed to keep going, still working part-time at the Institute, still writing articles, still thinking and functioning. His weakness and the need to stay close to home for the

frequent radiation sessions forced him to cancel his usual travel schedule, even the holiday stay in St. John that had been a family tradition for over ten years now.

Although he was still hoping that his condition would improve enough for some planned trips in the new year, he had no illusions about his ultimate prospects. "I have to die some year, and mine has been a pretty good life," he told a friend.[7]

"What does such a man think, confronted with death, a man with his head so full of ideas, so wise in so many directions . . . ?" wondered Lilienthal in his journal. "What goes through his mind, what goes on behind those eyes that were once so brilliantly blue, now rather bleary with pain and probably drugs? What does he think of the inevitability he faces?"[8]

One thing he thinks of, no doubt, is his past: choices made, accomplishments and failures, regrets and satisfactions. For Oppenheimer, a man whose past always hung over him like a leaden shroud, at least after his public downfall, such thoughts would be both dark and sweet. A hint of them comes in a letter to his old student David Bohm, who, after seeing the Kipphardt play and a television show on Los Alamos, became concerned that his old teacher and friend might be carrying an unearned and unfair burden of guilt.

In response, Oppenheimer wrote in part: "My own feelings about responsibility and guilt have always had to do with the present, and so far in this life that has been more than enough to occupy me." Yet, for reasons known only to himself, he cut those words out of the letter he actually sent.[9]

Perhaps his feelings were better encompassed by the words of another man, physicist Sir James Chadwick, who sent a concerned note to Oppenheimer at the end of the year. Chadwick reflected, "Now that I am getting old my mind turns too often to the mistakes I have made in the past—and not only in scientific work. I reproach myself but I do not grieve."[10]

One of the projects Oppenheimer had been looking forward to and had mentioned in several interviews was writing a history of twentieth-century physics. Excited publishers had already contacted him with offers, even though he hadn't seriously begun any work. "But," he admitted to Lilienthal, "I am not quite up to it now, don't

have the necessary gusto. . . . perhaps in two or three months I'll be better." Brave words that didn't fool Lilienthal for a second: "I don't really believe he thinks so."[11]

Lilienthal was right. Less than a week into the new year, Oppenheimer learned that the latest round of radiation treatments had done no good. Doctors decided to try chemotherapy, but there was little hope. Oppenheimer was declining rapidly; his hearing was now affected, and he could barely eat or speak. Kitty quietly asked Oppenheimer's long-time and faithful secretary, Verna Hobson, to get her a gun so that, in case the cancer spread to his brain, he could take matters into his own hands.

And yet Oppenheimer refused to succumb completely. Despite his condition, he attended a committee meeting at the Institute to select new fellows for the coming academic year. "Oppenheimer came to the meeting as usual, although he well knew that he would not be there to welcome the new members on their arrival," Freeman Dyson recalled. Although he could speak only in a tortured whisper, Oppenheimer had "done his homework" and managed to make his opinions known on the new candidates.

The meeting was on a Wednesday. Three days later, on Saturday, February 18, 1967, Robert Oppenheimer fell into a deep sleep from which he never awakened, and died later that evening. He was cremated two days later.

Officially, of course, according to the United States government, he was still a security risk.

The next day the passing of J. Robert Oppenheimer was front-page news around the world, beginning with *The New York Times*. "J. Robert Oppenheimer, Atom Bomb Pioneer, Dies," read the headline. "Physicist Cancer Victim—Censured and Later Honored by the AEC."

Even in death, Oppenheimer was a figure of ambivalence—a great man tainted by circumstance, somehow marked with darkness. The words "alleged association with Communists," "fundamental defects in character," and "security risk" were still irrevocably linked to his name, along with his admission to being "an idiot." The *Times* article featured a long, detailed biography and many photos, as befitting a public figure of Oppenheimer's status. But the mark placed there years ago by

William Borden, Lewis Strauss, and his other enemies remained—time, Fermi Award, and supposed "rehabilitation" notwithstanding.

Accolades, remembrances, and well wishes came in a flood to the family. David Lilienthal happened to be in Saigon on a visit as a special presidential adviser when he learned of Oppenheimer's death through an Associated Press reporter who contacted him for comment.

"The world has lost a noble spirit," he said, "a genius who brought together poetry and science. Those of us who were his friends and neighbors know that life for us will never be the same."[12] That was the official statement Lilienthal gave to the press, but to Kitty he wrote: "Out here, where violent death is an hourly occurrence, and the rumble of bombs commonplace, the death of so sweet and noble a man can't be reconciled with the beauty of a world he graced. How *much* it meant to me, those Saturday afternoon little visits. What a game and strong man; it is only the strong who can be as gentle and sensitive."[13]

Lyndon Johnson, the man who had disregarded political risk by personally giving Oppenheimer the Fermi Award when he could easily have avoided it, said he was "greatly saddened by Dr. Oppenheimer's death. . . . Dr. Oppenheimer was not only a great scientist but also a great humanitarian. He understood fully the implications of his work and did what he could to assure that the world would be a better place in which to live. The world will miss his genius."[14]

Oppenheimer's scientific brethren were especially affected. For Hans Bethe, it was "as if an older brother had died." AEC chairman Glenn Seaborg called his death "a tremendous loss. . . . he was one of the greatest theoretical physicists of this century." I. I. Rabi called Oppenheimer "fantastically magnetic, charismatic" and credited him with being "one of the greatest sources of scientific strength" for the United States. John Wheeler said that he couldn't "think of anyone else who could have brought that Los Alamos team together." Even the Japanese, in the person of physicist Dr. Hideki Yukawa, called Oppenheimer "a symbol of the tragedy of modern nuclear scientists."[15]

The New York Times editorialized that Oppenheimer was "an extraordinarily gifted man who led an extraordinarily dramatic life" and that for him, "the greatest disappointment of his life was probably the realization that he just missed ranking among the great immortals of nuclear physics. . . . his personal achievements in his chosen field were far

less important than those of a Fermi or a Bohr, let alone Einstein."[16] In this, *The Times* was inadvertently echoing some of Oppenheimer's former critics, including Senator Hickenlooper and even Haakon Chevalier, who claimed that he "made no fundamental contribution to his field."

But while it is certainly true that Oppenheimer never authored a paradigm-shifting discovery such as relativity or quantum theory, the present-day physicists who still employ techniques such as the Born-Oppenheimer approximation or the Oppenheimer-Phillips process might disagree that he made no significant contributions to physics. Former Institute for Advanced Study physicist Jeremy Bernstein believes that had Oppenheimer lived longer, and perhaps devoted more attention to physics in his later years, "the pioneering work that he and his students did on neutron stars and black holes would have, I am convinced, been widely honored, possibly by a Nobel Prize."[17]

Perhaps the reason such honors eluded Oppenheimer was that he tended to be too much of a generalist who "spread his intellectual energy too broadly," as Robert Serber said to Abraham Pais.[18] Pais, who had also worked with Oppenheimer at the Institute, believed that Oppenheimer was never completely satisfied with his scientific work.

Freeman Dyson agrees. "It's certainly the case that he was dissatisfied with himself, there's no doubt," he says. Dyson also shares Bernstein's opinion about the importance of Oppenheimer's early black hole research, published in 1939. "It was a fundamentally important piece of work that really nailed down black holes as something real." Yet Oppenheimer never followed up on the work, never developed it further, to Dyson's puzzlement: "For some stupid reason Oppenheimer never took any credit for that. It didn't even interest him. I found that very strange. I tried to talk with him about it sometimes, but he just said, well, I'm not interested in that anymore."[19]

So it would be less as a scientist than as a scientific leader, administrator, and intellectual that he would be remembered—and, always, as a controversial figure. None of the obituaries and articles and editorials marking Oppenheimer's passing could avoid the truth that, whatever one thought of him, his life, and his work, his name would never be as untainted as Einstein's, his legacy never as pure and idealized. If he was "the father of the atomic bomb," then he was just as much the "scientific

martyr to McCarthyism," the "twentieth-century Galileo/Dreyfus/ Faust," the "tormented, morally conflicted scientist."

Those complex and sometimes conflicting perceptions of him were in evidence even in his own memorial service, held on Saturday, February 25, on what was by all accounts a bitterly cold but clear, bright day. Coldness joining hands with brilliant light—a poetically appropriate setting in which to honor J. Robert Oppenheimer.

The commemoration began at his old home, Olden Manor, with a buffet lunch. Lilienthal was there, along with Lloyd Garrison, General Leslie R. Groves, George Kennan, the daughter of Albert Einstein, and most of the other important figures of his life: Nobel Prize–winning scientists, senators, poets, artists, statesmen. Notably absent were Lewis Strauss and Edward Teller, but that was probably just as well, considering the resentment and anger their presence would have evoked in some of those present, starting with Kitty Oppenheimer.

After the luncheon, the guests moved to Princeton University's Alexander Hall for the formal memorial service. Aside from the friends and colleagues who had begun the day at Olden Manor, Alexander Hall was soon packed with over six hundred others who had come to pay their respects. There was music: Igor Stravinsky's *Requiem Canticles,* chosen by Oppenheimer friend George Balanchine, director of the New York City Ballet. Although the Juilliard String Quartet was also present, the Stravinsky piece was played from a tape. Abraham Pais remembered the effect as *"extremely* eerie. An empty stage with but the chairs and music stands for a quartet . . . a lectern without speaker . . . and the new sounds of a Dies Irae coming from a big loudspeaker."[20]

When the music ended, Hans Bethe went to the lectern to deliver the first of three eulogies. Bethe spoke of Oppenheimer both as a scientist and as a government adviser, calling him "a leader . . . who brought out the best in us. . . . he did more than any other man to make American theoretical physics great."

Bethe was followed by Henry DeWolf Smyth, the physicist and former AEC commissioner who had cast the sole dissenting vote in favor of restoring Oppenheimer's security clearance in 1954, against enormous pressure from Lewis Strauss and the other commissioners. Smyth's presence at the service, not to mention his words, made clear that the security debacle would forever be linked with and help to define Robert

Oppenheimer's life just as surely as his leadership of Los Alamos. "Such a wrong can never be righted," Smyth declared. "Such a blot on our history can never be erased."

Finally there was George Kennan, the statesman and scholar whom Oppenheimer had brought to the Institute and defended when some of the faculty thought that he didn't belong there and lacked the sufficient eminence required of an Institute member. Kennan spoke of Oppenheimer both as scientist and administrator, and also as a human being. "He was a man of great erudition and discrimination in the humanities as well as in the natural sciences. . . . it is less well known . . . that he was also a man who had a deep yearning for friendship, for companionship, for the warmth and richness of human communication. The arrogance which to many appeared to be a part of his personality masked in reality an overpowering desire to bestow and receive affection. Neither circumstances nor at times the asperities of his own temperament permitted the gratification of this need in a measure remotely approaching its intensity; and in this too lay a portion of that strong element of tragedy which all who knew him sensed, I think, in his situation."

Oppenheimer's life, said Kennan, was "full of contrasts: of hope and disappointment, of conflict and harmony, of understanding and misunderstanding. It was a life full of pain and struggle." And yet, "Robert Oppenheimer's arm was one which, in this common, confused struggle, was always generously extended to those who wished to lean on it—extended, if in no other way, through the strength of his effort of understanding, and his readiness—indeed his eagerness—to share that effort with others."

Following the eulogies, the Juilliard String Quartet played two movements, the adagio and allegro, of Beethoven's Quartet in C-sharp Minor, no. 14, Opus 131, one of Oppenheimer's favorite pieces of music and chosen by himself for this occasion several months earlier. One of Beethoven's final compositions, its dark, near-impenetrable complexity, its abstractedness coupled with its deep emotional resonance, made it the perfect elegy for a man as darkly complex and impenetrable as J. Robert Oppenheimer.

After the service, widow Kitty and brother Frank held a quiet reception in the Institute for Advanced Study's new library, the one that

Oppenheimer had championed and seen through to completion. A few weeks later, Kitty took his ashes to St. John and, rather than scattering them in the water, dropped the urn into the sea, within sight of the beach cottage where they had spent so many happy times.

* * *

Oppenheimer offers no ready answers for this dilemma. "This is a world in which each of us, knowing his limitations, knowing the evils of superficiality and the terrors of fatigue, will have to cling to what is close to him, to what he knows, to what he can do, to his friends and his tradition and his love, lest he be dissolved in a universal confusion and know nothing and love nothing," he declares. "This cannot be an easy life. We shall have a rugged time of it to keep our minds open and to keep them deep, to keep our sense of beauty and our ability to make it, and our occasional ability to see it, in places remote and strange and unfamiliar; we shall have a rugged time of it, all of us, in keeping those gardens in our villages, in keeping open the manifold, intricate, casual paths, to keep these flourishing in a great open windy world; but this is, as I see it, the condition of man; and in this condition we can help, because we can love one another."[21]

An atomic scientist—the atomic scientist, the man who had built the bomb—talking about loneliness and beauty and loving one another? It could only have been Oppenheimer, and yet the Columbia address was markedly different from any of his previous public pronouncements. Despite its dark tone, or perhaps because of it, the address seemed to move many people and inspired a fair amount of commentary, and not simply because it had put Oppenheimer back into the public spotlight. Like so many of his pronouncements, it was enigmatic and deep, lending itself to the interpretative whims of those who heard it. Historian David Cassidy calls it "a portrait of intellectual despair much in keeping with the fragmented vision that he must now have had of himself as a scientist and a human being."[22] The New York Times published the speech in its entirety, calling Oppenheimer's words "wise and beautiful."[23]

The speech seems to be the words of an individual who has lost faith in the workings of the world, in the political, cultural, and moral systems humanity has devised to govern itself, and yet a man who hasn't quite lost his belief in the fundamental value of human interaction and congress on a more personal and direct level. No doubt Oppenheimer's words reflected the state of his mind and

heart as he recovered from his own personal ordeal, but he would never have thought to reveal his private pain in such a way. Not only would it be against his nature, but this was an age long before tell-all memoirs and juicy public confessionals were considered proper or expected, much less accepted as high culture. Whether he was subconsciously attempting to project his own pain onto the broader world canvas in his usual poetic and somewhat obfuscatory way, or whether he sincerely believed in the pessimistic assessment of human affairs that he presented in the speech, no one can say.

4-572 (Rev. 7-18-63)

OPTIONAL FORM NO. 10
MAY 1962 EDITION
GSA GEN. REG. NO. 27

UNITED STATES GOVERNMENT

Memorandum

TO : The Director DATE:

FROM : N. P. Callahan.

SUBJECT: The Congressional Record

Pages S2267-S2269. Senator Fulbright (D) Arkansas, stated
"J. Robert Oppenheimer is dead. Let us remember not only what his special
genius did for us; let us also remember what we did to him. - - - I ask
unanimous consent that an impressive and thought provoking obituary of
Dr. Oppenheimer, written by Alfred Friendly of the Washington Post, be printed
in the Record." The article indicated that "In November, 1953, William L.
Borden, former executive secretary of the Joint Atomic Energy Committee, who
had studied Oppenheimer's security file, wrote to FBI director J. Edgar Hoover
proclaiming that 'more probably than not J. Robert Oppenheimer is an agent
of the Soviet Union.' Hoover, in turn, sent the letter and Oppenheimer's file
to the AEC."

100 - 17828

14 MAR 2

In the original of a memorandum captioned and dated as above, the Congressional
Record for was reviewed and pertinent items were
marked for the Director's attention. This form has been prepared in order that
a copy of the original memorandum may be clipped, mounted, and placed
in appropriate Bureau case or subject matter files.

20

The Persistence of Dignity

Only a few days before the memorial service in Princeton, Henry DeWolf Smyth spoke at a meeting of the International Atomic Energy Agency in Vienna—a meeting that Oppenheimer, barring his illness and death, would probably have attended.

"It is sometimes said that we all had a sense of guilt," Smyth observed. "This is not true. We had a feeling of regret which is something quite different. We regretted that the laws of nature permitted the development of atomic weapons."[1]

There was no doubt that Oppenheimer, along with most of his other Los Alamos colleagues, shared that regret, and that he had spent the remainder of his life trying to come to terms with it in some way, and to help his country and the world do likewise. But for the public and press, intellectual regret and moral guilt were easy to conflate and confuse. By the time they were acknowledged and confirmed in the various remembrances, retrospectives, and tributes that followed in the months after Oppenheimer's death, the guilty/regretful scientist trope was irrevocably a part of the Oppenheimer image, the definition of how he would be remembered, as indelible as the "security risk" label had proved to be during his life.

About a year after Oppenheimer's death, Kitty completed the process of turning over his papers to the Library of Congress, so that what he had once called a "hideously complete archive" would be available to

historians and scholars. The papers contained correspondence, speeches, appointment books, clippings, declassified government records—about seventy-five thousand items, a collection that would be added to considerably in the following years. Fortunately for the library archivists, Oppenheimer had already organized the papers fairly well before his death, and they largely followed his own scheme in cataloging the material for the library.

But comparatively few people would ever delve into the real Oppenheimer contained, admittedly only partially, in the hundreds of archival boxes at the Library of Congress. For most of the world, the Robert Oppenheimer legend was already well established. It would receive another big boost when the Kipphardt play finally made its long-awaited, long-delayed American premiere, in the spring of 1968 at the Mark Taper Forum in Los Angeles. Oppenheimer was no longer around to try blocking the play, and Kitty wasn't interested in bothering to obstruct the production.

With the distinguished American actor Joseph Wiseman assaying the role of Oppenheimer with just the right tone of tormented dignity, the Los Angeles premiere enjoyed much the same accolades and enthusiastic response the play had garnered on the other side of the Atlantic. It was an event important enough for *New York Times* theater critic Clive Barnes to fly three thousand miles from his home base to see and review it personally.

"Oppenheimer emerges as a tragic fool and genius," he noted. Even though it was definitely "documentary theater," for Barnes "the forcefulness of the tragedy is enhanced by its historic truthfulness." Barnes concluded that "this is precisely the kind of play one would like to see on Broadway; perfectly conventional in its manner, but engrossing in its ideas and arguments and, at the very least, provocative in its basic concept."[2]

A year later, Barnes got his wish when the play made its Broadway premiere at the Vivian Beaumont Theater, again with Wiseman as Oppenheimer and most of the Los Angeles cast remaining. Both American versions contained a few interesting alterations, however: some of the character names were changed for the L.A. and New York productions. Thus, for example, I. I. Rabi begat "Jacob Lehmann" on the stage, not that anyone familiar at all with the case was confused by who was

supposed to be whom. But one critic found the name changes a "bizarre feature" of the play. "It seems that the real names were removed on the advice of lawyers, libel suits being feared." If such legal advice was valid, "then the laws obviously need changing to permit documentary drama to exist." But if that was true, why was it necessary to change some names and not others? Whatever the reasons, such "lawyers' games" highlighted the already troubled conflicts and tension between the reality of the case and Kipphardt's dramatic alterations of history.[3]

Barnes was just as enchanted by the Broadway production as by the American premiere in Los Angeles. "It is a talkative, stimulating and intellectually engaging evening," he wrote. He wondered how many people in the audience thought Oppenheimer vindicated by the play's portrayal of the hearing ordeal. Whatever impressions of Oppenheimer and his character they might take away from the work, the questions raised and addressed were worth contemplating. "It is good to have a play in town that offers a little nourishment for thought and discussion."[4]

Some of those directly involved in the hearing, now finally getting a chance to see the play after all the commotion over its existence, found it both fascinating and disturbing. David Lilienthal caught the Broadway production and felt it "a weird and personally distasteful experience" because of the unpleasant memories it stirred of "that half-nightmare of security phobia throughout my term as Chairman of AEC, and the later ugly persecution of Robert Oppenheimer." It also reminded Lilienthal of how he had been forced to apply those same measures of "false security" during his tenure at the AEC. Still, he thought the play "a surprisingly good construction of a drama out of facts still fresh in people's minds."[5]

Others found it less convincing. IAS faculty member Jeremy Bernstein, who had personally known many of the main characters from Oppenheimer on down, found "very little resemblance" to his friends: "Rabi, for example, came across as someone who might be at home managing a delicatessen."[6]

But the play was still only a play, acknowledged as a dramatic interpretation of truth rather than the truth itself, whatever its influence and effects on the Oppenheimer legend. Later in 1969 came the first major factual look at Oppenheimer since his death with the publication

of Philip Stern's book, now entitled *The Oppenheimer Case: Security on Trial.*

As the subtitle implied, and in accordance with the intentions he'd expressed to Oppenheimer some years earlier, Stern's focus reached much further than simply the Oppenheimer case itself. He used Oppenheimer's ordeal as a lens through which to scrutinize America's entire security and secrecy establishment—the hidden dossiers, the denial and granting of security clearances, the destructive power of arbitrarily applied criteria and evidence in the lives of American citizens. And although the book dealt with events of decades past, Stern made it very clear that the issues involved were wholly relevant to contemporary America, with the nation torn apart by dissent over an unpopular war. As Gerald Holton mentioned in *The New York Times Book Review:* "In the current atmosphere of high-level attacks on dissent, and in the battle to reassert civilian control over national destiny, the book may well provide a scenario for analogous events that are foreseeable for the early seventies"—an eerily prescient comment for a time when Watergate, officially sanctioned "dirty tricks" against political opponents, and White House "enemies lists" were just over the horizon.[7]

But Stern's signal achievement was writing the most detailed recounting and analysis yet achieved of the Oppenheimer security case. Stern traces the origins of Oppenheimer's downfall from its earliest seeds, including Oppenheimer's leftist meanderings, his political naïveté, and his knack for making friends and enemies, to the way in which the initially loose and vague forces opposing him came together steadily and inexorably under the direction of determined foes such as Lewis Strauss, Edward Teller, and military factions, slowly drawing around Oppenheimer a net of accusation and suspicion, until the Borden letter to J. Edgar Hoover provided the means to close and pull the net tight. And he demonstrates how Oppenheimer's own flaws and missteps contributed to his own downfall.

As we have seen, although he supported the project, Oppenheimer had declined to speak to Stern directly. But unlike any of the other Oppenheimer works published up to the time, Stern's book still benefited from the direct cooperation and participation of many of the principal figures on both sides of the case. Lloyd Garrison provided a lengthy account of his conduct of the hearing, which Stern includes verbatim in

an appendix. Even Roger Robb sat down with Stern for several in-depth interviews. When Stern asked him if, looking back on the entire Oppenheimer episode, he would do anything differently, Robb laughed and said he would probably not take the case at all. In a confidential account of his encounters with Stern he later provided to the FBI, Robb said that he told Stern that "having undertaken the case as a matter of public service and professional duty I had been libeled, slandered, and sniped at ever since and I was tired of it."[8]

The Oppenheimer Case enjoyed excellent reviews and was immediately recognized as an important work by critics and historians, but perhaps the best indication of its impact is that it had the power to rouse the aged Lewis Strauss out of retirement to complain about it. Responding to a review of the book in *Science,* Strauss claimed it gave "further currency to a pernicious myth"—essentially, that the AEC's condemnation of Oppenheimer had been in error and unjust.[9]

Strauss's letter to the editor was never published in *Science,* but the episode provides another example of how, even with Oppenheimer long gone (but still officially a security risk), Strauss found himself unable to let go, still desperate to have the last word, still refusing to admit any possibility of error, excess, or injustice in the Oppenheimer affair. He died in 1974, to the end stubbornly clinging to his belief in his own rectitude.

As the years passed and America struggled with fresh crises and conflicts beyond those of Oppenheimer's lifetime—with the persistent exception of the cold war and the omnipresent danger of nuclear Armageddon—Oppenheimer slowly, gently dissolved into the dimness of history, a process accelerated by the passing of important figures in his life.

While captaining her yacht on a worldwide cruise in 1972 with former Oppenheimer friend and colleague Robert Serber, with whom she had become involved in the years since Robert's death, Kitty fell suddenly ill as the craft passed Central America. She was hospitalized with an intestinal infection and an embolism in Panama City, deteriorated rapidly, and died on October 27, far from Princeton but closer to the Caribbean Sea into which her husband's remains had been cast over five years earlier. Her ashes were scattered in the same place. Like her husband, she had been only sixty-two years old at her death.

Daughter Toni had not led an easy life, suffering through several divorces and depression. Her father's past came back to haunt her in 1969 when she applied for a job as a translator at the United Nations. She couldn't get the required security clearance when an FBI background check exhumed Oppenheimer's never-cleared security-risk status. Eventually she moved to the comfort and isolation of St. John, and on one afternoon in 1977, alone and despondent, she hanged herself in the Oppenheimer beach cottage, only thirty-two years old.

Son Peter, estranged from his mother for many years, found a quiet life as a contractor and carpenter in New Mexico, having inherited his father's deep love and connection with that land. He still lives there today.

Oppenheimer's younger brother Frank slowly managed to emerge from the shadow of his own persecution and found his way back into physics. After teaching and doing research at the University of Colorado for a number of years, he went on to found one of the world's first "hands-on," interactive science museums, the San Francisco Exploratorium, in 1969, and ran the museum until his death in 1985.

In 1971, a group of Oppenheimer friends, colleagues, and Los Alamos residents joined to form the J. Robert Oppenheimer Memorial Committee. The committee planned to honor Oppenheimer by constructing "a quiet park at Los Alamos in the mountains of New Mexico as a site for a memorial sculpture to be dedicated as a symbol of the affection and esteem of those who will always remember him."[10]

The committee also established an annual series of lectures at Los Alamos in Oppenheimer's name. George Kennan gave the first of these in 1972, followed in subsequent years by luminaries including Linus Pauling, Hans Bethe, I. I. Rabi, and Murray Gell-Mann. The lecture series continues to the present, covering the entire universe of scientific and cultural matters, as wide-ranging and intellectually cosmopolitan as its namesake.

But the memorial park was never built. Instead, the committee decided that the money would be better spent—and that it would be more in keeping with the spirit and memory of Oppenheimer—to establish a science scholarship fund for promising high school seniors. Begun in 1984, the scholarship program also continues, and the committee continues to sponsor various events, publications, and other edu-

cational activities in Oppenheimer's name. Oppenheimer needs no formal, physical memorial, at least not in Los Alamos, where he continues to be ever present, both in the town and in the laboratory. Buildings, streets, even cafeteria sandwiches proudly bear his name.

The Oppenheimer Memorial Committee would not be the only custodians of Oppenheimer's memory and public image. Many books would follow Stern's, examining the security hearing and Oppenheimer's life. But it would not be until 2005 when a truly comprehensive Oppenheimer biography would appear, Kai Bird and Martin Sherwin's *American Prometheus: The Triumph and Tragedy of J. Robert Oppenheimer.* Awarded a Pulitzer Prize, Bird and Sherwin's work is generally recognized as the current gold standard on the subject.

Still, most scholars also note that, as historian Barton Bernstein declared in a 2004 centennial symposium at Berkeley, "Oppenheimer is not the kind of subject . . . for whom there will ever be a 'definitive' biography—too much of his life will remain subject to interpretive dispute."[11] The question of whether or not Oppenheimer was ever truly a Communist Party member, what was actually said in that kitchen in the "Chevalier incident," why Oppenheimer did and said such seemingly contradictory and self-damaging things—such are only a few of the issues that continue to perplex historians and fuel scholarly debates.

For the general public, however, such questions aren't even on the radar. Theirs is the Oppenheimer of basic history, the father of the atomic bomb, and most pervasively, the Oppenheimer of the popular media: film, television, fiction, and even theater.

In 1977, filmmaker Jon Else began working on a documentary film on Oppenheimer, entitled *The Day After Trinity.* Containing interviews with many of the then-living colleagues, friends, and even foes of Oppenheimer (including Haakon Chevalier), the film was released in 1981 and honored by an Academy Award nomination. *The Day After Trinity* highlights Oppenheimer in all his frustrating, elusive complexity. Even now, over twenty years after its release, it remains an invaluable and fascinating portrait, an indispensable document of the man.

A BBC miniseries in 1980 entitled *Oppenheimer* proved to be somewhat less satisfying, despite excellent performances from Sam Waterston as Oppenheimer and David Suchet as Teller. Producer Peter

Goodchild strove for accuracy and fairness, conducting extensive research and personally interviewing many principal figures. But like Kipphardt, he ultimately faced the conflict between truth and the practical necessities of creating what was, in the end, popular entertainment: events, conversations, personalities, had to be altered, added, or omitted for effect. To accompany the series, Goodchild penned a well-received Oppenheimer biography, but the series itself could only suffer a bit from the inevitable sacrifices of historical accuracy to dramatic effect.

To one degree or another, most of the fictional representations of Robert Oppenheimer since his death (even including an opera, *Doctor Atomic,* by the major American composer John Adams and director Peter Sellars)* are suffused with what has become the romanticized, idealized, iconic image of him: the tormented, guilt-ridden atomic scientist, the Bhagavad Gita–quoting philosopher, the tweedy intellectual who liked to make dense poetic statements. It's an image that's equal portions Jungk, Chevalier, Kipphardt, and Oppenheimer himself, mixed in with the press coverage pro and con, the record of the security hearing, the passionate proclamations of all his many defenders and critics over the past decades.

Like the man himself, it's contradictory, perplexing, confusing, and elusive. Truth and myth, accuracy and pretension: as Jon Else notes, "we have in fact a cascade of many public Oppenheimers. We get about two a generation. . . . Each of those public Oppenheimers is a construction." All of them contain some element of truth and myth, and yet they fail to come together, to focus sharply into one clear image of what might be called "the public Oppenheimer." Else observes, "You cannot fit him into meaning one thing. McCarthyism is a shorthand for just one thing. But the very fact that Oppenheimer is such a wonderful bundle of contradictions and conundrums is what makes it very hard for us to have a single public image."[12]

For some, even over half a century after his removal from public service, Oppenheimer remains the Security Risk, a figure ever stained with the mark of disloyalty and treason and official mistrust. A 2002

* Something that would no doubt have both greatly chagrined and amused the notoriously opera-hating Oppenheimer.

article about the security hearing published by this book's author in *American History* magazine roused one indignant reader to complain to the editor about Oppenheimer's "disloyalty" and "character flaws" in words that could have come from Fulton Lewis, Medford Evans, or any of the legion of critics who spewed forth anti-Oppenheimer columns, articles, letters to the editor, or warnings to the FBI in the 1950s. Some things, indeed, never change.

One of Oppenheimer's more neglected personas, and yet one that has proven more valuable and significant in the years since, was the role he created for himself as a freewheeling, globe-trotting, unofficial ambassador of science, the American scientific community, and the philosophies, goals, and objectives of the international scientific fraternity. Few others took up such a role during the 1950s and 1960s, and none with as much aplomb, energy, and dedication as Oppenheimer. Einstein was too old and frail by that time, and most other scientific figures of sufficient gravitas were hampered by their political or professional commitments and affiliations, unable or unwilling to speak completely openly because they were bound by security clearances, academic timidity, political hostility, or simple fear.

Ironically, as Oppenheimer frequently noted, while his removal from government and his position of power distanced him from the insider information that would make it possible for him to speak confidently on many issues, it also liberated him to express himself with a freedom he hadn't enjoyed as a government servant. He didn't have to worry about stepping on official toes when he commented on civil defense, nuclear testing, defense policy; he was as free to give speeches and make public pronouncements as any other American citizen. And while he might be criticized and condemned and called "disloyal" by Fulton Lewis and the *National Review* for speaking his mind, he couldn't be fired, suspended, or otherwise silenced.

While he never abused his freedom of speech, and never criticized American politics and policy as much as he could have (and as much as some believe he should have, given his position of moral authority and public celebrity), he did occasionally take advantage of the lack of an official muzzle on him, particularly in his later years. Perhaps one reason he never became a political gadfly and activist as did other scientists such as Linus Pauling and Leo Szilard was, for the initial years after the

hearing, some hope that his clearance might still be restored and an understandable reluctance to thwart that prospect. And in his last years, it was probably simple weariness, not to mention a certain cynical belief that nothing he might say would be heard and heeded by those in power, more than anything else that kept his tongue reined in. As former IAS member Stanley Deser says, "Grand old men often gravitate to the big picture and he would anyway only convince the converted."[13]

But even if Oppenheimer mostly avoided politics and tended more toward the broader, safer world of philosophy in his public words, his travels, lectures, and tours helped to bring science and the scientific viewpoint to the public and the world at large. By his skillful administration of the Institute for Advanced Study, he helped to build vitally important alliances and open communications among scientists, policymakers, and political figures all over the world.

In a world that is, as Carl Sagan once observed, "exquisitely dependent on science and technology, in which hardly anyone knows anything about science and technology," scientific diplomacy of the type pioneered by Oppenheimer is increasingly critical. The journal *Science* noted early in 2007 that "science diplomacy has played an important, if underappreciated, role in U.S. foreign policy over the past 50 years," and declared that "it is time to adopt science diplomacy for a new era." Aside from enhancing the international image of the United States, such efforts "promote education, economic growth, human well-being, and hope. . . . The fact that science is, and should remain, outside the realm of politics only makes scientists better suited for this task."[14] Contemporary scientists seeking an example of how such an effort might work could do worse than follow the model of Oppenheimer's travels and lectures of the 1950s.

Oppenheimer will remain one of those frustrating, elusive figures who will forever taunt us with unanswered questions and unresolved dilemmas. Lacking a single dominant public persona, such as a Washington or a Lincoln or even a McCarthy, he will continue to serve as a handy figure to be used for various agendas: the martyr of McCarthyism; the tormented atomic scientist; the 1930s leftist political radical; the sneaky, untrustworthy, disloyal Communist sympathizer; the heroic scientific genius who won World War II.

Even those who knew him closely disagree on Oppenheimer, who he was, the hows and whys of his personality. That his fall from grace profoundly changed him and indelibly affected the remainder of his life is certain. But friends and colleagues have never agreed on how. Did the security hearing "destroy" him, turn him into a shadow of his former self, the vibrant, energetic man who had led Los Alamos? Or did the experience of 1954 and the loss of his clearance change him for the better, make him into a more patient, thoughtful, serene, relaxed person? It's easy to find arguments on both sides from those who knew the man, and they can be equally convincing.

That ambivalence extends to feelings about the man himself. Abraham Pais wrote that he was convinced that a love-hate relationship was the right response to a person as complicated as Oppenheimer. Calling him "this man, so gifted, so tortured, so sweet, so cruel," Pais observed, "In all my life I have never known a personality more complex than Robert Oppenheimer. . . . More strongly than before I feel compassion for a man who could never find enough satisfaction with his signal achievements, who forever was compelled to reach for more. That, not the hearings, was his tragedy, and caused him to have a wretched life." Friend and colleague George Kennan simply wondered, "Could there, I wonder, be anyone harder to describe than he?"[15]

There's also no question that Oppenheimer could and did play to the audience as he saw fit. Freeman Dyson has remarked on Oppenheimer's talent for "self-dramatization," and Dyson was far from the only colleague to notice the trait. Jeremy Bernstein wrote, "I have often wondered whether a little of what people saw afterward [after the hearing] was something Oppenheimer wanted them to see."[16] Oppenheimer could put on a most convincing pose as a martyr and victim, but just as easily could play the stoic, unbending, silent but strong hero. In truth, he was both, in large parts and at different times.

In the twilight years of his life after the security episode, however, Oppenheimer did more than "prove that a security risk can survive," transform himself into a public poet-philosopher and roving ambassador of science, or merely keep the Institute for Advanced Study running. If he never found complete affirmation and redemption as a world-class scientist of Nobel caliber or a universally respected and sought-after public servant, if he never regained the official trust and

confidence of his own country, and if the stain placed upon his name by that country never quite washed off, he still managed to lead a conflicted, contradictory, quintessentially human life, filled with darkness and light, despair and hope, coldness and warmth.

His legacy as a scientist will never match that of his idol, Niels Bohr, or Einstein. He will always be a figure of unanswered questions, of controversy, of contention. His name will always be associated with and used as an example of one of the darkest eras in American political and social history, and forever tainted by that association. As Jeremy Bernstein observes, "With Oppenheimer there is no end to anything."[17]

But with all else that is positive and negative, good and bad, bright and dark, about Robert Oppenheimer, his final years also stand as an example of grace, courage, and basic human dignity in the face of injustice, contempt, and exile. That simple truth, as much as all the rest, remains part of the legacy of J. Robert Oppenheimer.

*　*　*

Although no one realized it at the time, probably not even Oppenheimer himself, the Columbia address was the first step in his evolution from the oracle of the atom to public philosopher-at-large, its elegiac tone providing a fitting coda to what was probably the most painful year in Oppenheimer's life. Whatever the "prospects in the arts and sciences" might have been, the prospects for Robert Oppenheimer at the end of 1954 were far from certain. How would his standing be affected by his public humiliation? He had been reappointed as director of the Institute for Advanced Study, at least, but what would that mean now? Would he be able to concentrate on his first and abiding love, science, and finally achieve something substantial that didn't involve building weapons? How would he deal with watching the United States and the Soviet Union continue on their shaky courses, "two scorpions in a bottle," as he had once called them, teetering at the edge of destruction, with him unable and unwelcome to participate by giving his counsel?

"Last year when I extended to you my best wishes for the new year I could never in my wildest dreams have forseen {sic} the series of cruel events which marked 1954," wrote friend and former AEC chairman Gordon Dean to Oppenheimer just before Christmas. "I do nevertheless at this time wish for you everything good and satisfying—the reestablishment of your good name, a

swelling in the ranks of your already countless admirers, much health and happiness."[18] *Oppenheimer no doubt wished the same, but whether those wishes would be realized was something no one could predict.*

Still, with the Columbia lecture, Oppenheimer had begun a slow and halting return to the public stage. He had demonstrated to the world that while beaten, he was perhaps not fully broken, and that he would still be heard from, that he had been humbled but not completely silenced. That fact was about to be even more significantly demonstrated. Shortly before the end of the year, Princeton was visited by two men from New York who were about to do their best not only to keep Oppenheimer alive in the public consciousness, but to introduce him to the American people in a way that they had never seen him before.

AFTERWORD AND ACKNOWLEDGMENTS

I didn't realize it until far too late, but there are few endeavors more intimidating than attempting to write a book, any sort of book, about J. Robert Oppenheimer.

First, one has to confront both the large volume and great quality of all that's been done before. Eminent historians, seasoned journalists, admiring (and not-so-admiring) colleagues, and even personal enemies have been writing books of all sorts about Oppenheimer since at least 1945, when he first burst upon the world's stage. Two of those volumes have been awarded Pulitzer Prizes (Richard Rhodes's *The Making of the Atomic Bomb* and Kai Bird and Martin Sherwin's recent *American Prometheus*), giving the Oppenheimer scribe a couple of very tough acts to follow.

So I decided that rather than trying to compete directly with those illustrious works by covering by-now-familiar ground (Oppie's early scientific work, his leadership of the Manhattan Project, his postwar career as a scientific adviser to the government, and the security hearing that stripped him of his vast power and influence), I would take a different tack. I would focus on a period of Oppenheimer's story that all the other books seemed to gloss over or dismiss briefly in a few closing paragraphs. They all seemed to end with Oppenheimer removed from public service and exiled to the Institute for Advanced Study in Princeton until his death in 1967.

What was the rest of the story? What happened to Oppenheimer in those remaining years of his life? How does a man recover and pick up the pieces of such a remarkable career and forge a new path for himself? Why did he apparently withdraw from the public arena instead of continuing to speak out more actively against nuclear testing and the arms race, as did many of his colleagues and friends—or did he simply find another, more subtle way to do so? Did the security hearing ordeal really "destroy" him, or is that simply a romanticism? How much of a "victim" was he, and how much responsibility did he himself bear for his own fate? Most puzzling of all: why did he ultimately refuse and rebuff the efforts of powerful allies and friends eager to officially and permanently clear his name and erase the stain on his reputation? Addressing these questions, I hoped, would serve to distinguish my book from all the others, at least enough to escape the "just another Oppie book" syndrome.

Still, that didn't do anything to assuage the other source of intimidation looming over me: the importance and magnitude of Oppenheimer as a historical figure—and even more than that, the elusiveness and ultimate enigma of the man himself. Not just historians and biographers, but even those who knew Oppenheimer personally and intimately, have remarked on his frustrating complexity, the sheer impossibility of truly understanding him. I'd heard and read such comments many times, but as I became more and more deeply immersed in my own research, I began to empathize with them more completely. Oppie is indeed elusive, indefinable: you realize that you'll never be able to fully pin him down, no matter what. You keep hoping that with more digging, more research, more thought and analysis, you'll somehow eventually stumble upon the right magic document or talk to the right person, and suddenly, in a blinding shock of *satori,* all the mystery will fall away, all the shadows will dissipate, and all the exasperating contradictions and conflicts of J. Robert Oppenheimer will come together in a beautiful, grand unified field theory of the man, in stark splendor and diamond clarity.

It doesn't happen. Instead, like the subatomic particles described in Heisenberg's Uncertainty Principle, J. Robert Oppenheimer himself can never, will never, be fully defined. Just when one aspect, one quality, of him seems conveniently pinned down and defined, another

remains maddeningly out of reach. And if you don't simply give up, you eventually learn to make an uneasy peace with the intractable ambiguity that is J. Robert Oppenheimer.

So now, having completed this project, I can finally make with reasonable confidence the same claim as all the other Oppie biographers: yes, I believe I do, in a way, sort of, in a certain light, through a fuzzy lens, understand J. Robert Oppenheimer a little more than I did before.

And, yes, I am also even more confused and confounded by him than ever. Such is the inescapable curse of the Oppenheimer student.

I say all this not by way of excusing any of my own inadequacies in capturing the man and his life in these pages, nor as an alibi for any errors of fact, which are entirely my own responsibility. My intent is merely to make clear that those looking for the final word on J. Robert Oppenheimer, those quixotic souls poring over all the texts on the man hoping to find *the* answer to his personality, the key to his soul, won't find it here. Or anywhere else, for that matter. No doubt, of course, the same is true for all of us—every human being, as Walt Whitman once observed, contains multitudes. But Oppenheimer's, perhaps, are simply more multitudinous than those of most other human beings.

One thing certain, however, is that at least a small multitude stands behind every author, and it's a distinct pleasure and privilege to acknowledge those that have stood behind me and beside me as I wrote this book.

As usual, the first person to wholeheartedly support and believe in the project was my agent, Michael Psaltis. Michael's enthusiasm for the book and his dogged efforts on its behalf were above and beyond the call of duty.

Every author hopes to find an editor who is sensitive to and understanding of one's own plans and aspirations for the work in question. It's a hope that's rarely realized, but somehow, I lucked out with Daniela Rapp, my editor at St. Martin's Press. From the beginning, Daniela was in tune with my intentions for the project and provided invaluable guidance and advice. Others who helped bring this book to life include the copy editor, Adam Goldberger.

The opportunity to meet one of my scientific heroes, Freeman Dyson, was one of the definite highlights of this project for me, and I will

not soon forget my time with this extraordinary man. He was most gracious and generous with his thoughts and impressions of Oppenheimer when we met in his office at the Institute for Advanced Study. Christine Ferrara and the librarians at IAS were also most helpful. Oppie's friends and colleagues Jack Steinberger and Stanley Deser shared their memories. Martin Sherwin, coauthor of *American Prometheus,* took time out to meet with me and discuss things Oppenheimer.

I must also acknowledge and thank profusely the impeccably professional, personable, and knowledgeable staff of the Manuscript Division of the Library of Congress, who cheerfully tolerated me for many months while I pored over the Oppenheimer papers at the Library. Likewise for the Special Collections staff at the Regenstein Library of the University of Chicago; Princeton University Library; and the American Philosophical Society in Philadelphia. John Gustafson of the J. Robert Oppenheimer Memorial Committee helped obtain photos.

Friends and family, including Amy Chamberlain, Linda Chamberlain, Kristina Finan, Jeff Harris, Jennifer Heimbach, Christie Henry, Leila Monaghan, Anne Osterman, Nancy Shepherdson, Denise Shubin, Judy Weightman, and Cheryl Wilmeth provided essential support, advice, encouragement, and (sometimes) gentle criticism. Suzanne Rosin provided all of the above along with valuable research and library assistance (and, occasionally, essential transportation). The always friendly and energetic staff of the Tuscany Café on Rittenhouse Square in Philadelphia never failed to keep me fully supplied with caffeinated sustenance as I worked at their back table for endless hours (or at least until closing time).

Whatever lack of conclusions or faulty certainties one may reach from studying J. Robert Oppenheimer, I have discovered at least one irrefutable truth: the serious attempt to understand him is an unparalleled and enlightening journey through the great complexities and profound depths possible in the human character. I hope this book has allowed the reader to share in that journey, while shedding a little light on the very human struggle represented by the life of J. Robert Oppenheimer.

NOTES

The J. Robert Oppenheimer Papers (JRO Papers) are contained in the Manuscript Division of the Library of Congress, Washington, D.C.

All FBI file excerpts in the text and chapter openings are drawn from the Federal Bureau of Investigation Personnel File on J. Robert Oppenheimer (100–17828), FBI Headquarters, Washington, D.C.

1. *The Scientist and the Reporter*

1. Joseph E. Persico, *Edward R. Murrow: An American Original* (New York: McGraw-Hill, 1988), p. 405.

2. Fred W. Friendly, *Due to Circumstances Beyond Our Control* . . . (New York: Random House, 1967), p. 70.

3. Friendly to JRO, November 3, 1954, JRO Papers.

4. Friendly, p. 71.

5. Quoted in Alexander Kendrick, *Prime Time: The Life of Edward R. Murrow* (Boston: Little, Brown, 1969), p. 376.

6. Friendly, p. 72.

7. Persico, p. 405.

8. Friendly, pp. 72–73.

9. Bob Edwards, *Edward R. Murrow and the Birth of Broadcast Journalism* (Hoboken, N.J.: Wiley and Sons, 2004), pp. 102–3.

10. Kendrick, p. 377.

11. Friendly, p. 73.

12. JRO to Edward R. Murrow, December 30, 1954, JRO Papers.

13. Friendly to JRO, January 2, 1955, JRO Papers.

14. Quoted in Friendly, p. 73.

15. Val Adams, "Dr. Oppenheimer to Speak on CBS," *New York Times,* December 31, 1954.

16. Friendly, p. 74.

2. *The Sage of Princeton*

1. Joseph E. Persico, *Edward R. Murrow: An American Original* (New York: McGraw-Hill, 1988), p. 406.

2. Joseph Alsop and Stewart Alsop, "Security Risk Hearing on Dr. Oppenheimer Begun by U.S. Board," *New York Herald Tribune,* April 13, 1954.

3. *The Price of Celebrity*

1. Fred W. Friendly, *Due to Circumstances Beyond Our Control . . .* (New York: Random House, 1967), p. 74.

2. Alexander Kendrick, *Prime Time: The Life of Edward R. Murrow* (Boston: Little, Brown, 1969), pp. 376, 378.

3. "Alien Act Scored by Oppenheimer," *New York Times,* January 5, 1955.

4. Philip Hamburger, "Television: Dr. Oppenheimer," *New Yorker,* January 15, 1955.

5. Lawrence Laurent, "Ed Murrow Has a Chat with Dr. Oppenheimer," *Washington Post,* January 1955.

6. John Crosby, "Oppenheimer Proves a Remarkable Man," *Chicago Sun-Times,* January 10, 1955.

7. "TV Presents a Famous Face and Mind," *Life,* January 17, 1955.

8. Fulton Lewis Jr., " 'Liberals' Whitewash Campaign," *New York Journal-American,* January 11, 1955.

9. Correspondence to JRO, JRO Papers.

10. W. H. Ferry to Paul Hoffman, Fund for the Republic Memorandum, February 16, 1955, Fund for the Republic Papers, Princeton University.

11. Notes of telephone call to JRO, January 19, 1955, JRO Papers.

12. Friendly, pp. 74–5.

4. *The Bleak Face of Unhumanity*

1. "Legion Protest Ignored," *New York Times,* March 26, 1955.

2. Edwin A. Uehling to JRO, February 9, 1955, JRO Papers.

3. Quoted in "Conant, Bush, Dean, Lilienthal, McCloy OK Oppenheimer," University of Washington *Argus,* February 26, 1955.

4. Students to JRO, February 17, 1955, JRO Papers.

5. "Pro Football Welcomed, but Oppenheimer Banned," University of Washington *Argus,* February 19, 1955.

6. "Guarding the 'Best Interests' of the University," *New Republic,* April 18, 1955.

7. Seth Neddermeyer to JRO, February 26, 1955, JRO Papers.

8. "Scientists Demur for Oppenheimer," *New York Times,* March 24, 1955.

9. *Congressional Record,* Senate, March 10, 1955, pp. 2158–59.

10. H. Stanley Bennett to H. P. Everest, March 18, 1955, JRO Papers.

11. JRO to John Manley, March 2, 1955, JRO Papers.

12. "Oppenheimer Would Talk at U.W.," *Seattle Times,* April 18, 1955.

13. Brooks Atkinson, "Two by Rattigan," *New York Times,* May 22, 1955.

14. JRO to Hayes C. Lamont, March 22, 1955, JRO Papers.

15. Richard G. Hewlett and Jack M. Holl, *Atoms for Peace and War: Eisenhower and the Atomic Energy Commission, 1953–1961* (Berkeley: University of California Press, 1989), p. 242.

16. "Dr. Von Neumann Backed for AEC," *New York Times,* March 9, 1955.

17. Kai Bird and Martin J. Sherwin, *American Prometheus: The Triumph and Tragedy of J. Robert Oppenheimer* (New York: Knopf, 2005), p. 507.

5. *A Great Open Windy World*

1. Harold Hughes, "Dr. Oppenheimer Tells of Search for 'Ultimate Shapes and Forms,'" *Portland Oregonian,* April 21, 1955.

2. "Little-Known Facts About Expert Told," *Oregon State Daily Barometer,* April 17, 1955.

3. James G. Welch, "Record Crowd Hears Physicist, Few Understand 'New Language'"; "Why Did They Go Hear Oppenheimer?" *Eugene Register-Guard,* April 21, 1955.

4. "Over Their Heads," *Portland Oregonian,* May 6, 1955.

5. Letters to editor, ibid., May 9 and May 11, 1955.

6. "Bomb Test-Weather Tie-In Doubted by Oppenheimer," ibid., May 2, 1955.

7. "Oppenheimer at Exeter," *Manchester Union Leader,* November 24, 1955.

8. "Phillips Exeter Boys Enlighten Oppenheimer," *Boston Sunday Herald,* November 27, 1955.

9. Robert Jungk to Joseph Barnes, September 30, 1955, JRO Papers.

10. Joseph Barnes to Robert Jungk, October 5, 1955, ibid.

11. Robert Jungk to Joseph Barnes, March 26, 1956, ibid.

12. Joseph Barnes to JRO, March 30, 1956, ibid.

13. JRO to Joseph Barnes, April 2, 1956, ibid.

14. Phone message to JRO, April 4, 1956, ibid.

15. FBI Memorandum, May 11, 1956, JRO FBI Files (100-17828).

6. *The Climate of Suspicion*

1. "Noted Physicists, Including Oppenheimer, Meet Here," *Seattle Times,* September 17, 1956; "Theoretical Physics Parley Opens at U," *Seattle Post-Intelligencer,* September 18, 1956.

2. Ginn correspondence: "Harvard Schedules Oppenheimer, Class Agent Quits in Protest," *Manchester Union Leader,* December 27, 1955; "Quits Harvard Council," *New York Times,* December 30, 1955.

3. Robertson letter: Quoted in FBI Memorandum, June 27, 1956, JRO FBI Files.

4. Arthur Brooks Harlow, Harvard "Veritas" Committee letter to alumni, March 23, 1957, JRO Papers.

5. Quoted in Gerald Gunther, *Learned Hand: The Man and the Judge* (Cambridge, Mass.: Harvard University Press, 1994), pp. 628–29.

6. "Tide Turning at Harvard?" New York *Daily News,* March 31, 1957.

7. "The 'Unfastidious' Position of Harvard," *National Review,* March 23, 1957.

8. "Truth at Harvard," *Toledo Blade,* March 29, 1957.

9. Letters to editor, *Harvard Crimson,* April 13, 1957.

10. "First Oppenheimer Harvard Lecture Packs 'Em in Despite Early Protest," *New York Times,* April 9, 1957; Craig Fleming, "Oppenheimer Says Reds Peril Liberty," *Boston Herald,* April 9, 1957; Mary Handy, "Oppenheimer Tells Harvard Audience Knowledge 'Open,'" *Christian Science Monitor,* April 9, 1957.

11. "Harvard Again Lights the Way," *Providence Journal,* April 12, 1957.

12. Mary Handy, "Oppenheimer Lights Way," *Christian Science Monitor,* May 27, 1957.

13. Interview with JRO by Louis M. Lyons, WGBH-TV Channel 2, Boston, May 1, 1957. Transcript, JRO Papers.

7. *A Sense of Panic*

1. John Mason Brown, *Through These Men: Some Aspects of Our Passing History* (New York: Harper and Brothers, 1956), p. 288.

2. Cohn excerpts: Victor Cohn, "Can a Security Risk Survive? Oppenheimer Tells for First Time of Fight Against 'Final Judgment,'" Minneapolis *Sunday Tribune,* June 16, 1957.

3. Paul Dickson, *Sputnik: The Shock of the Century* (New York: Walker, 2001), p. 112.

4. "Secrecy and Supremacy," *Washington Post,* October 11, 1957.

5. "Hagen Is Frank," *Washington Post and Times Herald,* October 14, 1957.

6. "Physicist Protests," *New York Times,* October 14, 1957.

7. "Oppenheimer Named to Legion of Honor," *Washington Post,* November 5, 1957; "French Decorate Dr. Oppenheimer," *New York Times,* November 5, 1957; Remarks by Edouard Morot-Sir at Legion of Honor ceremony, September 25, 1957, JRO Papers.

8. "Security?" *Washington Post,* November 8, 1957.

9. "Oppenheimer Case a Symbol," *Raleigh News and Observer,* November 6, 1957.

10. "A Nation's Gratitude," *Trenton Evening Times,* November 11, 1957.

8. *Rumblings of Redemption*

1. "The Sequel to Killian," *St. Louis Post-Dispatch,* November 13, 1957.

2. Robert Barkdoll, "Gardner Advises Look at Oppenheimer Ban," *Washington Post,* November 18, 1957; "Ask Return of Oppenheimer in Space Race," New York *Daily News,* November 18, 1957.

3. "The Oppenheimer Case," *Time,* December 2, 1957.

4. S. Miles Bouton Sr. to *New York Times,* November 5, 1957.

5. "Oppenheimer Gets Support on Rehearing," *Washington Post,* November 22, 1957; Frances Lewine, "Old Foe for Review on Oppenheimer," *Newark Star-Ledger,* November 22, 1957; "Murray Switches on Oppenheimer," *New York Times,* November 22, 1957; "Murray Asks Review in Oppenheimer Case," *New York Times,* November 23, 1957; "Murray Not Switching Oppenheimer Stand," *Washington Post,* December 9, 1957; "Murray Denies Switch on Oppenheimer Issue," *New York Herald Tribune,* December 9, 1957; "Murray Neutral on Oppenheimer," *New York Times,* December 9, 1957.

6. "Javits Proposes U.S. Reinstate Oppenheimer," *New York Herald Tribune,* December 2, 1957; "Finletter, Tracy Voorhees for Oppenheimer's Return," ibid., December 3, 1957.

7. "Ike's Aides Urge Recall of Scientist," *Washington Post and Times Herald,* December 8, 1957.

8. "2 Ike Scientists Want Oppenheimer Back," *New York Post,* December 6, 1957.

9. Ibid.

10. "Nixon Said to Find Oppenheimer a Risk," *New York Times,* December 23, 1957; "No Comment by Nixon: His Office Is Silent on Issue of Dr. Oppenheimer," ibid., December 24, 1957.

11. "Javits Proposes U.S. Reinstate Oppenheimer," *New York Herald Tribune,* December 2, 1957; "Murray Denies Switch on Oppenheimer Issue," *New York Herald Tribune,* December 9, 1957.

12. John O'Donnell, "Capitol Stuff," New York *Daily News,* December 9, 1957.

13. Warren Unna, "Oppenheimer Case: Change of Attitude Traced," *Washington Post,* December 26, 1957.

14. Fulton Lewis Jr., "Oppenheimer? Still Risk!" *New York Mirror,* January 19, 1958.

15. FBI Memorandums, November 6, 8, 13, 1957; December 13, 1957, JRO FBI Files (100-17828).

16. "Oppenheimer Still a Risk, Says Strauss," New York *Daily News,* January 9, 1958; "AEC Due to Keep Oppenheimer Ban," *New York Times,* January 9, 1958.

17. "Oppenheimer," Excerpt of presidential press conference, *New York Herald Tribune,* January 16, 1958; "No Review Planned of Oppenheimer Case," *New York Times,* January 16, 1958.

18. "Security or Science?" *Washington Post,* January 9, 1958.

19. Frank Altschul, "Oppenheimer Case Review," *New York Times,* January 13, 1958.

20. John F. Fulton to Frank Altschul, January 14, 1958, JRO Papers.

21. "My Day by Eleanor Roosevelt," *New York Post,* January 24, 1958.

22. JRO to George Kennan, December 19, 1957, JRO Papers.

23. JRO to Cyrus Eaton, December 18, 1957, ibid.

24. United States Atomic Energy Commission, *In the Matter of J. Robert Oppenheimer: Transcript of Hearing before Personnel Security Board* (Cambridge, Mass.: MIT Press, 1971). p. 270.

25. Ibid, pp. 468–69.

26. Ibid, p. 567.

9. *The Answer to Fear*

1. " 'Where Do We Fit In?' the Scientists Ask," *New York Times Magazine,* May 18, 1958.

2. *Where We Stand* program outline, CBS News, JRO Papers.

3. Howard K. Smith, *Events Leading Up to My Death* (New York: St. Martin's Press, 1996), p. 261.

4. JRO to Edward R. Murrow, November 17, 1958, JRO Papers; Smith, p. 261.

5. Sig Mickelson to JRO, November 10, 1958, JRO Papers; JRO to Edward R. Murrow, ibid.

6. Dorothy Kilgallen column, no date, JRO Papers.

7. International News Service report, JRO Papers.

8. Louis C. Souder to JRO, February 3, 1958; JRO to Louis C. Souder, February 6, 1958, JRO Papers.

9. "Name School for Scientist," *Trentonian,* February 14, 1958.

10. Louis C. Souder to J. Edgar Hoover, February 20, 1958, JRO FBI Files.

11. "Township Names School for Oppenheimer," *Levittown Times,* February 14, 1958.

12. Ibid.; "Board Names High School for J. Robert Oppenheimer," *Trenton Evening Times,* February 14, 1958.

13. "School Board Lets Slip Show," *Bucks County Courier Times,* February 15, 1958.

14. "For Oppenheimer," Letters to the editor, ibid., February 19, 1958.

15. "Great Americans," ibid., February 28, 1958.

16. "Oppenheimer Issue Aired," *Trenton Times,* February 25, 1958; "Challenge Fails on Oppenheimer," *Levittown Times,* February 25, 1958; " 'He's a Scholar,' " *Princeton Packet,* February 27, 1958.

17. "School Name Probe Urged," *Levittown Times,* March 7, 1958.

18. "Oppenheimer Stays as Name of School," ibid., March 14, 1958; "Anti-Oppenheimer Faction Loses Fight over Name," *Trenton Times,* March 14, 1958; "Fight over Name Drags, Oppenheimer Tag Stays," *Trentonian,* March 15, 1958.

19. Mrs. Julia D. Carson, "Our Way of Life," Letters to the editor, *Bucks County Courier Times,* March 17, 1958.

20. "Von Braun Deplores Ban on Oppenheimer," *New York Times,* March 15, 1958.

21. Gerald Crowningshield, "Inside the School," Letters to the editor, *Bucks County Courier Times,* March 18, 1958.

22. "Proposal to Oppose School Name Nixed," *Levittown Times,* March 19, 1958.

23. JRO Hearing transcript, p. 726.

10. *The Otherness of People*

1. "Legion Post Opposes Name of School," *Levittown Times,* April 7, 1958.

2. "Alarming Slant," Letters to the editor, ibid.

3. Edmond J. Wilkins to JRO, August 11, 1958, JRO Papers.

4. Thomas J. Horan, President, LCA, to Harry Woodruff, Commander, American Legion Post 960, August 25, 1958, JRO Papers.

5. "Mrs. Roosevelt Backs School Name," *Trentonian,* August 24, 1958.

6. "Legion Warns on Defense Cuts, Demands Nation Be Strongest," *New York Times,* September 5, 1958.

7. Kenneth D. Munn, "Defends Oppenheimer," Letters to editor, *Trenton Sunday Times,* September 21, 1958.

8. "Board May Reconsider Choice of Oppenheimer," *Trentonian,* March 12, 1959; "Oppenheimer School Name Up for Vote," *Levittown Times,* March 12, 1959.

9. "Oppenheimer School Name Changed to Woodrow Wilson by Twp. Board," *Levittown Times,* March 13, 1959; "Reject Oppenheimer, Pick Woodrow Wilson," *Trenton Times,* March 13, 1959.

10. Mrs. John J. Mancewicz to JRO, March 14, 1959, JRO Papers.

11. Donald Munter to JRO, March 16, 1959, ibid.

12. *Miami Herald,* March 5, 1958.

13. David E. Lilienthal, *The Journals of David E. Lilienthal,* vol. 4, *The Road to Change, 1955–1959* (New York: Harper & Row, 1969), pp. 306, 308.

14. "U.S. Citing Oppenheimer in Move to Clear His Name," *New York Times,* April 5, 1963.

15. Gray Board findings: JRO Hearing transcript, pp. 998–1021.

16. Harold P. Green, "The Oppenheimer Case: A Study in the Abuse of Law," *Bulletin of the Atomic Scientists,* September 1977, p. 58.

11. *A Good Augury*

1. John W. Finney, JRO hearing transcript, p. 837.

2. "Strauss Now at Odds with Many in Capital," *New York Times,* May 11, 1958.

3. "Commerce Secretary Strauss Follows a Familiar Pattern," *Louisville Courier-Journal,* March 16, 1959.

4. Richard Pfau, *No Sacrifice Too Great: The Life of Lewis L. Strauss* (Charlottesville: University Press of Virginia, 1984), pp. 230–31.

5. Ibid., p. 231.

6. Strauss excerpts: Lewis L. Strauss, *Men and Decisions* (New York: Popular Library, 1963), pp. 391–97, 400.

7. Bernice Brode to JRO, 1959 (no specific date), JRO Papers.

8. "Strauss Asserts Critic Is Biased," *New York Times,* May 2, 1959.

9. Pfau, pp. 234–35.

10. Ibid., p. 233.

11. Ibid., p. 236.

12. Ibid, p. 242.

13. Ibid.

14. "Exit Strauss," *New York Times,* June 21, 1959.

15. Senator Clinton P. Anderson to Verna Hobson, phone message, June 29, 1959, JRO Papers.

16. Lloyd Garrison to JRO, July 1, 1959, ibid.

17. JRO to Lloyd Garrison, July 13, 1959, ibid.

12. *A Kind of Humanity*

1. Benjamin Lease, "Oppenheimer and Chevalier Collide in Ungracious Novel," *Chicago Sun-Times,* November 8, 1959; Lewis Gannett, "A Bitter 'J'Accuse' Written as a Novel," *New York Herald Tribune,* October 25, 1959; Michael Amrine, "Physicist Under a Microscope," *Washington Post,* October 25, 1959; "Oedipus at Los Alamos," *Time,* November 2, 1959.

2. Kai Bird and Martin J. Sherwin, *American Prometheus* (New York: Alfred A. Knopf, 2005), pp. 563–64.

3. Charles Thorpe, *Oppenheimer: The Tragic Intellect* (Chicago: University of Chicago Press, 2006), p. 266.

4. "Fire at Oppenheimer's," *New York Times,* April 11, 1960.

5. Bird and Sherwin, p. 408.

6. Freeman Dyson, interview with author, February 2, 2006.

7. Abraham Pais, with supplemental material by Robert P. Crease, *J. Robert Oppenheimer: A Life* (New York: Oxford University Press, 2006), pp. 143, 275.

8. Harold Taylor to JRO, October 16, 1959, JRO Papers.

9. Thorpe, p. 269.

10. "Oppenheimer to Give Series of Talks Here," *Asahi Evening News,* September 6, 1960.

11. J. Robert Oppenheimer, "The Future of Civilization in the Scientific Age," lecture at Bunkyo Public Hall of Tokyo, September 21, 1960, JRO Papers.

12. "Dr. Oppenheimer Gives Lecture in Kyoto University," *Mainichi Daily News,* September 15, 1960.

13. "1,000 Hear Oppenheimer Give Talk," *Asahi Evening News,* September 19, 1960.

14. Earle Reynolds to JRO, September 16, 1960, JRO Papers.

15. "Oppenheimer Met by American Youth," *Mainichi Daily News,* September 18, 1960.

16. Oppenheimer, "The Future of Civilization."

17. John Mason Brown, *Through These Men* (New York: Harper and Brothers, 1956), p. 277.

18. Hearing transcript, pp. 1047–65.

19. *New York Daily Mirror,* June 30, 1954.

13. *Honor and Respect*

1. "Oppenheimer Backed," *New York Times,* March 27, 1961.

2. Strauss letter and FBI memo: JRO FBI Files.

3. JRO FBI Files.

4. JRO to Nicolas Nabokov, December 18, 1961, JRO Papers.

5. "Oppenheimer Says Concern Is Best A-War Deterrent," McMaster University *Silhouette,* February 2, 1962; "Father of the A-Bomb Now Sorry It 'Grew Up,'" *Hamilton Spectator,* January 30, 1962; "Oppenheimer Defends Scientists' A-bomb Role," ibid., January 31, 1962; "Rushed Into A-World, Oppenheimer Says," "Standing Room Crowds Hear Nuclear Physicist," *Toronto Globe and Mail,* January 30, 1962.

6. C. R. Vann to JRO, October 16, 1961; JRO to Vann, October 23, 1961, JRO Papers.

7. Arthur M. Schlesinger Jr., *A Thousand Days: John F. Kennedy in the White House* (Boston: Houghton Mifflin, 1965), p. 684.

8. Max Lerner, "Nobel Lords," *New York Post,* April 30, 1962.

9. "49 Nobel Prize Winners Honored at White House," *New York Times,* April 30, 1962.

10. Lerner, "Nobel Lords."

11. *New York Herald Tribune,* April 30, 1962.

12. Howard Margolis, *Science,* May 4, 1962.

13. "Eggheads at the White House," *New York Post,* April 30, 1962.

14. *San Francisco Chronicle,* May 1, 1962.

15. *National Review,* May 15, 1962.

16. John C. Devlin, "Teller Is Mute on Oppenheimer; Has TV Show Delete Question," *New York Times,* April 16, 1962.

17. Fred Friendly to JRO, November 1, 1962, JRO Papers.

18. John Mason Brown, *Through These Men* (New York: Harper and Brothers, 1956), p. 288.

14. *Charity and Courage*

1. Robert Coughlan, "The Tangled Drama and Private Hells of Two Famous Scientists," *Life,* December 13, 1963.

2. "An American Phoenix," *Boston Globe,* April 6, 1963.

3. "A Prize Well Won," *New York Times,* April 6, 1963.

4. John W. Finney, "Capital Is Silent on Oppenheimer," *New York Times,* April 6, 1963.

5. "AEC to Honor Oppenheimer," Associated Press, April 5, 1963.

6. "For Services Rendered," *Washington Post,* April 6, 1963.

7. "The Fermi Award," *Boston Herald,* April 6, 1963.

8. "Oppie's Comeback," *Newsweek,* April 15, 1963.

9. "Never a Word of Bitterness, Resentment," Oak Ridge (Tenn.) *Oakridger,* April 19, 1963.

10. Leo Szilard to JRO, April 10, 1963, JRO Papers.

11. John Lansdale to JRO, April 15, 1963, ibid.

12. I. I. Rabi to JRO, April 5, 1963, ibid.

13. Edward Teller to JRO, no date, ibid.

14. Lewis Strauss to JRO, April 6, 1963, ibid.

15. William F. Buckley, "The Oppenheimer Play," *National Review,* April 23, 1963.

16. Stanton Evans, "At Home," ibid., May 14, 1963.

17. "Award Makes Partial Amends to Atom Scientist Oppenheimer," *National Observer,* April 8, 1963.

18. "An American Phoenix," *Boston Globe,* April 6, 1963.

19. "Redeeming the Oppenheimer Case," *Christian Science Monitor,* July 30, 1954.

20. Marquis Childs, "Oppenheimer File Is Opened Again," *Washington Post,* April 15, 1963.

21. "Rehabilitation?" *Nation,* April 20, 1963.

22. "U.S. Citing Oppenheimer in Move to Clear His Name," *New York Times,* April 5, 1963.

23. Federation of American Scientists, Memo from General Counsel to Council Members, April 10, 1963, JRO Papers.

24. "Scientists Seek Oppenheimer Clearance Action," *Washington Post,* April 9, 1963.

25. *Congressional Record,* July 11, 1963, quoted in FBI memo, JRO FBI Files; "JFK Is Asked to Clarify Status of Oppenheimer," *Washington Post,* July 4, 1963.

26. "Hosmer Asks Oppenheimer Ban," *New York Times,* July 4, 1963.

27. Marlene Dietrich to JRO, JRO Papers.

28. "Morality USA," *Look,* May 1963.

29. David Lilienthal, *The Journals of David Lilienthal,* vol. 5, *The Harvest Years, 1959–1963* (New York: Harper and Row, 1971), pp. 440, 520.

30. *Christian Science Monitor,* June 19, 1954.

31. "Laborite Would Invite Oppenheimer to Britain," *New York Times,* June 4, 1954.

32. "Dr. Oppenheimer Discusses Future," *New York Times,* July 4, 1954.

33. George F. Kennan, *Memoirs, 1950–1963* (New York: Little, Brown, 1972), p. 21.

15. *Darkness and Light*

1. David Lilienthal, *The Journals of David Lilienthal,* vol. 5, *The Harvest Years, 1959–1963* (New York: Harper and Row, 1971), pp. 522–23.

2. Felix Frankfurter to JRO, November 22, 1963, JRO Papers.

3. "New Hickenlooper 'No!' on Oppenheimer," *New York Herald Tribune,* November 30, 1963; Associated Press, "Hickenlooper Scores Selection of Oppenheimer for Award," *Trenton Times,* December 1, 1963; United Press International, "Oppenheimer Salute Stirs New Furor," *Trenton Times,* December 2, 1963; "Oppenheimer's Record: Science Writer Answers Senator's Criticism of Fermi Award," *New York Times,* December 26, 1963; "Hickenlooper Protests to AEC over Award to Oppenheimer," *New York Times,* November 30, 1963.

4. Lilienthal, *Journals,* vol. 5, pp. 528–30.

5. "Oppenheimer's Remarks," *New York Times,* December 3, 1963.

6. Drew Pearson, "Washington Merry-Go-Round," *Washington Post,* December 12, 1963.

7. " 'Brotherly Spirit,' " *Newsweek,* December 16, 1963.

8. Edward Teller, *Memoirs* (Cambridge, Mass.: Perseus Publishing, 2001), p. 465.

9. Lilienthal, *Journals,* vol. 5, p. 529.

10. Philip M. Stern, with Harold P. Green, *The Oppenheimer Case: Security on Trial* (New York: Harper & Row, 1969), p. 457.

11. " 'Brotherly Spirit,' " *Newsweek,* December 16, 1963.

12. Kent Biffle, "Dallas Defended by Oppenheimer," *Dallas Morning News,* December 17, 1963.

13. Fred Friendly to JRO, December 4, 1963, JRO Papers.

14. John W. Finney, "Fermi Prize Faces Curb in Congress," *New York Times,* March 8, 1964; "AEC Will Alter Fermi Prize Plan," *New York Times,* July 5, 1964.

15. "Dr. Oppenheimer's Award," *New York Times,* December 3, 1963.

16. JRO to Dean Sanford S. Elberg, University of California, March 10, 1964, JRO Papers.

17. William Boquist, "Oppenheimer's Return to UC," *San Francisco Examiner,* April 24, 1964.

18. David Perlman, "Oppenheimer's Vision," *San Francisco Chronicle,* May 1, 1964.

19. "Boom Town Revisited," *Newsweek,* June 1, 1964.

20. JRO phone statement, October 16, 1964, JRO Papers.

21. Friendly to JRO, July 8, 1964; transcript of JRO interview, August 14, 1964, JRO Papers.

22. C. P. Snow, "A Down-to-Earth Aerial Act," *Book Week,* November 29, 1964.

23. Howard Simons, "Bohr's Motives Misunderstood, Oppenheimer Says," *Washington Post,* December 7, 1964; Charles Thorpe, *Oppenheimer: The Tragic Intellect* (Chicago: University of Chicago Press, 2006), p. 272.

24. "Memorandum to File," July 19, 1954, JRO Papers.

25. Jack Lotto, " 'Shadows' Guard Oppenheimers," International News Service, April 25, 1954.

16. *The Public and the Private*

1. Joyce A. Evans, *Celluloid Mushroom Clouds* (Boulder, Colo.: Westview Press, 1998), p. 27.

2. Quoted in William Lanouette, *Genius in the Shadows* (Chicago: University of Chicago Press, 1992), p. 362.

3. JRO to Heinar Kipphardt, October 12, 1964, JRO Papers.

4. Heinar Kipphardt, *In the Matter of J. Robert Oppenheimer,* trans. Ruth Speirs (New York: Hill and Wang, 1968), pp. 126–127.

5. JRO to Heinar Kipphardt, October 12, 1964, JRO Papers.

6. "The Oppenheimer Case," *Times* (London), October 13, 1964.

7. Katherine Clark, "Stage Version of Scientist's Case Is European Hit," *Washington Post,* September 9, 1964.

8. Jean-Pierre Lenoir, "Oppenheimer Play Staged in Germany," *New York Times,* November 3, 1964.

9. JRO to Heinar Kipphardt, October 12, 1964, JRO Papers.

10. Michael Josselson to JRO, October 22, 1964, JRO Papers.

11. Sterling Seagrave, "Play About Him Draws Protest of Oppenheimer," *Washington Post,* November 9, 1964.

12. JRO, statement to press, November 11, 1964, JRO Papers.

13. "Playwright Suggests Corrections in Text of Oppenheimer Drama," *New York Times,* November 14, 1964.

14. "German Drama," *Washington Star,* no date.

15. " 'Scenic Report,' " *Newsweek,* November 16, 1964.

16. "The Heretic as Hero," *Washington Post,* November 13, 1964.

17. Robert Oppenheimer, "The Hero Objects," ibid., November 20, 1964.

18. "German's Play on Oppenheimer Is Performed for Paris Critics," *New York Times,* December 15, 1964.

19. Thomas Quinn Curtis, "Paris Gets Play on Oppenheimer," *New York Times,* December 15, 1964, international edition.

20. "The Oppenheimer File," *Variety,* January 13, 1965.

21. "Oppenheimer Play Stirs New Dispute," *New York Times,* December 27, 1964.

22. "German Play About Oppenheimer Called Unfair by the Scientist," United Press International, January 10, 1965.

23. Cynthia Grenier, " 'The Oppenheimer File' in Paris 'Tendentious,' " *New York Herald Tribune,* December 15, 1964.

24. "A Rush of Science Plays," *AAAS Understanding*, Spring 1965.

25. JRO to John Roberts, February 22, 1965, JRO Papers.

26. Robert H. Montgomery Jr. to John Roberts, March 11, 1965, ibid.

27. JRO to Lloyd Garrison, October 7, 1965, ibid.

28. "Dr. Oppenheimer Prefers the French Stage Version of the Case," *Times* (London), January 15, 1965.

29. JRO to Heinar Kipphardt, December 16, 1965, JRO Papers.

30. JRO to J. Edgar Hoover, July 17, 1954, J. Robert Oppenheimer Papers, Library of Congress.

31. JRO to Katherine Russell and Verna Hobson, July 21, 1954, JRO Papers.

32. *New York Post,* September 5, 1954.

33. David Lilienthal, *The Journals of David Lilienthal,* vol. 3, *The Venturesome Years, 1950–1955* (New York: Harper and Row, 1966), pp. 614–15.

17. *Responsibility and Guilt*

1. Haakon Chevalier to JRO, July 23, 1964, JRO Papers.

2. JRO to Haakon Chevalier, August 7, 1964, ibid.

3. JRO and Lloyd Garrison, notes of phone conversation, March 18, 1965, ibid.

4. Jeremy Bernstein, *Oppenheimer: Portrait of an Enigma* (Chicago: Ivan R. Dee, 2004), p. 132.

5. Howard Simons, "Scientist Tizard Led Way for 'the New Priesthood,'" *Washington Post,* August 18, 1965.

6. "Fame by Association," *Newsweek,* August 30, 1965.

7. Alistair Cooke, "Getting Burned in a Chain Reaction," *Book Week,* August 22, 1965.

8. "An Indictment of the Men Who Made the Bomb," *New York Times,* October 12, 1958.

9. Edward Condon to JRO, June 30, 1954, JRO Papers.

10. "Oppenheimer Will Keep Institute Post," Associated Press, July 1, 1954.

11. Lewis Strauss to Charles Lauritsen, June 24, 1954, JRO Papers.

18. *The Sad Account*

1. Charles Thorpe, *Oppenheimer: The Tragic Intellect* (Chicago: University of Chicago Press, 2006), p. 275.

2. William Laurence, "Would You Make the Bomb Again?" *New York Times Magazine,* August 1, 1965.

3. "Trinity Plus Twenty," *Newsweek,* July 19, 1965.

4. "Dr. Oppenheimer Interview," *CBS Evening News with Walter Cronkite,* August 5, 1965, transcript, JRO Papers.

5. "Alpha or Omega Was 20 Years Ago," *Washington Post,* July 11, 1965.

6. JRO to *New York Herald Tribune,* April 16, 1965, JRO Papers.

7. *The Day After Trinity* (film, 1980), directed by Jon Else. DVD distributed by Image Entertainment, Chatsworth, Calif.; 89 min.

8. Ibid.

9. Kai Bird and Martin J. Sherwin, *American Prometheus: The Triumph and Tragedy of J. Robert Oppenheimer* (New York: Alfred A. Knopf, 2005), p. 578.

10. Freeman Dyson, interview with author, Institute for Advanced Study, February 2, 2006.

11. Stanley Deser, correspondence with author, March 28, 2006.

12. JRO to Sam Leidesdorf, April 15, 1965, JRO Papers.

13. Institute for Advanced Study press release, April 24, 1965, ibid.

14. "Oppenheimer to Retire as Head of Institute for Advanced Study," *New York Times,* April 25, 1965.

15. John Corry, "Visit to an Intellectual Hotel," *New York Times Magazine,* May 15, 1966.

16. Freeman Dyson, interview with author, Institute for Advanced Study, February 2, 2006.

17. John J. McMackin to Institute for Advanced Study, April 25, 1965, JRO Papers.

18. "Oppenheimer to Retire as Head of Institute for Advanced Study."

19. "Things Were Never the Same Again," *New York Times Book Review,* July 18, 1965.

20. Quoted in Lansing Lamont, *Day of Trinity* (New York: Atheneum, 1965), p. 302.

21. JRO to Kenneth Bainbridge, February 19, 1966, JRO Papers.

22. Philip Stern to Jerome Wiesner, JRO Papers.

23. Quoted in Philip Stern, *The Oppenheimer Case: Security on Trial* (New York: Harper and Row, 1969), p. xi.

24. Ibid., p. x.

25. JRO to David Bohm, November 19, 1966, JRO Papers.

26. Fred Friendly to JRO, May 4, 1965, ibid.

27. "Dr. Oppenheimer Discusses Future," *New York Times,* July 4, 1954.

28. "Oppenheimer Gets Pyramid Club Honor," *New York Times,* October 22, 1954.

19. *Quartet in C-Sharp Minor*

1. David Lilienthal, *The Journals of David Lilienthal,* vol. 6, *Creativity and Conflict, 1964–1967* (New York: Harper and Row, 1976), pp. 234, 255.

2. Freeman Dyson, *Disturbing the Universe* (New York: Perseus, 1979), p. 81.

3. James M. Olson, *Fair Play: The Moral Dilemmas of Spying* (Washington, D.C.: Potomac Books, 2006), p. 152.

4. "Record of Congress for Cultural Freedom," *New York Times,* May 9, 1966.

5. "Banned Play on U.K. Stage," *New York Herald Tribune,* October 20, 1966; "Dispassionate View of the Oppenheimer Case," *Times* (London), October 18, 1966; "In the Matter of J. Robert Oppenheimer," *Daily Mail* (London), November 29, 1966; "Scientist Who Had Scruples," *Daily Telegraph* (London), November 29, 1966.

6. JRO to Poul Anderson, October 27, 1966, JRO Papers.

7. Quoted in Peter Michelmore, *The Swift Years: The Robert Oppenheimer Story* (New York: Dodd, Mead, 1969), p. 254.

8. Lilienthal, vol. 6. *Creativity and Conflict,* p. 300.

9. JRO to David Bohm, December 2, 1966, JRO Papers.

10. James Chadwick to JRO, December 29, 1966, ibid.

11. Lilienthal, vol. 6, p. 324.

12. "Oppenheimer Praised as Theoretician and Teacher," *New York Times,* February 20, 1967.

13. Lilienthal, vol. 6, p. 387.

14. "President Praises Oppenheimer Genius," *New York Times,* February 21, 1967.

15. "Oppenheimer Praised as Theoretician and Teacher."

16. "Marshal of Science," *New York Times,* February 20, 1967.

17. Jeremy Bernstein, *Oppenheimer: Portrait of an Enigma* (Chicago: Ivan R. Dee, 2004), p. viii.

18. Quoted in Abraham Pais, *J. Robert Oppenheimer: A Life* (New York: Oxford University Press, 2006), p. 279.

19. Freeman Dyson, interview with author, February 2, 2006.

20. Pais, p. 305.

21. "Text of Oppenheimer Lecture Ending the Columbia Bicentenary," *New York Times,* December 27, 1954.

22. David C. Cassidy, *J. Robert Oppenheimer and the American Century* (New York: Pi Press, 2005), p. 345.

23. "The Wisdom of a Physicist," *New York Times,* December 28, 1954.

20. *The Persistence of Dignity*

1. Henry DeWolf Smyth, Remarks at IAEA Conference, February 22, 1967, Smyth Papers, American Philosophical Society, Philadelphia.

2. Clive Barnes, "Theater: Drama of Oppenheimer Case," *New York Times,* June 7, 1968.

3. Eric Bentley, "Oppenheimer Mon Amour," *New York Times,* March 16, 1969.

4. Clive Barnes, "Theater: Oppenheimer Case as Drama," *New York Times,* March 7, 1969.

5. David Lilienthal, *The Journals of David Lilienthal,* vol. 7, *Unfinished Business, 1968–1981* (New York: Harper and Row, 1983), pp. 109–10.

6. Jeremy Bernstein, *Oppenheimer: Portrait of an Enigma* (Chicago: Ivan R. Dee, 2004), p. 156.

7. Gerald Holton, review of *The Oppenheimer Case: Security on Trial,* by Philip Stern, *New York Times Book Review,* January 4, 1970.

8. Roger Robb, Memorandum to FBI, July 21, 1967, JRO FBI Files (100-17828).

9. Harry Kalven, "Judgment: The Oppenheimer Case," *Science,* February 20, 1970; Strauss draft of letter to Kalven, July 17, 1970, JRO FBI Files (100-17828).

10. J. Robert Oppenheimer Memorial Committee brochure, JRO Papers.

11. Barton J. Bernstein, "The Puzzles of Interpreting J. Robert Oppenheimer, His Politics, and the Issues of His Possible Communist Party Membership," in *Reappraising Oppenheimer: Centennial Studies and Reflections,* Cathryn Carson and David A. Hollinger, eds. (Berkeley: Berkeley Papers in History of Science, University of California–Berkeley, 2005), p. 106, n. 62.

12. Jon Else in "Oppenheimer in Film: A Transcript," ibid., pp. 362, 380.

13. Stanley Deser, correspondence with author, March 28, 2006.

14. Kristin M. Lord and Vaughan C. Turekian, "Time for a New Era of Science Diplomacy," *Science,* February 9, 2007.

15. Abraham Pais, *J. Robert Oppenheimer: A Life* (New York: Oxford University Press, 2006), pp. xxii, 139; George Kennan, *Memoirs,* vol. 2, p. 18.

16. Jeremy Bernstein, *Oppenheimer, Portrait of an Enigma,* p. 194.

17. Ibid., p. 141.

18. Gordon Dean to JRO, December 23, 1954, JRO Papers.

SELECT
BIBLIOGRAPHY

These are the major book-length works I found most useful in writing this volume. All other sources, including newspaper and magazine articles, interviews, original papers, etc., are referenced in the notes.

Bacher, Robert F. *Robert Oppenheimer 1904–1967*. Los Alamos, N. Mex.: Los Alamos Historical Society, Monograph 2, 1999.

Bernstein, Jeremy. *Oppenheimer: Portrait of an Enigma*. Chicago: Ivan R. Dee, 2004.

Bethe, Hans. *The Road from Los Alamos*. New York: American Institute of Physics, 1991.

Bird, Kai, and Martin J. Sherwin. *American Prometheus: The Triumph and Tragedy of J. Robert Oppenheimer*. New York: Alfred A. Knopf, 2005.

Boskin, Joseph, and Fred Krinsky. *The Oppenheimer Affair: A Political Play in Three Acts*. Beverly Hills, Calif.: Glencoe Press, 1968.

Boyer, Paul. *By the Bomb's Early Light: American Thought and Culture at the Dawn of the Atomic Age*. Chapel Hill: University of North Carolina Press, 1994.

Carson, Cathryn, and David A. Hollinger, eds. *Reappraising Oppenheimer: Centennial Studies and Reflections*. Berkeley: Office for History of Science and Technology, University of California, Berkeley (Berkeley Papers in History of Science, Volume 21), 2005.

Cassidy, David C. *J. Robert Oppenheimer and the American Century*. New York: Pi Press, 2005.

Casti, John L. *The One True Platonic Heaven: A Scientific Fiction on the Limits of Knowledge*. Washington, D.C.: Joseph Henry Press, 2003.

Chevalier, Haakon. *Oppenheimer: The Story of a Friendship*. New York: George Braziller, 1965.

Curtis, Charles P. *The Oppenheimer Case: The Trial of a Security System*. New York: Simon and Schuster, 1955.

Dyson, Freeman. *Disturbing the Universe*. New York: Basic Books, 1979.

———. *Weapons and Hope*. New York: Harper and Row, 1984.

Goodchild, Peter. *Edward Teller: The Real Dr. Strangelove*. Cambridge, Mass.: Harvard University Press, 2004.

————. *J. Robert Oppenheimer: Shatterer of Worlds.* New York: Fromm International, 1985.

Herken, Gregg. *Brotherhood of the Bomb: The Tangled Lives and Loyalties of Robert Oppenheimer, Ernest Lawrence, and Edward Teller.* New York: Henry Holt, 2002.

Jungk, Robert. *Brighter Than a Thousand Suns: A Personal History of the Atomic Scientists.* New York: Harcourt Brace Jovanovich, 1958.

Kipphardt, Heinar. *In the Matter of J. Robert Oppenheimer.* Translated by Ruth Speirs. New York: Hill and Wang, 1968.

Lamont, Lansing. *Day of Trinity.* New York: Atheneum, 1965.

Lanouette, William. *Genius in the Shadows: A Biography of Leo Szilard, the Man Behind the Bomb.* Chicago: University of Chicago Press, 1992.

Larsen, Rebecca. *Oppenheimer and the Atomic Bomb.* New York: Franklin Watts, 1988.

Lilienthal, David E. *The Journals of David E. Lilienthal.* Vol. 3, *Venturesome Years, 1950–1955.* New York: Harper and Row, 1966.

————. *The Journals of David E. Lilienthal.* Vol. 4, *The Road to Change, 1955–1959.* New York: Harper and Row, 1969.

————. *The Journals of David E. Lilienthal.* Vol. 5, *The Harvest Years, 1959–1963.* New York: Harper and Row, 1971.

————. *The Journals of David E. Lilienthal.* Vol. 6, *Creativity and Conflict, 1964–1967.* New York: Harper and Row, 1976.

————. *The Journals of David E. Lilienthal.* Vol. 7, *Unfinished Business, 1968–1981.* New York: Harper and Row, 1983.

Major, John. *The Oppenheimer Hearing.* New York: Stein and Day, 1971.

McMillan, Priscilla J. *The Ruin of J. Robert Oppenheimer and the Birth of the Modern Arms Race.* New York: Viking, 2005.

Michelmore, Peter. *The Swift Years: The Robert Oppenheimer Story.* New York: Dodd, Mead, 1969.

Oppenheimer, J. Robert. *Atom and Void: Essays on Science and Community.* Princeton, N.J.: Princeton University Press, 1989.

————. *The Flying Trapeze: Three Crises for Physicists.* New York: Harper and Row, 1969.

————. *The Open Mind.* New York: Simon and Schuster, 1955.

————. *Science and the Common Understanding.* New York: Simon and Schuster, 1953.

————. *Uncommon Sense.* Boston: Birkhauser, 1984.

Pais, Abraham, with supplemental material by Robert P. Crease. *J. Robert Oppenheimer: A Life.* New York: Oxford University Press, 2006.

Polenberg, Richard, ed. *In the Matter of J. Robert Oppenheimer: The Security Clearance Hearing.* Ithaca, N.Y.: Cornell University Press, 2002.

Rabi, I. I., Robert Serber, Victor F. Weisskopf, Abraham Pais, and Glenn T. Seaborg. *Oppenheimer.* New York: Charles Scribner's Sons, 1969.

Regis, Ed. *Who Got Einstein's Office? Eccentricity and Genius at the Institute for Advanced Study.* Reading, Mass.: Addison-Wesley, 1987.

Rhodes, Richard. *Dark Sun: The Making of the Hydrogen Bomb.* New York: Touchstone, 1996.

————. *The Making of the Atomic Bomb.* New York: Simon and Schuster, 1986.

Rouze, Michel. *Robert Oppenheimer: The Man and His Theories.* Translated by Patrick Evans. New York: Paul Eriksson, 1965.

Schweber, S. S. *In the Shadow of the Bomb: Oppenheimer, Bethe, and the Moral Responsibility of the Scientist.* Princeton, N.J.: Princeton University Press, 2000.

Stern, Philip M., with Harold P. Green. *The Oppenheimer Case: Security on Trial.* New York: Harper and Row, 1969.

Teller, Edward, with Judith L. Shoolery. *Memoirs: A Twentieth-Century Journey in Science and Politics.* Cambridge, Mass.: Perseus Publishing, 2001.

Thorpe, Charles. *Oppenheimer: The Tragic Intellect.* Chicago: University of Chicago Press, 2006.

United States Atomic Energy Commission. *In the Matter of J. Robert Oppenheimer: Transcript of Hearing Before Personnel Security Board and Texts of Principal Documents and Letters.* Foreword by Philip M. Stern. Cambridge, Mass.: MIT Press, 1971.

INDEX